ORDINARY HEROINES

Transforming the Male Myth

Nadya Aisenberg

GW00455524

Continuum • New York

1994

The Continuum Publishing Company
370 Lexington Avenue, New York. NY 10017

Copyright © 1994 by Nadya Aisenberg

Printed in the United States of America

Library of Congress Cataloging-in-Publication Data

Aisenberg, Nadya.
    Ordinary heroines : transforming the male myth / Nadya Aisenberg.
        p.   cm.
    Includes bibliographical references.
    ISBN 0-8264-0652-1
    1. Women in literature. 2. Heroines in literature. 3. Sex role in literature. 4. Social change in literature. 5. Women and literature. 6. Literature, Modern—20th century—History and criticism. I. Title.
PN56.5.W64A37 1993   93-44438
809'.93352042—dc20   CIP

Acknowledgments will be found on pages 230–232, which constitute an extension of the copyright page.

The Spirit of Ruin

If peace had been a possibility in the heroic world,
would Achilles have dragged Hector's wounded body
in the dust, lashed to his chariot wheel,
boasted he'd leave his enemy to vultures, dogs,
devour him himself? Could he, who prayed to War
to gorge him on the choking groans of men,
have judged the funeral games, honored his aging father,
husbanded the groves? Would he have been content
to prod white oxen as they trod white barley
on the threshing floor, and say of Troy,
"There was a world as well"?
If peace had been a possibility,
might he have joined the amorous couples
dancing on his shield, been neither god nor beast
but man, as when King Priam, risking all
to ransom Hector's body for the pyre,
moved wrathful Achilles, however briefly, to tears?

— *Nadya Aisenberg*

Contents

Acknowledgments

I would like to thank the friends and colleagues who have seen portions or versions of this manuscript and listened, read, and shared their knowledge with me: Marion Mainwaring, Miriam Goodman, Nancy Kassell, and Mary Anne Ferguson. Mona Harrington and Gillian Gill, with whom I belonged to a writer's group during the progress of this book, gave unstintingly of their time and critical attention and to them I owe a particular debt of gratitude. Marie Cantlon's encouragement and advice stood me in their usual good stead. My agent, Anne Edelstein, supported me with her enthusiasm for the work, and my research assistant, Alison Park, proved a most diligent and intelligent investigator. Pam Bernard provided valuable pictorial research. I would also like to thank Prof. Barbara Page of Vassar College for introducing me to the work of feminist film maker, Sally Potter. Kate Mattes of Kate's Mystery Bookstore, Cambridge, Massachusetts, provided help from her storehouse of knowledge.

My husband has been, as always, my staunchest ally, sustaining me through all difficulties between the idea and the end.

For work undertaken in residence I would like to express appreciation to the Villa Montalvo, Saratoga, California, January 1989; and the Macdowell Colony for the Arts, Peterborough, New Hampshire, 1992. Finally, the first draft of most of this book was written in the Writer's Room of the Massachusetts Artist's Foundation, and I want to acknowledge with gratitude the energy this facility, and the writers working there, afforded me.

Chapter 2 won Honorable Mention in the Kathleen Gregory Klein Popular Culture Competition. Chapter 5 was presented, in an earlier version, at the Alliance for Independent Scholars, 1989, and at the New England Women's Studies Association, 1990. A prior draft of Chapter 7 was presented at Vassar College and at the New England Modern Language Association in 1991.

Prologue

Of Women and Heroines:
Subjects in the Making

The key question for women now is no longer Freud's querulous "What do women want?" but "What can women *do* in their lives, in the stories of their lives?" To explore these related questions, I use literature as the instrument for calibrating women's position, since literature simultaneously reflects and forecasts the social world to which it is inextricably linked.

Contemporary poetry and fiction by women tell us a great deal about what women can do. The female protagonists we find in both poetry and fiction help us to understand the difficulties which beset composing a contemporary heroine. Through studying these writings, we will understand the paradox that though there is no dearth, and never has been, of courageous women, active women, spiritual women, women of leadership, the Hero has nonetheless been our culture's central symbol. Hence within our male-dominated culture we experience great trouble conceiving a heroine.

Whatever the difficulties, the creation of a new heroine is a crucial task facing us today. We need a new heroine with new strengths, new virtues, and new energies to play new roles because classical heroes and the heroic code they embrace have failed us badly. The paradigm of virtue that heroes like Aeneas, like Roland, and the heroic code—maiden-rescuing, dragon-slaying—represent has been destructive both to the individual and to Western culture. Yet because these heroes come to us from core texts in our education, we absorb them uncritically, store them in our unconscious.

They imprint values that still persist today in the deepest layers of Western culture's imagination. It is for a new heroine to challenge inherited touchstones of virtue.

Specifically, what must be exposed are the heroic emphasis upon physical courage, the hero's position as separate from his society, the premise of a god-given destiny—the hero as savior, that is—and most importantly, the prototype of the hero as warrior. At the outbreak of the 1991 Iraqi war, the *New York Times* placed President Bush in the company of other warrior Presidents Americans consider great—Washington, Lincoln, and Franklin D. Roosevelt. Honor depends not only upon brave deeds in this code, but also upon not losing face, not backing down. This interpretation of virtue has led us in the past, and is still leading us, to bloodshed as a reflexive response to conflict. Indeed, our response to domestic or foreign threat arises from the heroic view: act first, impose your will, think later. Male ideals of conquest have extended to the conquest of nature, posing a double threat: the extinction of the race and of the planet.

Examining the hero, we discover his essential narrowness which neglects concerns with community, negotiation, nature, human relations, and the enablement of individual destinies to flourish in their differentness. The heroic code is conservative in its essence, which means it does not commit itself to broad social issues particular to a time, such as the illiteracy, poverty and violence which permeate our society now. Rather, the heroic quest is single-minded—bring back the Golden Fleece, evict the Moors from Spain. It does not seek to establish agencies for improving the *salus populis*, the good of the people. We cannot accept the hero's will, following its course unswervingly and unquestioningly, as the final arbiter of our common destiny.

Moreover, because classical heroes are figures fulfilling a god-given destiny, they stand above and beyond their fellow men. In their very perfection, their larger-than-life, nearly-god identity, heroes are inimitable, and therefore disempowering to more ordinary men, inhibiting them from becoming leaders. Because heroes experience their destiny as god-bestowed, they are not concerned with enabling successors, who, like themselves, presumably have to wait upon election.

The failure of the heroic code to provide a workable model for leadership is most evident in the development of the so-called anti-hero of modern literature, the protagonist who is the hero's opposite: T. S. Eliot's Prufrock, who asks whether he dares to eat a peach, Saul Bellow's Augie March, whose adventures are merely seamy. However much the anti-hero may deplore heroic excesses, he is himself so limited, so tenuously functional, that he cannot stand as a replacement for the hero he has justifiably repudiated.

For women, today's heroine must also specifically address their lives. Recent studies in the psychology of women, such as *In a Different Voice* by Carol Gilligan, *Women's Ways of Knowing*, by Mary Field Belenky, Blythe McVicker Clinchy, et al., *Composing a Life* by Mary Catherine Bateson, and *Writing a Woman's Life* by Carolyn Heilbrun, all suggest that women's voices and developmental experience differ from those of men. Women need a heroine who will speak of this experience in a voice that rings true to them, so that the image we receive and the image of what we want to be are, for the first time, one. Women are creating new images of themselves, and, finding little help in canonical history, they look to literature for the new heroines they seek and are in the process of becoming.

In the past, the hero dominated the heroine; in both life and literature, men were the active figures and women followed them, even within the fictional or operatic love plots where the heroine was a major protagonist. The images of themselves that women absorb from male-authored texts, from TV, from magazines, from advertising, and from film, exert an enormously disabling influence. Women's traditional place as passive, supportive, and awaiting a romantic destiny, is reinforced by the fact that women's contribution is omitted from the long record of historical achievement handed down by men. Women therefore have seen themselves as inferior. The disproportionate degree to which women more than men suffer from emotional disorders such as anxiety, anorexia, depression, and agoraphobia can be traced, in large measure, to their gendered roles as subordinated beings. But women's lives have changed radically, and are still changing. In unheard of numbers, women are entering spheres previously reserved for men and, at the same time, are reshaping their private lives. Looking for a heroine is a most timely task.

Women are in a position, perhaps for the first time, to think beyond the goal of equality and to implement feminist values that have never prevailed in our culture. Beyond the great importance the heroine attaches to the individual life, she is deeply committed to a more humane society. She is forward-looking, since she is trying to forge something which doesn't exist yet. She remains a responsive leader of the society from which she has emerged, an ordinary woman endeavoring, nevertheless, to tackle extraordinary problems. In all these ways, she distinguishes herself from the hero. Significantly, she substitutes moral courage and a moral voice for the hero's physical courage and sense of predestination.

As we go in pursuit of the new heroine, we confront immediately the traditional, overwhelming dominance of the hero whose identity has obscured hers. She is a new heroine, then, in the sense that her outline is just emerging from the huge shadow cast by the hero. Until now it has been almost impossible to discuss the heroine without reference to the hero, as if she were merely the obverse side of his coin—she taking definition simply from what he is not. Partly as a result of this negative definition, there exists no archetypal heroine to set alongside the archetypal hero, nobody we can summon from the depths of our unconscious as the original, the prototype. Eve is not the heroine of the Genesis myth; Jocasta's role in the Oedipus myth is to be married and to die by her own hand in reaction to the graver fault of her son/husband. Men have provided the vision of destiny that moves women through space and time, and consequently, through genres that don't speak for them and images that don't reflect them. What women do, in literature and in life, has remained largely invisible, because in a man's world women's place is to be invisible. Characteristically, women are anonymous or generic protagonists. As we find woman's voice and create visual symbols which truly represent woman, a new heroine emerges.

When we talk at all of women's representation, whether voice or image, we begin from a long-standing condition of lack, of absence. That women are unrepresented—the "Blank Page," the *tabula rasa*—is indicated by the degree to which the experience of one sex is made the interpretive key to the understanding of both sexes. Thus, Roland Barthes, in *The Pleasure of the Text*, argues, like Freud, for the centrality of the male Oedipus myth. "Doesn't every narrative lead back to Oedipus? Isn't storytelling always a way of searching for one's origins?"[1] To the second question we may well answer "yes," but as to the first, whose story are we telling? Though feminist theorists reject or seriously qualify Freudian Oedipal theory, the Oedipus story, because it is the central male narrative, is assumed to be the normative narrative for *both* sexes. Just as there was no archetypal heroine to set beside the archetypal hero, so there is no female narrative comparable to the Oedipus narrative. Despite the efforts of poets like Anne Sexton and Sylvia Plath, Electra and Psyche simply haven't entered the mainstream to the same degree that Oedipus has; there isn't a similar recognition of their plots as basic to our understanding of human conduct. Substantively, then, women cannot tap into a historical formulation of their own developmental quest. Indeed Adrienne Rich maintains that because women were never told to study their own lives, they are excluded from the traditional conception of serious developmental process.

We are all taught in school that the war between the Trojans and Greeks was fought over Helen, and that the raging quarrel between Achilles and Agamemnon was over Briseis. But the story of the Trojan War became an epic of heroes; the *Iliad* leaves Helen and Briseis to one side. Even when male authors wrote in the personae of Helen and Briseis and Dido, their heroines are heroines *manqués* playing restricted roles. Women have always been excluded from the male heroic plot. How can women even decide what heroism is, or could be, or *should* be, when the examples that instruct us represent only half the society? "What would happen," Christa Wolf asks, "if the great male heroes of world literature were replaced by women? Achilles, Hercules, Odysseus, Oedipus, Agamemnon, Jesus, King Lear, Faust, Julien Sorel, Wilhelm Meister?"[2] These were our texts, our heroes! What transference was required for women to identify with these men! Nor did books specifically written for women supply missing heroines: the correct assignment for women, as presented in conduct books, popular "family" magazines, hygiene manuals, social science studies, was the maintenance of order and domestic virtue. Further, the absence of women from the issues of law, annals, history, in which male figures establish the organization and written recording of what is supposedly all *human* experience, creates serious questions about where women can find authority that validates them, and enables them to develop into heroines.

Women's lack of representation, and the overshadowing of heroine by hero reveal themselves if we probe basic terminology. Both terms, hero and heroine, trail myriad qualifications and exceptions, both cultural and temporal, in their wake. Yet because we still resort to these loose and inaccurate terms, we must bear with their shifting meanings and try to understand their implications. They are engrained in our cultural thinking and carry forward notions of gender imbalance.

First, hero and heroine are inexact terms because they seem equally weighted but are not so: They are, rather, hierarchical. They designate in fact the heroine's lack of stature and autonomy. The suffix "-ine" denotes the diminutive, the very term is a variation wrung on the masculine noun. The dictionary defines a heroine as a "woman of qualities like those of a hero"—she is, at best, a similacrum of someone male. By this definition, the heroine can never be the hero's equal. As the term is generally understood, the heroine can more properly be described as the leading female protagonist; the hero is the leading male protagonist and more. We impute to the hero qualities of "nobility," "largeness of scale," "valor," "illustriousness;" we speak of the "heroic age," of "heroic poetry," of "the heroic couplet." These broader applications suggest the nature of the hero is "more." Small wonder that feminist critics experience discomfiture with the word "heroine" and feel the need to redefine it or qualify it. They reject its diminution.

The hero feminist commentators have in mind when they distinguish heroine from hero is the classical, archetypal hero—the tragic or epic hero,

a man of nobility and importance, of superlative, even transcendent courage. They are referring to heroes with a capital *H*: Aeneas, Hector, Achilles. This Hero is even now the model we summon when we think of west-
erns, war movies, comic strip supermen; he persists in the solitary hero of
Hemingway's *The Old Man and the Sea.*[3] Some exceptional women fit into
this same category: Medea, an early example of the Terrible Mother (she
kills two sets of children!), who is also a sorceress; and Electra, who helped
her brother Orestes avenge their father's death. These women share this
extra-ordinariness; we might say they are Heroines with a capital *H.* They,
like Heroes, believe in an abstract honor and in god-given destiny. But the
overwhelming majority of legends, myths, and fairy tales depict heroic adventures, not heroinic ones. Down to *The Three Musketeers* and Captain
Ahab, it's a man's world in the literature of the past.

The fact that we possess neither an archetypal heroine to set beside
the archetypal hero nor a female narrative which commands the same instant recognition as the Oedipus story, speaks worlds about the relative
positions of the sexes outside literature, in society. It shows how unequal
those terms really are. Women have been a footnote in history, handmaidens
in literature. Only recently have Shakespeare's sisters been unearthed.[4] Because of this, looking at the position of ordinary women in literature, heroines with a small *h*, rather than only at exceptional Heroines like Antigone,
serves my purpose.

In the large-scale effort now underway to recover women's contribution to culture, their voices, their images, we discover a counter-narrative
for the new heroine to set in motion. Very different values sustain hero and
heroine. Were the heroine to be as dominant a protagonist as the hero, she
would still act differently. Hero and heroine belong not only to separate
sexes, but to different worlds. The conventional terminology of hero and
heroine, distinguishing the characters by sex, has obscured this. To avoid
confusion, Lee Edwards invents the term "female hero," using the myth of
Psyche as her paradigm; Susan Morgan employs the phrase "feminine heroic" to define a set of feminist values which she perceives as opposing male
heroics in nineteenth-century British novels; Starhawk, the feminist spirituality leader, creates the term "heras."

The lack of terminology to describe a heroine in her own right reflects
the basic lack of female subjectivity, or selfhood. A woman is not seen, nor
does she see herself, as a subject, the I, the mover, as in "the subject of the
sentence." She is, rather, the object, the me, the reflection. Constituting a
self may seem an old-fashioned aim given that postmodernist thinking
emphasizes deconstruction, not construction. But what the postmodernist

theorists have done in challenging the claims of the old certainties and virtues is to break down established boundaries for the heroine, specifically the boundaries of gender identity and gender hierarchy.

Walter Benjamin describes the loss of boundaries and limits graphically in his collection *Reflections,* that prescient text of postmodern experience. This memoir or remembrance is a commemoration of the obliterated. In his essay "A Berlin Chronicle" the philosopher pictures himself middle-aged, wandering through the streets of Berlin, the city of his childhood, map in hand, but utterly lost. The streets he knew intimately are destroyed, and he sees in the destruction of landmarks the destruction of all of his former life, the cultural assumptions of his young world. The death of the middle class, the advent of World War I and beyond, the rise of communism, render his map useless. Consulting memory as a guide, he discovers an unreliable jumble of ill-assorted impressions. Benjamin concludes that where his own past should be, there is a circle of fragments. There is no epistemological certainty, but only indeterminacy.

What this means for the heroine in both literature and life, is that within the deconstructed text (book or life), character and plot are both destabilized. Space opens. Genre itself becomes unstuck. From all these beginnings, the heroine picks her path through a vastness of rubble which, when intact, formed monuments of obstruction, heroic artifacts. Now, as the example of Benjamin demonstrates, the real has become flux. This is the heroine's river of time. The heroine represents the sex traditionally defined as amorphous, fluid, imperfect, changing. She represents the sex which boasts no monumental, universal totality. Walter Pater and Mikhail Bakhtin intend this characterization derogatively. Jacques Derrida labels her "disorderly," a highly significant term I shall revert to in the Epilogue. I see the heroine, exactly because she is herself a subject-in-process, as the apposite protagonist for our postmodern time. She is, in some sense, a postmodern heroine.

Furthermore, if postmodernist notions of fragmentation and partiality supercede prior notions of universality and totality, no one speaker can presume to speak for all. There can be no "normative" speech. Discourse cannot be univocal as the heroic voice typically is. The heroine, excluded from the hero's plot and the heroic voice within that plot which believes in an unchanging and external reality, can insert her voice for the first time and tell her/story. Difference can challenge his/story, in this new multivocalic, multiplicitous discourse. Without women's contribution, society as a whole is governed by a unitary view and deprived of richness and complexity, the polyphony of diversity. And her stories will vary by time, race, class and region.[5] The new heroine is aware of this, and it gives her a special kind of moral authority derived from social conscience and self-awareness. The new voice is polyvalent, demanding new genres. Reality itself becomes subject to interpretation; there are alternative realities. Which genre contains the "truth?" What is the relation of "truth" to fiction? This is the point at which genre and gender intersect, a point with which postmodernism is not specially concerned, but feminist thinking is.

Thus, at the same time that Lacan and Derrida are questioning genre boundaries, the boundaries of the body and between bodies are breaking down. Psychologist Jessica Benjamin's term "intersubjective space" describes this new perception of reality. Each area of questioning, genre and gender, interacts with the other. Certain modes of psychoanalytic theory, such as object-relations theory which asks "What is feminine?" and "What is masculine?" are also mapping this new cartography. The postmodern characteristic of inclusiveness loosens stylistic categories, thereby facilitating the creation of texts at once more novel and more accessible, fusing high and low diction, fantasy and reality. New genres emerge for which names such as "fici-fact" or "meta-fiction" are found. In the past, genre followed gender in hierarchy; women were unrepresented in the most honorific genres, epic and tragedy. But as new genres appear which represent new senses of the self and the world, and the self in relation to the world, women compose and enter them.

I do not wish to imply that current literary invention has been the exclusive province of women writers, but authors such as Djuna Barnes and Angela Carter use it to an end different from that of men: to express what Jane Marcus calls "the obscene laughter of the oppressed."[6] We cannot isolate "truth" any more than we can specify "reality" or purify genre.

Feminism shares with postmodernism a quest crucial for the emergent heroine, the struggle to find something beyond current epistemes. Indeed the very term "postmodern" gives off an aura of uncertainty, defining a condition only in terms of what is past, of what it comes after, declaring the present, and therefore the future, as necessarily open. I welcome such openness rather than perceive it as a cause for anxiety. When Jane Flax titles the final chapter of her *Thinking Fragments* "No Conclusions," her choice may disallow certainty but it allows the heroine for today to ask, "What will have to be done?" rather than "What was done in the past?" or "Who did it before?" Flax's book title echoes Walter Benjamin's discovery that his past is a circle of fragments.

Suddenly, we are no longer talking about limits and boundaries, but about beginnings, about change. Now we are in the heroine's world. Postmodernists may simply observe and report a historical moment, but for feminists, this moment is opportunity. Even so, the task the new heroine faces will not be easy. When we talk of destabilizing gender identities, we are disturbing one part of an ancient and powerful legacy, we are engaging in enormous cultural conflict. The breaking of boundaries, incurring the possibility of hybridization, has been anathema to western Judeo-Christian culture for millennia, going back, as Marcus points out in "Laughing at Leviticus," to Old Testament injunctions concerning separation and purity. We have constructed and refined and maintained for centuries strict lines defining cultural categories, whether animal/human, male/female, homosexual/heterosexual, Christian/Judaic, Native American/Caucasian. The *Iliad*, to return to classical regulation, says the hero's authority is vested in the honor "dividing man from beast, hero from host." The hero is defined by exclusionary means, by separateness. Any attempt to break these boundaries has been perceived as an act of subversion, because boundaries are established upon the premise of superiority. Boundaries have to *do* with the preservation of power, with hierarchy.

So, while the postmodernist has opened the way with strokes of the pen, the heroine must struggle not only with the imaginings of her future self but with the hold of conventions that require subservience, conventions backed by the power to punish subversive acts. Before I begin to trace the heroine's new stories, therefore, I look closely at the old forms and their strictures against freedom.

1

Of Heroes and Heroines

Of arms and the man I sing.

—*Aeneid*, Virgil

How could a woman ever know what the heroes felt,
what spurred them to war and battle?

—H.D.

Three traditional forms of confinement for the would-be heroine are space, time, and genre. The first, space, instantly provides a contrast between the hero, whose god-given destiny most frequently impels a literal and meta-phoric quest journey, and the heroine, whose circumscribed state, also literal and metaphoric, inhibits adventure. The heroine, operating within narrow bounds, has difficulty claiming a public space, a stage from which to air her views.[1] Further, genderization also denies her the space of solitude in which to develop selfhood and to grow in ways that would in turn strengthen her contribution to the community. Finally, traditional gender views of woman's space lead to debilitating passivity; the fairy tale princess awaiting the rescuer from the outside world becomes the contemporary victim of agoraphobia. As gender roles become less rigid, the heroine's re-lation to space alters accordingly.

Space

The classical Hero's movement is Departure/Initiation/Return. Bruce Chatwin observes in *Songlines* that the trajectory of Ché Guevara's career follows the classical heroic path. He notes that by those criteria, the Cuban warrior never put a foot wrong. The classical Hero separates himself from the society in order to rescue it; in fact, he is uniquely qualified to save it, which is why he acts alone. The Hero's actions serve as a lofty example for all those (men) who necessarily fall short of emulating him. There is a dangerously thin line in the heroic code between the insuperable task of emulating a hero and, failing that, merely awaiting one.

The Hero undergoes perils and overleaps hurdles, acquiring prizes (the Grail, the Golden Fleece, the answer to a riddle) so that his society may be restored and redeemed. Thus, the Hero and his journey are ultimately incompatible with a democratic and individualistic view of human experience: the concern of the Hero is not self-fulfillment but a god-given destiny. (This is a complex point, however; a story of male development, or *Bildungsroman*, is assumed either to have already taken place or to be taking place simultaneously on another level while the Hero acts for the community.) In fact, the Hero is distinguished from merely being the central male protagonist by the fact that he receives the validation of the community and its rewards, including, frequently, the waiting heroine.

Regarding this, Elaine Showalter comments that even R. D. Laing, who has made important contributions to feminism, characterizes the psychotherapist as the guide in what Laing characterizes as "a transforming journey that is archetypally epic, heroic, and masculine, a psychic pilgrimage more exotic and perilous than the voyages of Ulysses or Kurtz."[2]

He makes this comment despite the fact that psychiatry, as a relatively recent discipline, boasts scores of illustrious women practitioners. If the journey, then, is archetypally male, the heroine, in contrast, is space-bound. Even when her confinement is metaphoric rather than actual, her destiny has been to mourn, to wait, to sacrifice, to support: Penelope, wily weaver, kept importunate suitors at bay for twenty years while, suitably tucked away "in quarters" among her women, she awaited the return of her husband; Andromache, widow of Hector, was simply allotted to one of the victors after the sack of Troy. They are heroines without capitalization. We can read Eurydice's failure to regain the world of light as a metaphor for women's stalled entry into the public space, the limelight. So, too, the traditional heroine confined in chateau, dungeon or tower, awaits liberation by an outside agent, the hero. Even the brave Heroine Alcestis, who offers her life in place of that of her weak-kneed husband, is only rescued from that final sacrifice by a superman, Hercules.[3] This is only another way of saying that the heroine's identity conventionally has been measured by her position in relation to a man.

Because the Hero projects an active line, moves in a linear progression, like Spenser's knight "pricking on the plaine,"[4] while the heroine's space is static, sexual difference inscribes itself in the flow of the narrative. Would Odysseus, a comic Hero, have been a Hero if he had, instead of a world to explore, the limited opportunity of one of Grace Paley's survivors? After all, the comic Hero traditionally voyages toward something new. Both Max Horkheimer and Theodor Adorno find Odysseus to be a self-defining, autonomous subject and the *Odyssey* a tale about the development of *human* subjectivity. Even with a comic hero such as Odysseus, the normative experience for coming into a self is held to be male, whether female development resembles it or not.

Confronting a vacancy where a fully realized, empowered Heroine should be standing, and also bearing in mind my original question—"What can women *do* in their lives, in the stories of their lives?"—I turn to the romantic heroine in literature. I will explore her impact on the problem of female doing, because she, more than any other single type of heroine, has impressed herself upon ordinary women's imagination. She also provides the greatest possible contrast with the Hero.[5]

Expectant, passive heroines, typified by the protagonists of many eighteenth and nineteenth century novels and operas, are unsalvageable stock characters who cannot carry women forward yet have proven surprisingly difficult to jettison. For the romantic heroine, destiny is romance, successful or unsuccessful. This heroine personifies the absence or presence of individual identity; she has great difficulty conceptualizing an active or individuated role for herself. The contemporary poet Gillian Clarke adapts an old Irish ballad:

> The minstrel boy to the war has gone,
> But the girl stays.
> To mind things. She must keep. And wait. And pass time.

Clarke's poem reflects a highly gendered Irish society, in which the female speaker longs to work with the men in the fields but can only bring their tea. From her domesticity, she stretches toward a broader world:

> In the airing cupboard you'll see
> a map, numbering and placing
> every towel, every sheet.
> I have charted all your needs.[6]

As Clarke introduces metaphors of travel and cartography, the speaker constructs a voyage of her own imagining.

The hero acts, while the heroine is acted upon. (In an interesting way, the two male protagonists in *Waiting for Godot* by Samuel Beckett take on the traditionally female role of waiting for deliverance by an outside agent.) The romantic heroine, even when situated at the novel's center, remains primarily a supporting character. Within the novel's framework she most frequently broadens her scope by attachment to a male character. Aristotle's *Nicomachean Ethics*, which states that animals and women cannot participate in the moral life, expresses the moral philosophy that rationalizes this conduct. The Renaissance was not so enlightened that it did not believe women's subordination to be based in "natural law" and therefore a "truth." As Milton had earlier counseled, "Man's life for God; hers for God in him." (What Milton preached, he practiced in his own family life!)

By this reasoning, women are excluded from rule-making, decision-making and equal participation in public affairs. How can they be heroes, or heroines? Romantic heroines reinforce and echo the economic and political disenfranchisement of women in the world outside literature. They can lend definition to a contemporary heroine no more than can the hero or anti-hero, as we shall see.

What are these stock women romantic characters permitted to do? Although Flaubert has been credited with inventing the modern novel, he did not invent a modern heroine. Flaubert may have been a realist, portraying the futility and frustration of sexual passion, but Emma Bovary lives as a romantic heroine. Her very excess and abandon mark her as such. She does not turn a retrospective and appraising eye upon her fate. She rushes headlong upon a course that ends in her suicide; she steals her husband's money to support her (unworthy) lover.

If, to return to our question, we ask what Emma Bovary can *do*, the answer is she can live and die for love. She can play out a romantic formula. We may urge sympathetically that all her senses are deprived of fulfillment: neither her husband Charles nor her drab, small town of Yonville can provide any sensory delight; her imagination is starved for beauty. She violates the codes of her stifling and tasteless milieu and commits adultery because her body represents the only means of extending her limits. It is the only apprehension of beauty she has.

We may even admire Emma's refusal to settle for a life without excitement, generosity or risk. This said, we nevertheless see in her the weakness which, in fairness, may be observed in all romantic heroines: she lacks scope. Although Flaubert may have said, "I *am* Emma Bovary," the fact remains that he is the writer, she the character. She does not become the author of her life. Judging from the verbal abuse with which Flaubert greeted the literary output of his own mistress, Louise Colet, he would hardly have granted Emma the control implied in authorship. As Andreas Huyssen points out, Sartre analyzed Flaubert's identification with Emma Bovary as part of a neurotic fantasy. Could Emma have said, in reverse, "Flaubert, c'est moi"? If so, presumably she would not have had to resort to suicide; Flaubert didn't.

Rebellion in Emma's case is individual, and remains personal; she does not receive any mandate from her society. Her aim is gratification. Significantly, she lacks the ethical or ideological motivation of many of her male counterparts, the heroes of nineteenth century novels. Her dying request for a mirror reflects supreme self-absorption and symbolizes the narcissism that has governed her actions. This narcissism prevents the reader from according her full tragic marks. As Henry James sums it up, Emma Bovary remains "too small a thing."

The death of each individual is not *per se* a tragedy, and even the deaths of romantic heroines may be insufficient to raise them to classical heights. Ben Jonson wrote, "The tragic hero will evoke admiration, not compassion." But it is compassion we feel for the cramped destinies of Emma Bovary, with her provincial circle and closed carriages, and Anna Karenina, who, symbolically, doesn't take the train out, only the way out. Love, the cause for which they die, is perceived by society as less worthy than duty or war; these heroines have misplaced their allegiance, made the ultimate sacrifice for an inappropriate end. The values of the romantic heroine and those of her society are at odds. The fact that she does not receive the validation of the community establishes her status as a lesser figure, and reveals the society's inacceptance of love as a heroic ideal. A private emotion, love confers nothing on the city-state.[7]

In the *Aeneid*, Dido remains true to her own moral code by committing suicide when her lover leaves her behind. Love does not make Dido the mover though she is Queen of Carthage, and Aeneas does not die for love of her. Rather Aeneas, prompted by duty, moves on from the space of love, the static, tarrying place, to found Rome; Dido is an obstacle to his heroic quest. Dido's plight complies with Nancy K. Miller's definition of the female space as the place from which the male plot is suspended. Despite the emotional intensity that Vergil grants Dido, she dies early; only Aeneas' plot developing through six more books, conforms to the heroic code. Though Dido may be a tragic heroine, she does not dictate the plot. It seems only when both male and female protagonists (Romeo and Juliet, Antony and Cleopatra, Tristan and Iseult) die for love, is the asymmetry of duty/love corrected, compelling the protagonists' sacrifices and the author's serious attention.[8]

If we turn to a character who does not die for love and who, as the creation of a liberated and strongly intellectual woman we might (naively) expect to be powerful, what do we find? Dorothea Brooke, the heroine of George Eliot's *Middlemarch*, is an admirable woman of noble ideals. She seeks fulfillment not in self-regard but in social purpose. She marries the pedant Casaubon under the mistaken impression that his scholarship is an intellectual enterprise of vast proportions.

When she becomes aware of the sterility of her husband's project, she transfers her quest for moral significance to the physician Lydgate and his public hospital scheme. Even those heroines who have intimations of a significant quest beyond the romantic confines of their feminine worlds do not know how to activate their quests except by attaching themselves to male figures.

Although Dorothea Brooke was created by an author who in her own life defied the rules imposed by her culture, Dorothea's search for a significant life is frustrated. She remains a traditional heroine. Her romantic destiny grants her a second chance: a happy ending. Casaubon dies and Dorothea marries Will Ladislaw. Despite Dorothea's moral sensibility, she must still conform to the romantic formula: die or marry. The first is not a happy ending; the second all too readily is assumed to be one. We may say of *Middlemarch* that it reflects a shift in sensibility, but its feminism lies not so much in the creation of new dimensions for its heroines as in the failure of its male characters to become heroes. *Middlemarch* is modern, that is, in its deconstruction of the hero and heroics. With Dorothea, we move away from the Aristotelian definition of tragedy to a much more modern sense of tragedy as waste, a sense reflected here in the social tragedy of genderization. Perhaps we should be looking at Lydgate when we search for change.

Part of the project of twentieth century women authors has been to disconnect women characters from the all-consuming and subsuming Love Plot. This stock plot has had a disastrous effect upon the imagination of adolescent girls, who, as they mature, discover the extreme difficulty of recreating in their own lives either the successful or unsuccessful dénouements of the literary romance. In the past, heroism for women has consisted for the most part in a struggle to wrest something for themselves within the illiberal definitions of their space.

Women's inability to carve out a place for themselves is intimately linked to their general condition of economic dependence. No one knew this better than women authors like Charlotte Brontë, George Eliot, or Jane Austen. Though Jane Austen has been faulted for taking no notice in her novels of the Napoleonic war that engaged her country while she wrote, she is far more than the miniaturist she is too often labelled. Her books, like those of Eliot and Brontë, confront a major issue: the emphatic connection between money and power, and women's distance from both.

Many critics of *Pride and Prejudice*, both male and female, have impugned Elizabeth Bennett as mercenary. Part of the appeal of Darcy's estate, Pemberley, however, is metaphoric; the huge prospect his property commands offers Elizabeth a sense of extension, of scope. Mansfield Park similarly attracts Austen's Fanny Price. Dorothea's beneficence waits upon her widowhood; she inherits money with which she can be a benefactor. Stendhal's eponymous heroine, Mina de Vanghel, can flee the stifling atmosphere of Königsburg and get to Paris by herself, because she is independently wealthy and can pay for the journey she believes will be the beginning of a new life. Though in fact Mina is caught by romantic destiny in the end of the novel, and dies for love, as romantic heroines are wont to do, her control over her funds enables her to exercise *choice*. We recall Emma Bovary's profligacy and her path to ruin.

The desire to transcend constraints of many sorts motivates such stock stage and film figures as the tom-boy, Shakespeare's cross-dressing Rosalind and Portia, or characters portrayed by actresses like Judy Garland, Marlene Dietrich, and Katharine Hepburn. Women cross over into male space, where they can enjoy an identity less restricted economically, sexually, and vocally. As we will see later, costuming provides unique opportunity for masking sexual identity.

Turning next in our consideration of space to the focus of solitude, defined here as the *space* around the self, we can sharpen our understanding of how literature differentiates heroes from heroines. An integral stage of male initiation rites is to remove the aspirant from the nurture of female society to a place of seclusion with other male members of the tribe, be it Greek gymnasium or African kraal.[9] Across geographical and cultural boundaries, the seclusion of the initiate is a prerequisite for the progress from boyhood to manhood.

The hero's condition is an active solitude. Is it a prerequisite for the heroine as well? Female characters' separation from the matrix of domesticity and connection is still largely relational; it remains personal and, for that reason, does not conduce to a position of leadership. For the female protagonist whose self-awareness still cannot be taken for granted, "surfacing," to use Margaret Atwood's word, may be all we can expect. This surfacing actually parallels the movement of a *Bildungsroman*, and a *Bildungsroman* always remains an individual's story.

Her solitariness, when it does exist, is often depicted as boredom, itself frequently a symptom of rage and isolation. The wives in Ibsen's *A Doll's House*, Evan Connell's *Mrs Bridge*, and Sue Kaufman's *The Diary of a Mad*

Housewife exemplify this unhappy solitude. Theirs is solitude without a quest, the depression and loneliness portrayed fictively in Marilyn French's *The Women's Room* and clinically in Maggie Scarf's *Unfinished Business*. So many proscriptions prevent women from attaining creative solitude that literary accounts of this struggle, such as Virginia Woolf's *A Room of One's Own*, Kate Chopin's "The Story of an Hour," and Charlotte Perkins Gilman's "The Yellow Wallpaper," are, sadly, still relevant. Women feel guilty for wanting solitude.

Furthermore, the social definition of women as primarily relational has been so internalized that the condition of solitude itself is interpreted differently by men and by women, as Miriam Greenspan points out in *A New Approach to Women and Therapy*: "The fear of being alone heads the list of female terrors. . . . Unlike men, who often think of being alone as a . . . prelude to adventure, women view aloneness as deprivation and abandonment. Aloneness and loneliness are seen as synonymous. . . . Solitude is a male virtue, a female affliction."[10] Thus, while some women feel guilty for desiring solitude, others feel rejected and depressed when solitude becomes their lot, because relation has been impressed upon them as the proper womanly mode. In either case, the relationship between women and solitude is problematic.

Contrasting hero and heroine, we see that whereas solitude is a given for the hero, women seeking solitude are seen as unnatural. The space of the woman, then, is not only static in contradistinction to the active line the hero pursues, but also does not function as the ground from which she can launch her heroinic adventure, the stage after survival, or "surfacing."[11]

Currently, a strong attempt is being made to validate a creative solitude for women, one of contemplation and the movement into subjectivity; May Sarton, Anita Desai, Gail Godwin, Anita Brookner, Annie Dillard and Mary Gordon have all written of the necessity of solitude both for their work and for their heroines' lives. Doris Lessing's heroine, Jane Somers, sighs when her niece moves into her apartment: "When Jill moves in here, my life will become shared. It is the end of lovely solitude. Oh, oh, oh, I can't bear it, I can't. Oh, how I do love being alone, the pleasures of solitariness. . . ."[12] Although in this particular novel the heroine comes to retract this view of solitude as precious, for the reader it represents an ongoing conflict: women, having only recently arrived at any feeling of entitlement to solitude, find it a hard-won gift to relinquish. Yet, if women are to be heroines of any sort, they need to have available to them the *lebensraum* that nurtures spiritual, intellectual, and creative selves, the amplitude of space that men and heroes have always claimed.

Curious contradictions are at work. As with so many gender-based distinctions, it is clear that female relatedness and male solitude are not equally prized modes of being by our culture. Men define even the kind of relatedness women may choose. In Charlotte Brontë's *Shirley*, the heroine exchanges the more customary romantic plot (male/female dyad) for a life in which relations and friends bring fulfillment. However, Brontë shows in the course of the novel that making this exchange without broad social acceptance of her choice simply martyrs the heroine.

The lesson, still true today, is that our society *values* males' lack of attachment, seeing it as a sign of maturity, while it perceives a female code of relational attachment as a sign of immaturity. Forging relation is seen as *not-production*; it is non-reimbursible, women's work.[13] The psychologist J. D. Broverman, working with other clinicians, found that the model of maturity for *both* sexes is male.[14] Women receive a confusing message: Society prizes the typically male lack of attachment and criticizes women's relational mode as 'immature' at the same time that it faults women who desire the detachment of some solitude.

Psychologist Jean Baker Miller, however, suggests that society as a whole would be better off if attachment were viewed as a strength rather than a weakness. The Hero, and patriarchal culture for the most part, still see it completely as a weakness. Since maturity is defined as a progress toward separation, the values of the heroine which endorse attachment render her a less valuable, less plausible contributor to the society, a less significant person than the Hero.

Here again, looking at this opposition of the values of attachment and non-attachment, as before with the opposed virtues, love and honor, we see a conflict arising from divergent male and female perceptions of how the self should relate to society. Appreciating the nature and extent of this conflict is crucial to any consideration of hero and heroine, because these antagonisms indicate a radical difference in values. This is not to imply that the self should, ideally, exist exclusively in relation to others. It should instead be individuated *and* socially connected; women and men need separation *and* intimacy. The heroine must alter her spatial relation to society, and hope to establish a model for both sexes.

Looking next at the relation between the heroine and Time, we note at the start that the heroine's tardy arrival in a contemporary scenario has distinct advantages. First, she does not have to disentangle herself from the heroic notions of virtue currently falling into general disrepute. Growing alienation of the individual from government and the rich from the poor, along with the exposure of venality in high places, has fueled this rejection of traditional heroic virtue. Second, the heroine can develop her own persona without regard to the anti-hero, a figure who arose because of the hero's failure but is himself an inadequate replacement for that character. Looking around her now for a quest that is meaningful today, the new heroine can search on her own, freed from these two crippling *dramatis personae*. Lastly, the heroine brings to her quest a different sense of Time, not linear but cyclical or myth-oriented, like that of many indigenous peoples. Appearing late, then, she escapes association with a failed code.

Time

The fact that any contemporary heroine enters the scene late certainly has a formative influence upon her typology; our age has a democratic and individualistic view of destiny, antipathetic to the traditional heroic view and to the epic that recounts the Hero's exploits. Moreover, postmodernism, part of the contemporary heroine's cultural background, is anti-elitist, and orients itself toward democratic art. Many conditions suggest that our culture is ready to validate an ordinary heroine.

In the modern world, a major breakdown of traditional thinking and beliefs about the hero occurred about the time of World War I, and with this breakdown, a now-familiar anti-hero emerged. As in the case of the terms hero and heroine, the term anti-hero is more complicated than first appears. The anti-hero is self-absorbed and marginalized, and is often a bumbler, of unremarkable physique and fragile psyche. Sometimes, intelligence creeps in as his substitute for valor.

The prominence of the anti-hero in literature reflects shifts in cultural attitudes other than the movement toward democracy and individualism. Thackeray's *A Novel Without A Hero* went from being the exception to being the rule. Our *zeitgeist*, faced with the possibility of nuclear warfare, harbors a deep suspicion of the "heroics" typified by abstract nouns such as *glory*, *honor*, *chivalry*, whereas honor or esteem is vital for the warrior-Hero and in the classics, gives him transcendence. Thus Hector, battling Achilles in the *Iliad*, entreats the gods to grant him not life, but a mighty deed, so he may not die ingloriously.

Hemingway's *A Farewell To Arms*, its title capturing the post-World War I disillusionment with war, addresses the hero's burden. It reaches back to classical times to respond to the Aeneid's resonant opening line, "Of Arms and the Man I sing." Martial abstractions that pertained to the notion of individual combat have been rendered hollow and obsolete by terrorism, missiles, bombers, submarines, tanks, flamethrowers, and tear gas.

Critics such as Seán O'Faoláin in *The Vanishing Hero: Studies in Novel-*

ists of the Twenties, Paul Fussell in *The Great War and Modern Memory*, and more recently, Modris Eksteins in *Rites of Spring: The Great War and the Birth of the Modern Age* document the actual passing of heroic language. Heroism with a capital *H* requires abstraction, as Nancy Hartsock observes. The language of male virtue became so closely identified with machismo, bravado, the inability to compromise, the undertaking of needlessly competitive or merely egotistical exploits, and the acceptance of the convention of boasting that regularly accompanies such exploits, that the discrepancy between the real experience of war and the abstract rhetoric that supposedly described it, grew insupportable. The film exposé of the Vietnam war, *Born on the Fourth of July*, treats this subject. Male rhetoric, military or political, carries within it risks of a combative, senseless, dehumanizing, atomizing future.

When we look, on the other hand, at anti-heroes, we see that the situation alters, but the plot still falters. The anti-hero, unfortunately, does not pit himself against heroism, but is, rather, at his worst, victimized, and at his best, ineffectual. Thus, both hero and anti-hero disqualify themselves as agents for change: the hero desires to restore the past order; the anti-hero is capable only of self-regard.

The death of the anti-hero Willy Loman is the suicide of a victim; but would he have ranked as a tragic hero if he had survived, and lived out his life in a long wallow of sameness? Or is he, as Susan Gubar said of Edith Wharton's Lily Bart, not a tragic figure but a societal fact? Willy Loman epitomizes the modern tragedy of waste we spoke of earlier. He marks the shift from hero-as-savior to non-hero, the character whose actions bring disgrace or downfall (in the salesman's case, to his family), the marginal destroyer.

Men, it seems, think in terms of the binary opposition of Hero and anti-hero because they are caught in outmoded definitions of manhood rooted in primitive models of physical strength, physical courage, and toughness. Like many of the oppositions established by a binary system of thought, this polarity leaves us with a Hobson's choice: the warrior Hero, active John Wayne; or the peace-loving anti-hero, passive Woody Allen.[15] Those are the two principal and equally unacceptable personae that men offer to society.

Now that we do not need hunters and hand-to-hand warriors, what will define manhood? The hero who lives by his sword, or dies upon it, cannot serve as the model for a mature society, yet we still retain the primitive idea of "baptism by fire." Our society has not accepted alternative models that relate manhood to a maturity valuing restraint, moderation, judiciousness, compassion. Try to list heroes characterized by such qualities in recent fiction and poetry; the paucity of such examples is distressing. Because male virtues are based on an obsolescent model, men are caught between the roles of hero and anti-hero and are apprehensive about securing a male identity at all. The new men's consciousness-raising groups, misogynistic and drum-beating, display a nostalgia for the heroic role. Where are male protagonists at some midpoint between these antithetical characters? Henry James' Strether in *The Ambassadors*, and many other Jamesian men, manifest the compassion and finely-tuned sensibilities usually attributed to women. But they are also unimpassioned and renunciatory and remain within intensely private lives. Neither heroes nor anti-heroes, they still fail to provide a paradigm for a contemporary heroine, if indeed any male character can.

Since the heroine, however, has traditionally been excluded from male education and male enterprise, she has escaped being schooled to be a Hero. The unlooked-for benefit of her exclusion may be that she can honor criteria of maturity different from the "manly" virtues. Such a notion brings extraordinary freedom. For example, in the light of the Heroic code we may read a random act of violence as a purposeful, justifiable event. But once we reject this code, we can see how male values transform violence and death into intoxication and ecstasy: ". . . [his] head was split open, and the coursing blood had stained his white beard. . . . The old man had fought well. . . . And so he had died a fitting death, in the wild turmoil of Life's hunt, where red huntsmen pursue red game through forests where Death and Desire are profoundly entwined. . . ." So writes the German novelist and World War I hero, Ernst Junger, in his novel of World War II *On the Marble Cliffs*.[16]

Certainly, the Heroic code informed the kamikaze pilots of World War II, and in fact the derivation of the code from classical times onward shows an undeviating romance with death. Robin Morgan argues that terrorism is a contemporary manifestation of heroics, and evaluating the justice of this remark, we remember our earlier definition of the Hero as a man with superlative, even transcendent *physical* courage. Nancy Hartsock reasons persuasively that heroism is the male answer to the meaninglessness of life in the face of mortality. Thus, she continues, Sarpedon in the *Iliad* asserts that "a man becomes a hero because he cannot be a god."[17] Yet, paradoxically, heroism and death are inextricably intertwined because the hero overreaches himself to gain immortality through honor and risks death as a matter of course. The hero thinks in supernal terms. In so doing, he loses touch with his community. As the hero aspires to be a god but cannot become one, so the ordinary man aspires to be a hero, but cannot become one. To hold out for the perfect, for the ideal, is to desert the imperfect reality of humanity.

In Carolyn See's recent novel, *Making History* (the title is meant to be read ironically), the male protagonist, Jerry, is driven mad by the ideal of perfection, the perfectability of life, his/story. His wife, Wynn, however reminds him that the American notion that nothing is so bad it can't be fixed leads to an impossible interpretation of the world of real human beings. That is her/story. Separation between ideal and real is a paramount difference between the traditional hero and the new ordinary heroine.

Yet, having abandoned the notion of the Heroic as risking and approving death, what conduct can we endorse for the heroine as its replacement? Can we say, for example, that the ability to survive or to endure is sufficient to characterize a heroine? For example, there were courageous and valiant women who settled the west, and whose stories are finally being recounted. The recent book *Body and Soul*, by Carolyn Coman and Judy Dater, profiles the lives of little-known, real-life women whose extraordinary endurance redefines for women what is heroic. Especially in the Third World but also among ethnic minorities in the Americas and Europe, women's lives are subject to a range of hardships which many feminists believe qualify these women as heroines. In this view, survival and endurance are enough. At this point, we need to assert the pluralism of feminism, the diversity of voices and definitions. Paula Gunn Allen, for instance, sees the endurance of Native American women as making them "spirit-warriors." Perhaps special traditions are required to give that endurance voice. Perhaps we should see endurance as resistance, elevated by the joy which punctuates Gunn's stories of austerity.

The vexing question of scope for the heroine, however, still hangs around the edges. Would Odysseus be a hero if he did not possess an extraordinarily agile intelligence engaged in the vast comedic experience of life? In endorsing the position that endurance and survival are the stuff of heroines, we risk the danger of abetting the long tradition of self-sacrifice and redemption through suffering in women's roles, in life and literature. But if we think of resistance, of "spirit-warriors," we may be able to circumvent that trap. The configuration of the heroine depends upon race, class, and gender, even within the confines of contemporary western culture. But we need not strive for a unitary voice to produce a heroine. Although the hero spoke with a unique voice, the ordinary heroine, like Anita Hill, like Nobel peace laureate Rigoberta Menchú, or the Navajo spokeswoman Roberta Blackgoat, has one among the many voices of diversity.[18]

Society is experiencing a quest for a quest; this, too, determines what women can do. And in those fortunate countries where survival is not *the* overwhelming problem, the new heroine can ask "How shall we live our lives?"or "What does our society want?" Angela Carter's novel *Love* looks back wistfully to the idealistic sixties, and asks, "Where now?" Susan Morgan argues in *Sisters in Time* that while the female leads of Victorian novels brought new values to their plots, the values of the Victorian male hero were already anachronistic. If we do not want force to be the instrument of international relations it now regularly is, if our quest is to save the environment, to provide adequate health care for our citizens, to rebuild a productive society, it is irrelevant to sing of arms and the man. The *Iliad*, the first of many great books of western literature to celebrate the honor to be won in warfare (though acknowledging the stupendous cost), offers no alternative definitions of heroism. As we reflect upon the epic past with skepticism and trepidation, we may see redefinition of protagonists and plots as a reprieve, even a last chance.

Our hopes for a new model for the heroine lies in the fact that she may have a better understanding of her life than the hero, for whom will is all. A post-romantic heroine does not have passively to await—or accept—a destiny-shaper; we can become shapers ourselves.

In the light of the failure of epic, tragic, or anti-heroic conduct to serve the contemporary heroine's conception of her life, the science fictions (in postmodernist language, meta-fictions) of Doris Lessing and Joanna Russ, or the fantasies of Angela Carter, can be read as fictional strategies undertaken to permit new realizations of feminine destiny. This involves a significant shift from the past of the epic, or the present of tragedy, to the future tense of fantasy. Time entered our discussion first when we asked what it means to live in the postmodernist world, to be alive at this very moment, to have a sense of life as fragmentary, a sense of genre as "anything goes." But there is a second sense of time operative here, the sense of time different genres offer. The Hero's tragedy is short-lived; in his present he faces and embraces death. This is why so many Heroes, like Macbeth and Othello, seem rash or impetuous.

Nancy Hartsock reminds us that the classical hero *as warrior* ceases to think of the future because he must stake everything on the success of the moment. The heroine, with a vision of change, has, by contrast, a futuristic sense of time. Like the postmodern artist and writer, the new heroine works without established rules, formulating in the present what needs to be done. Her actions are more improvisatory because she has not inherited the legacy of male goals: to win a princess, to be initiated into a fraternity, to defeat a mythical beast, to carve a glorious name for herself.

These distinctions bring us to yet another sense in which the heroine's relation to time differs from that of the hero. Though myth is commonly thought to be plot-directed, proceeding through linear time, in fact it can

be interpreted as occurring in cyclical time, relating incidents which, re-
peating themselves endlessly without a strict beginning, middle, and end,
can be entered from any point. Obviously the natural world is the prime
example of this time—seasons, days, hours—which is timeless. In her sear-
ing vision of an Armageddon between the sexes, Angela Carter's Tiresian
character reflects: "Oedipus. . . had a sensible desire to murder his father,
who dragged him from the womb in complicity with historicity. His father
wanted to send little Oedipus forward on a phallic projectory (onwards and
upwards!); . . . [wanted him] to turn his back on the timeless eternity of
interiority."[19] The "timeless eternity" which Carter contrasts to the Oedipal tragedy of sequential events is generally conceded to be feminine in its
mythical and cyclical view of time.[20]

Are there heroes whom time has not invalidated, or some whose qualities the heroine can emulate with profit? Where can she look for anteced-
ents? Not, without great selectivity as we have shown, to her own romantic
plot, though she might do worse than glance at the heroines of Stendhal,
the author singled out by Simone de Beauvoir as the most feminist of the
male novelists of the nineteenth century.

For the heroine in the making, though, two protagonists, the comic
hero and the humanitarian hero, possess qualities, and function in ways that
she may adapt. Let us look first at the more important of the two, the comic
hero. Comedy is pragmatic; it is about policy, not about extremity, which
dictates the epic or tragic hero's exploits. Extremes and the choices which
lead to them are not the new heroine's way; for this reason, she also rejects
the excesses of romantic heroines. Indeed, contemporary heroines perceive
such extremes as abnormal and extravagant, exceeding social necessity. Thus
women writers like Fay Weldon, Doris Lessing, and Angela Carter turn to
the mock-heroic, parodic.

Pragmatic comedy considers the good; once individual death is not an
exalted goal, we have space and time to explore ethical practices and codes
by which we can live. In his study comparing tragedy and comedy, Albert
Cook makes the provocative observation that supra-human aspiration is
incompatible with ethical behaviour in society. Comedy, unlike tragedy,
focuses on a broad social unit, at a minimum the family, more frequently
the society at large. Society is also the primary concern of the new heroine.
The lens of comedy, to which spectacle itself belongs, is a wide-angle lens;
it does not spotlight the individual, her honor, her fame. In this, comedy
fits the character of the contemporary heroine, who does not view her destiny as god-given, or herself as vastly differentiated from the group.

For our purposes, then, one of the most significant differences between tragedy and comedy lies in their models of character. First, the comic hero is, by convention, bourgeois, while the tragic hero is of important rank. From comedy, then, we can take an idea of a heroine not limited by class structure. Second, the tragic hero falls or dies, while the comic hero lives and succeeds. This means that, like the heroine, he looks to the future. He journeys toward the new. The contemporary heroine, who aims to improve society rather than to exercise individual will, to emphasize moral above physical courage, to stress the joyfulness of life rather than its death-wish, is prefigured by the comic hero.

The task that still faces her, however, is shaping her own social criticism. That is, the mode, but not the specific targets of male comedy and of its hero, is useful. In fact, comedy, especially satire, notoriously has made women its butt; the perennial theme of the battle of the sexes, as in *The Taming of the Shrew*, is reincarnated in Edward Albee's *Who's Afraid of Virginia Woolf?* Now that women are writing comedy and satire they are creating new images which offer women alternatives to stereotypic gender roles such as the shrew. To understand fully the powerful grip of gender identities and gender roles, we must see them as part of a much larger system which carries strict prohibitions against transgression—one that encodes taboos against incest, homoeroticism, miscegenation, even, as we have noted, against hybridization of creature/kinds. One means by which we express what is otherwise taboo is through comedy. Comedy *is* transgressive. Thus Toni Morrison, for example, explains the practice of blackface in minstrelsy as enabling what is taboo to be spoken, as a release from law and the punishment inflicted for speaking out. For women, circus, carnival, masquerade, those sub-genres of comedy which share an emphasis on the body and trespass across gender boundaries, are particularly useful for deconstructing gender definitions.[21] If the archetypal hero is essentially conservative, these comic modes in the hands of women enable the heroine to be essentially subversive.

What of the heroes closer to our own time, a hero with a lower case *h*? How does a heroine stand in relation to great-hearted humanitarian heroes like Pierre of *War and Peace*, to the 'good men' of Jane Austen: Edmund Bertram, Knightly, and Wentworth? The goals of these heroes resemble in some ways those of the contemporary heroine, particularly in the fact that both visualize a self in its working relation to society. However, important caveats prevent the heroine from modelling herself faithfully upon them. First, in this case as in all others, there is the fact that genderization is going on. Humanism is patriarchal humanism. Speaking of Tolstoi's Pierre, what of his great love, his wife, Natasha? First a flirtatious, inarticulate girl, then a brood-mare who represents mystical Mother Russia, the Earth-Mother. The humanitarianism of these heroes does not preclude paternalistic thinking; the women in their stories still live in a male world and are identified as mothers, sister, sweethearts, daughters.

Moreover, these benevolent heroes are in general in a position to bestow money and employment, whereas the benevolent heroine takes calves' foot jelly to the sick! (And even then she is ridiculed for charitable works, as Dickens savages Mrs. Jellyby in *Bleak House*, depicting her family as pitifully neglected, sacrificed to the ego that drives her public spirit.) Even when the benevolent heroine is not attacked, she is ignored, says Susan Porter. Both the benefactor and the indigent women who are assisted have been disregarded by a "historiography that has perpetuated both male orientation and class bias."[22]

The second reason these benevolent male characters are not finally acceptable to the new heroine inheres in the concept of benevolence itself. Think, for example, of the innumerable *anonymous* benefactors in the novels of Dickens: Pip's benefactor in *Great Expectations* or Esther's benefactor in *Bleak House*. Some of them, like the Cheeryble brothers, even go so far as to operate in disguise. They operate behind the scenes because Dickens believes they must unobtrusively slip good into a capitalistic, class-ridden society, presented as cruel and implacable. Jean Valjean in Hugo's *Les Misérables* is an outstanding example of the indictment of such a society against which the benevolent hero himself can do relatively little. Benevolence can only patch up social inequity; it has never succeeded in making itself unnecessary.

Reaganomics has divided the United States into two differentiated nations: rich and poor, the same division that characterized Victorian industrial England, as Disraeli noted. We have lived through the failure of the Enlightenment to bring about its promised progress based on belief in rationality, an inviolable "truth," science, a stable self. Quite the contrary, we have witnessed the Holocaust and Hiroshima; our times are encapsulated in a Theater of the Absurd, a Theater of Cruelty, drawing the attention of cultural interpreters like Theodor Adorno. In the face of the evidence, the contemporary heroine realizes that benevolence fails; it remains a worthy personal effort, but it is not an effective policy. Furthermore, even though these humanitarian heroes are benevolent, they retain power, they act as *dei ex machina*.

So a contemporary heroine may require a "brave new world" *she* imagines and defines. As the Chinese poet Bao Dei wisely wrote:

in fact what is hard to imagine
is not darkness but dawn.[23]

The heroine may stand for positive values—relation, flexibility, compassion, mediation—unacceptable to the inherited views of tragic and epic heroes and unavailable to anti-heroes too disabled to be a moral voice. (In fact, the heroine's search actually proceeds in the very circumstances that gave rise to the anti-hero.)

What remains in our day for the heroine is the truly valorous task of finding a moral explanation and a moral significance within contemporary disbelief. This is the "quest for a quest" mentioned earlier. A heroine, distinct from hero or anti-hero, may be propelled by a vision, equally intense and committed to change, of opening the society to feminist values. She has different ways of knowing, different ways of arriving at moral judgments, different ontological perceptions. Both because she is new, and because she is different, she just may be the only protagonist left standing to whom the society can look.

Genre

Revisionist work by feminists is now under way in many disciplines, including law and medicine. For our purposes, the new literary genres which women are creating illuminate the strong connection between gender and genre, and the consequent necessity for women to create new forms, new structures, to express their experience and their different sense of the self and its best relation to society.[24] Here, in contemporary literary innovation, postmodernism's intermixing of genres and levels of language, with its predilection for magic realism and fantasy, meet feminist concerns.

There is a comic irony in the fact that the essentialist concept of women, (that there is *a* woman's "nature," and that that nature is unstable) can be turned to our advantage. What is held against us, a disposition or openness to change, has enabled us to create new worlds to inhabit, zones of our own. Literature becomes a tool of resistance. Genres conceived as masculinist can be broken apart, innovatively shaped to new perceptions, as the old ones were originally shaped to relate male experience.

The story of women's development is circular; therefore, structurally as well as substantively, male texts with a linear quest characteristic of the older sense of narrative fail to authenticate women's experience. Women's own development, characterized as interrupted, parenthetical, and marked by paradox, has required experimentation with literary forms in which to locate difference. That is, women do not foresee acquiring subjectivity by replacing heroes with heroines within a male epic or tragedy, with acts of physical bravery as milestones, taking place in time which is successional. But rejection of this model is a result of more than a gendered position. It stems as much from *both* sexes calling into question criteria of authenticity as from women's historical exclusion from this world. In our modern world neither women *nor* men find emotional resolution in large-scale, ideal figures functioning in coherent stories held together "by war and murder and homicide and the heroic deeds which accrue to them," as Christa Wolf phrases it.[25]

Coherent stories simply do not correspond to our experience of life. Postmodernism actually lends feminist experience unofficial credence. Moreover, an improvised form is suitable for a heroine who is herself improvisatory. Joanna Russ suggests a replacement of the organization of the heroic epic by a lyric organization: "the organization of discrete elements . . . around an unspoken or thematic or emotional center . . . its principal of connection is associative."[26]

Such a style, as it unfolds in the prose of Dorothy Richardson, Virginia Woolf, James Joyce or Alain Fournier, among many others, corresponds to psychological processes of memory, understanding, and knowing. These writers employ a temporal sense based on Henri Bergson's perception of time as having psychologically individuated duration. A lyric organization finds the device of stream-of-consciousness or interior monologue congenial; the purportedly factual march of events is superceded in lyric by the epiphanies of individual interpretation.

Constellated or clustered time and perception, emblematized in the staccato register and idiosyncratic typography of T. S Eliot's *The Wasteland*, replaces linear time. This is not, of course, a feminist innovation but a modernist one. Yet, viewing the richness of feminist writing during the past several decades, Molly Hite claims that the innovations in narrative form found recently in feminist writing are more daring than even postmodernist experimentation.[27]

Such comparison is overstated, but there is no doubt that form in feminist writing has been as avant-garde as its content has been anti-establishment. This distresses many readers who see plot as the spine of fiction, the page-turner. But the fact is that many postmodern novels, feminist and not, do not rely heavily on plot and employ techniques which belong more characteristically to poetry.

In general, modern and postmodern considerations of genre inevitably impinge upon considerations of time as flux and space as interiority. At these two points, aesthetic concerns and the perception and presentation of "feminine nature" intersect. As Mary Russo points out, Mikhail Bakhtin has defined the female aesthetic in *Rabelais and His World* as that of a grotesque body, which is "open, protruding, extended, secreting," in opposition to the classical male body, which is "monumental, static, closed, and sleek." Woman is, in other words, "process and change," abhorrent to classical aesthetics which desired a finished idealization of the material body.[28] Since the idea of the hero originated for us in classical civilization, it is no wonder that the male is, in both narrative and visual art, the figure of perfection. Walter Pater ranks masculine aesthetics as superior to feminine aesthetics precisely because he holds this same view of their difference. Accordingly, the male aesthetic is: "the spirit of construction as opposed to what is literally incoherent or ready to fall to pieces, and in opposition to what is hysteric or works at random, [it is] the maintenance of a standard."[29]

This difference has far-reaching implications because commentators like Bakhtin and Pater identify women with an aesthetic which is disruptive and imperfect, and therefore inferior. We need to ask whose truth informs this aesthetic ranking of the sexes, even if, for the sake of argument, we grant the simplistic idea of a "feminine nature." Aesthetics, too, is gendered.

Is being fixed and finished—an unchanging 'standard' of aesthetics—a code we *wish* to endorse? It implies that art corrects the mutability and imperfections of life, and life is left to contain them. Pater's definition of a female aesthetic shows why the heroine is not valued enough to be accepted as hero, but on the other hand, Pater's "perfection," his aesthetic idealization of the male, reveals at the same time why a heroine wouldn't *want* to be the hero. Is not one of the hero's flaws that he is flawless? Can art exclude the ugly or the changeful without removing itself from humanity? Simply, Pater's description of ideal form resembles strongly the description of the heroic character—resistant to change and aspiring to the god-like. On the other hand, Pater's aesthetic derogation of the female indicates an essentialist view of women. If women are viewed as essentially "unstable" (Pater's word), if that is their nature, then hysteria is the pathology toward which they will 'naturally' incline, the predictable outcome of their condition of being. Even the name of the illness, *hysteria*, derives from the Greek root for womb, *hystera*.

When we juxtapose Pater's *aesthetic* analysis with Elaine Showalter's analysis of hysteria, perceived and treated in the nineteenth century as a woman's disease, we see the convergence of aesthetic judgement and medical judgment in a common denigration of what is assumed to be female. Showalter reports that hysteria's "fits, fainting, vomiting, choking, sobbing, laughing, paralysis and the rapid passage from one to another suggested the lability and capriciousness traditionally associated with the feminine *nature*" (emphasis added).[30]

Not until shell-shocked male soldiers returned home after World War I was the idea that hysteria was a gender-specific malady gradually laid to rest. In fact, such a view was used to justify the reality of women's medical repression in the nineteenth century, as substantial documentation attests.[31]

Michel Foucault sees the pseudoscientific nineteenth century theoreticians, particularly its sexologists, as suppressing women's social realities. In his own *History of Sexuality*, he terms this the "medicalization of the anomalous." Caroll Smith-Rosenberg believes that hysteria in women, which is a kind of social disruption, erupts to challenge rigid controls placed upon women's sexuality. The symptoms that signal hysteria can perhaps be understood as the dramatic extrusion of women's social reality, the perception of them as anomalous and requiring control, unstable of nature. The dichotomy important to mark, then, is between male fixity and feminine flux.[32]

Both the aesthetic judgment demeaning women and the essentialist and reductive concept of a "female nature" are being reinterpreted more positively by feminist thinkers. Thus in her recent *Subject to Change: Reading Feminist Writing*, Nancy K. Miller argues that the very notion of process is built into feminist thought, itself always evolving. Reflecting the same idea, Rachel Blau Du Plessis entitles one of her books *Writing Beyond the Ending: Narrative Strategies of Twentieth Century Women Writers*. Writing is viewed as process, as are women themselves.

The constructive consequence these critics foresee is that when new artistic structures express as much human experience as the heroic narrative, tragic or epic, women will have a place to write and to act. For example, the feminist visual artist Nancy Spero incorporates into her collages the printing technique of repetition (that is, her collages are arranged not just spatially but temporally, the same design elements recurring at intervals), making the whole composition into a kind of theme and variation, theme and variation. Her conception emphasizes flux, suggestive of cyclical, natural time, like mythical time. She interposes mythical female figures among contemporary ones: Heroines from the past, ordinary heroines from the present. Her collages flow on, and may be entered by the viewer at many different points. (Indeed, the collage, like the quilt, may be peculiarly expressive of how many women view their experience, since both are composed of overlapping, unboundaried, elements.)

Miller's book documents a resistance to closure in feminist writing which I read as antithetical to the traditional narrative of the hero, its unitary voice, its conservative values. Feminists have had to change prevailing definitions of genre in order to enter a world created for and judged by men, and recounting their actions. As recently as 1975, the Homeric scholar James Redfield contended in *Nature and Culture* that the Homeric world view embodies mature understanding of *our* world more than any other text.

This glorification of war in the postmodern world? And is there presently *any* unified world view? This judgment in a multicultural world? The Homeric world celebrates heroes and their deeds. The doctrine of universalism, contained here in Redfield's "*our* world," doesn't recognize the infinite differences of which the world is composed; it subsumes difference, whether of gender, race, or class. To achieve unity is necessarily to repress difference, often violently.

We can see literary corollaries to the idea of woman as adaptable, as a plastic medium, in the fictional flow of Ursula Le Guin, whose fantasies, combining fiction, poetry, journal and illustration, correspond to no traditional genre; in Gertrude Stein's "Somagrams," as Catharine Stimpson has dubbed them; Alice Walker's *The Temple of My Familiar*, the novel as feminine myth; Monique Wittig's *Les Guérillères* (which, drawing on the drama of the Amazons, defies categorization); or Jeanette Winterson's fable, *Sexing the Cherry*.

The most striking example of such stylistic innovation in the service of feminist representation is Julia Kristeva's "Stabat Mater." Each page of this work presents graphically first her personal account of the experience of childbirth, both pain and joy, and then the official Christian doctrine of maternity (the Suffering Mother, or Stabat Mater) and its absorption of femininity. In this way, Kristeva simultaneously develops and juxtaposes an existential account and an historical analysis; and the first, personal account, disrupts the linear progression of the second. Kristeva claims this poetic language is transformative, dividing and multiplying "the truth."

What the foregoing strongly suggests about genre is that the expression of women's values, the feminist desire for changes which will implement those values, together with the flexibility of women's nature itself, generate new literary structures. Although the identification of woman with process may have led to the stereotype of woman as fickle or even hysterical, we still should take it as a hopeful sign that women are open, perhaps predisposed, to change. The improvement of society depends upon sweeping change, and the mandate of the contemporary heroine is to be an agent for change.

Our heroines, then, belong to comedy in its largest sense, that of being profoundly committed to the human world and its betterment, to making it, in Dante's phrase describing the arena of comedy itself, "pleasant, prosperous, and desirable." Before any of that can happen, women have to become subjects of their stories, stories silenced and warped by past gender roles and gender hierarchy. Literature shows us how and where we are now in the process of inventing ourselves. Looking next at selected contemporary novels, we will see how women move through their lives, through their scripts, through what I term Woman/Space.

2

Woman/Space

Time and Space are Real Beings
Time is a Man Space is a Woman

—William Blake

But the role of pastoral heroine
Is not permanent, Jack. We want to get back to the meeting.
—"Two," *Pro Femina*, Carolyn Kizer

Woman is space-defined in two perceptual modes: the biological and the social. Biologically, she contains the space of sexual reception, the womb-space. As the grower of seed, the source of life, she is, like "Mother Earth," receiver of the seed. Moreover, woman's sexuality does not reside in an extruding sexual organ but in a place of entry. Thus the female body signifies interiority in the biological definition of woman/space. As poet Lucille Clifton writes: "i entered the earth in / a woman jar."

Socially, space also shapes a woman's definition, her gendered sense of her identity. Women are projected into a domestic space, which is again an interior space, a space which contains the container, and within which the activities of the household are enacted. Sandra Lee Bartky, in an essay, "Foucault, Femininity and Patriarchy" cites remarkable evidence of this relation of women to space:

> In an extraordinary series of over two thousand photographs, many candid shots taken in the street, the German photographer Marianne Wex has documented differences in typical masculine and feminine body pos-

ture. Women sit waiting for trains with arms close to the body, hands folded together in their laps, toes pointing straight ahead or turned inward, and legs pressed together . . . Men on the other hand, expand into the available space; they sit with legs far apart and arms flung out at some distance from the body. Most common in these sitting male figures is what Wex calls the "proffering position," the men sit with legs thrown wide apart, crotch visible, feet pointing outward, often with an arm and casually dangling hand resting comfortably on an open, spread thigh.[1]

Although both woman as earth-goddess, whose function is fertility, the space of germination, the principal aspect of the biological definition of woman/space, and her antithesis, woman as "angel in the house," spiritualized love in the social, gendered definition, seem at first glance to designate roles equal to if not privileged over man's, in fact both positions impose severe and damaging constriction and isolation. Mary Daly remarks, "The journey of woman becoming is breaking through the maze—springing into free space, which is an a-mazing process."

This role constriction profoundly affects narrative conventions and, through these, general cultural attitudes. Teresa de Lauretis argues in "Desire in Narrative" that implicit in narrative structure itself is the establishment of polarities, one of which is sexual difference, and that the movement of narrative discourse "specifies and even produces the masculine position as mythical obstacle, or simply, the space in which movement occurs."[2]

She posits that space, the female plot-space, presents a boundary through which a character, the male linear hero, moves. For example, freeing an imprisoned heroine becomes the hero's quest (as in the fairy tale *Briar Rose* where the flower is guarded by thorns from its de-flowering). Freeing the body from its guarded and inaccessible position becomes a synecdoche for the capture of the woman's secret. Here once again we see narrative resolution for the woman as either marriage or death; when the Prince takes Beauty for his bride, the story effects closure, as does the story of Bluebeard when he kills his wives one by one upon the fulfillment of his desire.

Moreover, although the male body is represented as capable of individual acts of violence and destruction, our culture does not extrapolate from this an ineluctable moral destiny for men. For women, the equation of biology with destiny is not individual, but collective and generic.

Wendy Lesser, commenting on the biological destiny of women relates it to male fears:

Melville's odd story ["The Paradise of Bachelors and the Tartarus of Maids"] is in part about the degree to which women are imprisoned by their biology. . . This story is also about men's fear of women's bodies, their terror of being lost and enclosed in that deep gorge. The profound desire manifested in the Oedipus complex is the other side of a profound fear—that a man *will* have to reunite with his mother, go back down into the womb from which he came.[3]

The biological definition of woman/space, sexist as it is, promotes highly ambivalent emotions in men. The character of the "good mother" is no more powerful than, and is but one step away from, that of the wicked step-mother. Observing this ambivalence toward women, Mary Daly in *Gyn/Ecology* maintains: "Within a culture possessed by the myth of feminine evil, the naming, describing, and theorizing about good and evil has constitued a maze/haze of deception."[4] The 'bowers' in Edmund Spenser's Renaissance allegory, *The Faerie Queene*, typify this mazy place, at once a place of de-lightful promise and a place of sexual threat.

The difficulties women experience today shedding both the sexual and the social definitions of woman/space may be gauged by the prevalence of anorexia nervosa/bulimia and agoraphobia—the respective pathologies of these social definitions—among women today. The widespread existence of these pathologies indicates how injurious our cultural assignments are.

The anorectic woman, challenging the biological definition, attempts to minimize the space her own body displaces by denying it food. This ef-fort, which results not only in be-*littling* her, but often in amenorrhea, can produce, then, a physical denial of her sexuality. She not only eliminates her womanly appearance, appearing boyish or at most, girlish in her out-lines, but may render herself truly incapable of procreation.

Many feminist theorists (Elaine Showalter and Noelle Caskey, for ex-ample) have pointed out that anorexia may represent a desire not to desire, to suppress the sexuality of the body and attain a more spiritual condition. For this reason, it has been termed "Holy Anorexia" by Caroline Bynum. In the lives of the saints the desire to transcend the flesh seems historically to have taken the form of flagellation in men and of fasting in women. Both may be forms of self-punishment for experiencing desire. There is also a non-spiritual and gendered self-denial effected by anorexia: the daughter, brought up to embrace a sacrificial role in human dynamics, goes to the length of literally effacing herself.

Lastly, in any consideration of anorexia today, we must remember our legacy of Victorian literary heroines, who are typically weak, hungry, deli-cate, often sick.[5] There are, of course, physiological and biomedical com-ponents to these eating disorders but they do not obviate the necessity to probe the psychological maladjustments of women to the demands of their acculturation.

The pathological extreme of the gender definition of woman/space is

agoraphobia, the disease in which the woman so internalizes the social definition of her limited space that she becomes literally unable to leave it. The
world outside looms as threatening and unsafe. Entering that world neces-
sitates taking leave of a familiar territory in which she is centered and centralized to enter a realm where she has little cultural identification.

Departure, then, requires establishing her autonomy, and going psychologically unprotected. She leaves the patriarchal protectorate, but suffers marginality. Thus the widespread contemporary search on the part of
both sexes for "roots" in a generally mobile and immigrant-based America
is particularly difficult for women, much of whose history has never been
recorded. The flood tide of recent biographies about women testifies to
women's search for lives which can guide them through the strangeness of
male history that certainly was never *Herland*, Charlotte Perkins Gilman's
feminist utopia.

Both anorexia and agoraphobia are predominantly women's diseases.
The Darwinian psychiatrists of the nineteenth century viewed women's
emotional illnesses (especially hysteria, neurasthenia, and anorexia) as out-
growths of women's new freedom and independence. Their solution was
for women to retreat, to take cures, rests, milk baths, to eat special soothing
diets, not to read (!) or get excited. Though the treatments were faulty, bi-
ased, even cruel, and based as much upon premises of women's moral and
intellectual inferiority as upon ignorance of what was to become the science of psychopharmacology, we must still look to issues of freedom and
independence to account for many of the same symptoms today.[6]

Consideration of six contemporary novels and their female protagonists will indicate how the dynamics of spatial definition work in fiction,
and how freedom and constraint operate to define the women in the novels, and reflect metonymically the current social status of women.

Fiction is especially appropriate as a means of understanding woman/
space, because novel reading, and to some degree even novel writing, have
traditionally been viewed as a woman's province, inhabited by Hawthorne's
"damned horde of scribbling women."[7]

The novels to be discussed (*The Good Mother* by Sue Miller, *Ironweed*
by William Kennedy, *A Fairly Good Time* by Mavis Gallant, *Illumination Night*
by Alice Hoffman, *Housekeeping* by Marilynne Robinson, and *Nights at the
Circus* by Angela Carter) represent a progression upward and outward from
the womb-defined maternal pathos of *The Good Mother* to the space-defy-
ing flights of the aerialiste in *Nights at the Circus*.

The title of the first novel, *The Good Mother*, by Sue Miller, resonates
with the collective historical charge of the good mothers so prevalent in

religion and mythology, the Great Mother Demeter, to take an obvious example. The novel turns on the axis of a confrontation between erotic and maternal love; the resolution occurs through the mother's self-abnegation, thus keeping it strikingly close to the resolutions of older sentimental novels such as *Stella Dallas*, though the central character in Miller's novel, the divorced Anna Dunlap, is updated with a Cambridge "pad" and an emancipated dress code.

The dénouement tells us that motherhood remains the only sanctioned outlet for women's sexuality, now as for Anna Karenina. The narrative arranges itself unselfconsciously and unconditionally around Anna Dunlap's supervening concern for her daughter; there is never a point in *The Good Mother* in which the title is used ironically, its burden of connotations acknowledged. Rather, the bogeywoman of the "bad mother" stalks the book.[8]

As the novel opens, mother and daughter are spending a few weeks alone together in the country before moving to the new apartment necessitated by the divorce. We learn the child's name, Molly, immediately; we learn the name of the ex-husband, the name of the town in which they've rented a cottage. But we don't learn Anna's name when the book commences; rather, her identity is established through the relentless series of "Mom's" with which the child's conversation is peppered. In fact, we don't learn Anna's name until the conclusion of the chapter. It is almost as if her name were superogatory information: we know her as "the good mother," the function subsuming the name.

Likewise, motherhood makes her body invisible, displacing her own desires with her concern for her child. As Jessica Benjamin notes about the maternal female body, the woman is either "mother" or "other": "The mother's sexual feelings, with their threat of selfishness, passion and uncontrollability, are a disturbing possibility that even psychoanalysts would relegate to the 'unnatural.'"[9]

Furthermore, though Anna Dunlap has left her husband, which might tempt us to see her as initiatory and self-propelled, the new context of her divorced life is still shaped by motherhood—mother and daughter share food, outings, conversation, companionship. Indeed, at the outset of the book, Molly, three years old, is her mother's *sole* companion, and the reader is left in no doubt that Anna arranged this, wanted this. Barely emerged from the womb-space, Molly is now the epicenter of the gender space.

In an incident which occurs near the book's beginning, Anna, who requires a notary's signature for some divorce papers, chases one down on the outskirts of the town—a queer recluse, harboring a large assortment of stray cats. While she goes inside to obtain his signature, Anna leaves three-year-old Molly asleep in the car. The situation is extremely tense for the mother—the man is censorious, she's arguing, at the point of tears, against a deadline for the return of the papers—and when she finally gets back to the car, she finds Molly distraught. The child has been attacked and clawed by the notary's undomesticated cats. What Anna is doing for her own well-being (leaving a loveless relationship, obtaining a divorce) is rigged by the author to be the direct cause of injury to her child. Dunlap believes she is not "strong enough, good enough to do this alone."[10] From the beginning, then, the notion of sacrifice defines the mother who struggles to 'deserve' the child.

After Anna moves with Molly to Cambridge, she begins a new relationship with a lover, who is described rapturously as both fulfilling for her and warm and understanding toward the child. Notwithstanding this, when Anna is threatened by her ex-husband and his second wife with a custody suit because of this lover, she relinquishes him and hence her own desires, in order not to jeopardize the case. It is clear to the reader that erotic desire without procreation is inimical to the gender definition of woman/space, or to phrase it more precisely, that non-reproductive sexuality requires punitive treatment. The cultural convention of dichotomizing reproduction and eroticism makes the problem of resexualizing the persona of the mother, any mother, particularly difficult. (In our culture, we can never forget the unique mother, the Virgin Mary, who emblematizes an absolute separation of function.)

Anna loses custody despite her sacrifice, and when Molly's father and his second wife move the child to another city, Anna immediately moves too; she gives up her job, her apartment, her friends, to move alone to a strange city. She chooses an apartment whose best qualification is that it is near Molly. In fact, following her daughter she enacts the subordinate role which ordains that wives traditionally follow husbands. One relational tyranny has merely replaced another; Anna is hostage to her child.

Not only does Anna finally relinquish her lover, but when they are still together he taxes her with the complete absence of any passion for her work; she makes clear to him that she lives in a totally 'relational' mode, and that work does not involve, for her as for him, a passionate relation. Though each brings intensity to their mutual relationship, only the male brings the same intensity to his work. Her 'relational mode' means that she is 'good' (nurturant) with the rats in the laboratory where she holds a routine job, stroking and feeding them, handling them in soothing ways so they don't bite or get excited. By contrast, his work is creative: he is a painter.

When Anna gives up her lover, then, we witness a betrayal within the sphere she claims as most important, as central to her nature, the relational sphere. Her daughter is the only passion of her life. This has its basis in cultural tradition firmly enough established that feminist theorist Julia Kristeva takes both Freud and Lacan to task ("Des Chinoises") for repressing the figure of the mother who has sexual pleasure. In *The Good Mother* the limited expression of female sexuality is safely restored to the womb.

The author places in an (unnecessarily) uncompromising and melodramatic opposition the duality of the woman as desiring, erotic, (the subject organizing the field of vision) and the woman as biologically determined (motherhood, the object of desire). But of course melodrama itself is a genre heavily populated by women characters, since it requires a vulnerable central figure, a potential victim. Albeit the absence here is that of the child and not the lover, *The Good Mother*, which purports to bring the reader a contemporary radical insight into the understanding of women's nature through pitting maternal against erotic love, still concludes on the old note of the pathos of absence. The pathos of absence which pervades the book is what makes it highly reminiscent of the women's films known as "the weepies." And indeed, at the finish, the "good mother" has lost husband, lover, and child in a melodramatic sweep.

Thus, though Anna Dunlap in the course of events moves from marriage to a divorce of her own seeking, though she moves from one city to another, these moves do not engender a self-directed life; she does not succeed in projecting herself into a spatial relation of subjectivity. Her moves do not correspond to the stages of a novel of male development.

Ironweed by William Kennedy has a male protagonist, Francis or "Franny" Phelan for its central character, but also employs an important woman character, Helen, who is relevant to our consideration of woman/space. The novel is enacted within a context of flop houses, tent cities, bars, park benches. If we look at the space through which Helen moves, it is largely *exterior* space, because her poverty leaves her homeless, makes her an itinerant. (Franny and Helen's circular route around the city cannot fail to recall the rings of *The Inferno*.) It seems a far remove from the enclosure of domesticity. Unmarried and childless, she lives roughly, among men, and without the security of the next meal.

But whereas Franny, her ex-lover and male counterpart, out of a profound sense of guilt toward his family, has *chosen* not to return to the fixed abode in which his former wife and his son still live, Helen's peregrinations are reflexive, a response to the magnetic attraction that Franny exerts upon her. Her passage through the book is grim and *involuntary*. Helen, unlike Franny, also a down-and-outer, has no subjectivity, does not even possess a surname, lives the life of a vagrant, alcoholic, sick, and penniless.

Through the hardships of her unwished-for circumambient days, Helen retains a vision of an earlier domestic interlude with Franny. His emotional instability, his religious scruples about divorce, his bouts with drunkenness, have not tarnished her sentimental memory of their shared domestic space: "We had a beautiful apartment up on Hamilton Street. We had all the dishes anybody'd ever need. We had a sofa and a big bed, and sheets and pillow cases . . . We had flowerpots full of geraniums that we kept alive all winter long . . . And we had an icebox crammed full of food . . . It was Haviland china, the very best you could buy . . . solid mahogany chairs . . . my beautiful upright piano."[11] We learn, in fact, that this idyll lasted only a few months, perhaps only six weeks, before Franny drank up all their money.

A former radio singer, Helen is persuaded in her present debilitated state to give an impromptu performance in a bar in which she, Franny, and some friends are drinking. The bar, tellingly, is called "The Gilded Cage."[12] The direct relation between the motif of imprisonment and the male gaze is evident in the lines of her song, "And her beauty was sold / For an old man's gold" from "She's Only a Bird in a Gilded Cage." Helen, choosing songs with sentimental lyrics—"He's My Pal," "My Man"—possesses what the author describes as a "lifelong devotion to forlorn love," or, one might say, to the inside of a gilded cage. Yearning for their old apartment, keeping in her carryall old newspaper clippings about Franny's baseball stardom as well as his old penknife, his old razor, she is always prepared to recommence their former life.

This woman, wandering around the anonymous city is nearly anonymous herself. She, like Anna Dunlap, is surrounded by the pathos of absence. She dies alone with her mementos in a rented hotel room. Her swelling abdomen, the result of a cancerous growth, is a false, fatal pregnancy. Though Helen is granted moments of beauty, even transcendence, she is an almost final diminishment of her queenly name.

The female character on her own, like baggage left behind in a rented room, is a familiar one in fiction. In the novels of Jean Rhys, for instance, the very titles echo displacement: *Good Morning, Midnight*, and *After Leaving Mr. Mackenzie*. Rhys' psychological fictions depict with chilling clarity the hapless fate of women untrained to support themselves in the larger society. Her women move with such lethargy and are so victimized, willless and helpless, that they seem hardly to move at all.

A Fairly Good Time by Mavis Gallant belongs to this category of novels about abandoned women. A young female protagonist, deserted by her husband, traipses across Paris ineffectually trying to make sense of her singleness. As an American, the strangeness of her new position accentuated, she is doubly an outsider. An inordinate amount of the description in this novel is devoted to dwelling places, apartments and houses (containers). Shirley,

Gallant's protagonist, becomes a frequent guest in other people's apartments and houses, enacting the same destiny that prompted Alicia Borinsky to describe Jean Rhys as drawing a "detailed picture of the woman as guest."[13]

Literally flitting from perch to perch, unable to impress her identity upon the domicile which still seems to bear her husband's imprint, Shirley scrutinizes her landlady and her neighbors who inhabit the contiguous interiors comfortably, as if they were clues to the interpretation of her space, and by extension, her life. Though Shirley never understands, indeed even denies the truth of her abandonment, the apartment becomes ghost-ridden and claustrophobic.

For Gallant, Rhys, Anita Brookner, and many other women novelists, the gender definition of woman/space as domestic space, however lavish or elegant, does not prevent its turning into the place of betrayal.[14] In *A Fairly Good Time* there is such a conflation of married life and the apartment that it almost seems as if the husband has committed a separate act of desertion toward the apartment.

Shirley "kills time" waiting for word from her husband, or for his return; she is a direct descendant of all the Victorian heroines waiting for lovers who will free them from trivial pursuits and carry them into wider spaces. Time is not women's element to manipulate; they fill the space of their days, but can only murder time.[15] Shirley, too, like Anna, like Helen, exists in the pathos of absence. For instance, in her effort to reinstate some measure of domestic attachment, however tenuous, she trudges through Paris on frequent visits to the home of her ex-husband's family; though they dislike her, she forces herself into their midst, even imagines having an affair with one of them, blindly but persistently attempting to insert herself into another domestic space.

The condition which I term "the pathos of absence" expresses the emptiness and negativity which also characterize Freudian and Lacanian definitions of women's sexuality as lack. In these novels the central characters are apprehended by the reader in relation to some *one* missing, as women's sexuality in Freudian and Lacanian interpretation is understood in relation to some *thing* missing, the male sexual organ.

Jean Rhys' women, Shirley in *A Fairly Good Time*, and most of the female protagonists of Mona Simpson's and Edna O'Brien's novels never achieve subjectivity. Such women don't present definitions of themselves alternative to the biological one; and though they move from place to place, they do so as flotsam, not by re-forming the larger social shape. They are formulations of both sexual and social woman/space; "the pathos of absence" stamps them as pathetic.

In Alice Hoffman's novel, *Illumination Night*, the protagonist, Vonny, is married, has a child, and lives in the country with her marginally employed husband. Vonny is a potter and, significantly, Vonny keeps her potter's wheel, her tubs of clay, and other supplies on the sun porch attached to their home, whereas her husband retires to a distinct male work space, a woodshed outside to do his work.

Furthermore, although the details about handling clay are convincing enough for the reader to credit Vonny's familiarity with the medium, her craft plays such a minor role in the development of either plot or character that the reader finds herself forgetting it. Her work does not afford either the reader or Vonny herself a fuller notion of her identity, or purposefulness.[16] Although pottery may be more expressive of Vonny than Anna Dunlap's laboratory job was of Anna, it nevertheless has no narrative function.

In the course of the novel, Vonny's latent agoraphobia (the growing gravity of the illness is not fully explained) reaches the point where she is literally unable to step outside the house, which has become her only "safe place." Yet at the inception of the novel Vonny complained about her husband's choice of this home—its deficient stove, its sagging steps. But she completely internalizes this space, domesticates it, identifies with it. The space, in turn, seems to cannibalize her.

As her phobia worsens Vonny seeks help, variously, from a therapist, a minister, and finally from self-help books which offer coping strategies. And as she begins to improve, her husband becomes her "safe person," a position he finds both irksome and gratifying. He is the someone whose presence enables her to do things she can't undertake alone. He functions, in this way, as the instrumentality of her subjectivity, too close, for the reader's comfort, to heroes who rescued maidens in distress.

Vonny's final release from the captivity of agoraphobia results from the necessity to find her small son who has strayed away from their yard. Although since her illness she has only driven in her husband's presence, she forces herself outside and into the car to search for the child. She finds her son, fortuitously saved from the car accident that killed his playmate. Though an adolescent girl and an elderly woman participate peripherally in the process, husband and son are the major agents of Vonny's regaining any signification.

Despite Vonny's restored health she remains a passive figure, and the vitality of her action—leaving the home finally and driving the car—is dissipated by the very structure of the novel. The author chooses not to conclude the novel with Vonny's narrative, but instead focuses upon another character, The Giant, whose role is allegorical and tangential to Vonny's life. This structure reinforces the reader's sense that though Vonny has surmounted her illness, she has a very limited subjectivity to reclaim. The atmosphere of the novel leaves us unconvinced of the growth of the central character; her triumph seems, rather, to have been dependent, as in so many fairy tales, upon magical happenings and helpers.

Although agoraphobia presents a heightened dramatization of the difficulties women encounter directing spatial relations outward, it is only the extreme degree to which this is true in *Illumination Night* that is pathological.

In her book-length study of women's films of the forties, *The Desire To Desire*, Mary Ann Doane arrives at conclusions about woman/space that are as relevant for fiction as for cinema:

> Space is constricted in the woman's film, usually to the space of the home. The opposition between inside and outside in relation to the house attains a significance which it rarely reaches in other genres. . . . In this narrowing of space the most humble object signifies. . . . In a patriarchal society, women's genres are characterized by a kind of signifying glut, an overabundance of signification attached to the trivial. In the woman's film there is a hypersignification of elements of the domestic—doors, windows, kitchens, bedrooms. . . . In watching a woman's film, one actively senses the contraction of the world attributed to the woman, the reduction of meaning and its subordination to affect.[17]

This is precisely what prevails in *The Good Mother*, *A Fairly Good Time*, and *Illumination Night*. (*Ironweed* is not a "woman's novel.") But in the three novels cited above, the reader is surfeited with trivial detail—what kind of sandwiches were packed for the picnic, at which moment the clothes were transferred from the washer to the dryer, what brand of aspirin is purchased. It is as if all these details, *en masse*, confer an authenticity not just upon the texture of the story but upon the female protagonist herself. These brand names are summoned to impress the protagonist's presence upon the day, as if she is comprised of these details.

Such shadowy self-identity makes a transition into public space seem hazardous; what individuated self can the character project? What in Doane's "narrowing of space" will provide the female protagonist with the vision of destiny necessary to move her actively through space? Or move her to pass through boundaries which, as Jessica Benjamin writes, she herself is perceived as *constituting* within the dynamics of male subject/female object relations?

If we visualize the sense of space invoked by melodrama, a predominantly female genre employing a centripetal action focussed on the cowering or trapped central figure of the woman, frequently even spotlit (as in Degas' painting "The Interior" with its suggested melodrama of rape), and then visualize the space of the Western, a male genre, in which the hero rides centrifugally through wide openness out to the perimeter, the contrast in spatial relations between the sexes becomes clear.

Anna Dunlap traverses the few blocks between her small apartment and the apartment in which her daughter is being kept away from her; Shirley meanders around Paris and vaguely supposes she and her ex-husband will see each other —where?—in dreams and recollections, in a secret, interior place. Vonny, returned to a functional state, knows that her agoraphobia will always lurk beneath her surface, and that she will remain hostage to the gender definition of woman/space.

The second group of three novels—*Housekeeping*, *Surfacing*, and *Nights at the Circus*—offers a variety of conditions under which new definitions of woman/space may be imagined. *Housekeeping* by Marilynne Robinson presents a fresh narrative line by taking a traditionally male viewpoint and successfully transferring it to a woman character, thereby challenging long-held assumptions about female nature.

For Sylvie, Robinson's female protagonist in this novel, it is domestic space that proves intractable and mysterious. Set the task of bringing up her dead sister's children, she finds in herself no instinctive knowledge. The house, symbol of domesticity, becomes under her regime a chaos of old magazines, broken window panes stuffed with newspaper, half-emptied tins of food. She is so removed from male definitions of woman/space, of boundaries, that she encourages her nieces to play hookey from school in order to go exploring the outlying countryside on their own, as she does. Her relationship to her own nature is inextricable from her relationship with Nature.

The neighbors, critical and suspicious, do not understand Sylvie any more than she understands them. But Sylvie's is not the garden variety of neglect; the neighbors don't see that, but the reader is meant to. In Sylvie, Robinson dramatizes a kind of consciousness different from that of the bourgeois women living nearby. The author does not represent Sylvie as selfish, insensitive, or cruel, but as compassionate and autonomous. She simply blunders, inept, in this domestic setting to which she never adapts.

She is drawn to the remote, to an uninhabited island offshore to which she rows, the unknown destinations toward which the train whistle beckons. That train whistle has sounded for countless young men, and is an earmark of the *Bildungsroman*. But for women, restricted by biological and gender definitions which control them, escape has never acquired rituals.

The lack of traditional rites of departure may explain Sylvie's final act of arson: she not only flees from the house into beyond, but destroys it as a final gesture of obliterating inside-outside separation, or inside as it is home-defined.[18] She retains "inside" as the emotional haven of love, "travelling on" with one of her nieces, but rejects the traditional interior spaces of maternity and of the home. In fact what saves this novel from the facile identification of "the call of the wild" with personal freedom, is precisely the rarity of such identification by women. Sylvie works in temporary jobs in order to earn the money that will enable her to move forward; husbandless, loverless, childless, she is nevertheless *not* defined by the pathos of absence, because she is able to project her own subjectivity, almost always a male function, as the narrative action. Riding the boxcars, also a traditionally male activity, she is joyous.

One sign of the novel's departure from conventional perceptions of woman/space is how little the reader is told about Sylvie's life prior to her sudden appearance in the novel. Was she once married, as she claims? Why didn't she have children? What jobs did she have? Where did she live before? She moves around with very little baggage, both literally (arriving at her nieces' home with one suitcase, no suitable clothing for the cold weather, no wallet), and metaphorically. She is not embedded in a matrix. Her hoard of washed, empty tin cans makes a mockery of bourgeois provisioning. The rigid demarcation between interior and exterior space which is characteristic of domestic novels is meaningless to Sylvie; she's at home, natural, in a boat on the lake at night, or sleeping in the orchard.[19]

In *Housekeeping* the boundaries between inside and outside dissolve, creating instead a new perception of space that is continuous and fluid. The necessity to deconstruct prevailing notions of woman/space is an acknowledged goal of feminist theorists; Jessica Benjamin suggests, as we have mentioned, what she terms "Intersubjective Space," a perception of relations she opposes to the male construct of subject/boundary/object. Canadian psychologist D.W. Winnicott also rejects a strict division into interior and exterior space: "The interior of the body and the space between bodies form an elusive pattern, a plane whose edge is ever-shifting." In both Winnicott and Benjamin normative perception of inside/outside is moved closer to woman's own experience of the body as process and away from the male experience of boundary.

Housekeeping, then, questions assumptions about the social definition of women. What is fresh here is Sylvie's liberation from those desires all women are supposed, generically, to harbor, everything that the word "nest" implies. We can appreciate Robinson's innovation if we try to recall the names of other female itinerants in literature who choose that life, and are not merely abandoned into it. Sylvie, possessed of a wanderlust traditionally identified with men, like Ulysses wishes to embark upon a voyage that leaves "housekeeping" at home. (Ulysses manages this by leaving Penelope at home; his wrath at the suitors who cluster around his wife in his prolonged absence reveals a sense of entitlement few women characters are permitted.)

Helen, the hobo, in order to appear more respectable, buttoned her "good black coat" around her when she agreed to sing in the bar. Shirley, the deserted wife, tried to dress smartly, studying everyone's clothes as if they were totemic and she an anthropologist. But Sylvie's total inattention to dress is emblematic of her rejection of domesticity *within* the domestic novel; the gaze she casts is the gaze a subject directs toward her own field of vision. Her autonomy seems almost extravagant or hubristic within the domestic, enclosed, relational construct of woman/space; the tug between the two creates the tension which drives the novel. In the film made from *Housekeeping*, Sylvie's redefinition of context is so hard to convey that she emerged merely as "flaky."

The next novel introduces us to Fevvers, the irrepressible, polymorphous heroine of Angela Carter's *Nights at the Circus*. Fevvers' name alludes to her feathered wings; swan-like, they project from her shoulders, large and strong enough to make flight easy. To paraphrase Oscar Wilde, Fevvers succeeds through excess—wings sprout when she's an infant, literally breaking through the skin; her stature is enormous; her cascade of hair is forever escaping its pins and ribbons. Her appetite for wine, food, and sexual adventure equals that of Tom Jones, and she possesses what we customarily think of as a "masculine" hardheadedness about money.

Carter utilizes the picaresque narrative technique of Fielding and Defoe; even before Fevvers adopts the career of an aerialiste we see her escaping from dungeons and villains.[20] In Carter's parody of the genre we have a true "send-up." (The plot, that is, is a spoof, or "send-up," and Fevvers, as aerialiste, is quite literally "sent up" to perform.)

Travelling from London to Siberia with the circus, she experiences hilarious ups and downs, in her fortunes as well as in her acrobatic and sexual positions. Ironically, her theme song is "I'm only a Bird in a Gilded Cage," and that is exactly how she is displayed to the audience when the curtain rises on her circus act: she is inside a cage the bars of which she proceeds, with her unusual strength, to push aside, and from which she steps, reminding us of Helen's failure to open the bars of *her* gilded cage in *Ironweed*. And then this woman-wonder launches herself upon her own two—not feet—but wings. As a professional aerialiste, she literally launches a new heroine through the circumstance of being a swan-woman, breaking through the space barrier before Sally Ride did.

Fevvers' creation of new spatial definitions for herself through empowering morphological changes parallels that in Margaret Atwood's novel *Surfacing*. The language, tone, setting, and secondary characters are all very different in the two works; the similarity lies in the use of morphological change as a metaphor for presaging other change: the liberation of female protagonists from both sexual and social definitions of woman/space.

Briefly, Atwood's protagonist Anna, refuses to return to the mainland from an island in Canada on which she has been camping with her lover and another couple. They have all come to the island to search for her father, who has disappeared from the family cottage. This Anna, like the Anna of *The Good Mother*, seems to function in a completely reactive manner. Her work, commercial illustration, is presented, like Anna Dunlap's, as trivial. Her relationships have little foundation; at one point she remarks of the other woman with her, "She's my best friend—I've known her for two months." But then, when the dead body of her father has been found, and there is no further reason to stay on the island, she disassociates herself from her lover and her friends, and stays on alone. We understand this decision because as readers we have watched her recoil from progressive scenes of cruelty, mental and physical, inflicted within the novel on both humans and animals. The sexual arrogance which pervades the male conversation, and the display of male brute strength which characterizes the male/female relation in both couples, is paralleled by the book's dramatic presentation of the exploitation/rape of the island landscape.[21]

As the novel progresses, Anna perceives the other characters as being "halfway to a machine." She herself wishes to return to a more natural state, and consciously tries to feel her way back to a more elemental existence. She "goes wild." She begins to feel as if she's an animal ("there's no fur on my skin yet, it's too early") native to the island, not a visitor; her hair becomes matted, she goes naked except for the protection of a blanket; her diurnal rhythm changes; she uses no tools except her hands.

As she changes morphologically, like Fevvers she perceives space, and her own woman/space, differently. "I am not an animal or a tree, I am the thing in which animals and trees move and grow, I am a place [space]." She is natural space, yet Atwood would seem to distinguish this from just the space of germination, the container; it is without boundaries. As Sylvie in *Housekeeping* understands inside and outside as a continuum, so Anna knocks down the fences around the garden, understanding in her new self-awareness that nature should not be confined in human gardens, seeing confinement as evil. (Words denoting confinement, such as "trapping," operate on two levels throughout the novel, speaking metaphorically to Anna's condition, recalling the 'cage' metaphor, and speaking literally to the trapping of birds and animals which transpires on the island.) Not only are boundaries between inside and outside abolished, but, through shape-shifting, even boundaries between humans and other creatures. Finally, Anna evolves into uninterrupted, unconstrained space itself.

As the present tense, gerundive construction informs us, "surfacing," i.e., coming to the surface, is what Anna accomplishes in the novel; her motion toward awareness is the action of the narrative. The novel is a *Bildungsroman*. Significantly, "surfacing" assumes a prior submerged state from which it is necessary either to surface, or drown.

Looking at the expectations of the female characters in the first three novels and the second group of three, we can observe a definite change. Broadly, the first three are informed by subtraction, the second three by addition. For example, in *A Fairly Good Time*, Shirley, after the pivotal event of her husband's desertion, so unexpected and so puzzling, ransacks the apartment, vainly hoping to understand her husband's 'important' work or to discover a rival. She finds nothing that aids her development; she is less than she was at the opening of the story; in popular jargon, we might say "she hasn't a clue."

Atwood's heroine, on the other hand, searches her parents' cottage for *gifts* that will mediate between her own space and the unbounded space of the natural world. She *knows* she will find a helpful legacy, and, when she docs find it, she immediately recognizes its significance. Her father's gift is a map of Indian pictographs to be found on the island; her mother's, one of Anna's own childhood drawings, depicting herself as an infant in her mother's stomach, and a man opposite her who was God: "The gods, their likenesses: to see them in their true shapes is fatal, while you are human; but after the transformation they could be reached."

Both of these drawings, legacies, are inscriptions of an 'other' world beyond the cottage itself, its social boundaries, its particular temporality. The Indian map connects her to a lost history which she reclaims when, by "diving deep and surfacing," in Carol Christ's phrase, she finds the pictographs on submerged rocks; her own childhood drawing recalls her initial encounter with the blinding power of the gods, upon whom, in her transformed state, she may now gaze.

Guided by these gifts, she plans to remain in the forest (not even in the cottage), and there to raise her unborn child. In this she recalls Hester Prynne, who although she was banished to the forest, a social outcast, nevertheless represents the pole of freedom and organic growth in *The Scarlet Letter*. Anna intuits that she is pregnant, but whether she is carrying a child or giving birth to a new self, the reader can't, and needn't, be certain. We leave her in a solitariness necessary for creation.

These visions of Robinson, Carter, and Atwood are salutary and even exhilarating, and though they can hardly be prescriptive, they are at least more than cautionary; they succeed in expanding accepted woman/space definitions. The problem with embedded gender definitions such as we've been exploring is that they become sanctioned by custom; they are even spuriously seen as conferring worthiness upon women.

It is imaginatively comforting, not only for men but for some women, to take refuge in the idea of a perfect complementarity of the sexes accomplished through the provision of a womb, a breast—through what is circular and interior rather than temporal and linear—sealing or healing what in Blake's epigraph ("Time is a Man Space is a Woman") is presented as a polarity. (Even *narrative* closure is a pleasurable sensation, as we all know from our reading.)[22]

Furthermore, it is comforting, especially to the male, to perceive domestic space as preserving something pre-industrial and non-commercial, in which a holy labor takes place, a gift rather than a commodity. But this holy labor, as we all know, is unpaid and unrespected by the society at large. These ancient and charged sexual and social definitions of woman/space hallow inequality and prevailing gender hierarchy. Exclusionary, ruling out the possibility of change, they seriously handicap women attempting to change from object to subject, attempting to direct action through the narrative and not merely to account for its pauses, its still places. Old definitions restrain women who seek to move through space as their own gaze leads, and not like Marcel Duchamp's *Nude Descending a Staircase*, a specular object of cubist refraction.

3

Woman/Sight

The eye altering alters all.

—William Blake

Looking is a civilized substitute for touching.

—Sigmund Freud

There is a place where passion hides in order to explode a gaze.

—Eugenio de Andrade

"The Gaze" has been the subject of a spate of articles, lectures and books by feminists. Why is it so important? Is it first of all simply a matter, not simple at all, of finding both the language and the imagery to represent women's desire as well as that of men? For the gaze *is* male, and in itself constitutes gender positioning, the displacement of women's experience and her definition as "other." The gaze as it is traditionally composed raises related issues of fetishism ("For months my hand had been sealed off in a tin box," writes Anne Sexton in the poem, "The Touch"), of narcissism, of texts in which the woman is mis-seen and unseen, erased, invisible.[1] Women's gazes are socialized by the male gaze to be obedient to a particular line of vision. The coercion raises the correlative problem of the woman's body being commonly taken as synedoche for her whole being: her metonymic figure remains still to be discovered. This all means, of course, that the gaze is a political issue; we build social arrangements upon it. The gaze can function as a weapon upholding inequality; to correct it means to change woman from the object viewed to woman the subject viewer.

Finding precedent for unequal social arrangements in Grimms' *Fairy Tales*, Ruth Bottigheimer asserts in *Grimms' Bad Girls and Bold Boys*: "Norms buttressed by society and religion bind women of all degrees from poverty to majesty, and a woman's transgression of these norms results in profound deprivation of selfhood. . . [even] the possibility of death itself. A man, however, may ignore prohibitions without consequence."[2]

This is one reason the tales were such a productive text for Anne Sexton and Angela Carter to reinscribe in *Transformations* and *The Bloody Chamber and Other Stories*, respectively: transforming the events, Sexton and Carter subvert the traditional values fairy tales reflect (particularly the passivity of the heroine), replacing them with sexual energy.[3]

Literary or visual representations work both backward and forward; they arise from values and represent them, but they also solidify them by making them societal structures. As women have moved toward the will to self-representation instead of allowing male representation of them to signify lack, the remarkable absence of a female gaze has stirred much commentary and controversy.

In both photography and the visual arts the female body becomes the map on which the lines of male desire are drawn by the paintbrush, or, later, by the camera eye. The nude (always female) in Western painting is important enough to be considered a major genre of its own.[4] Margaret Miles points out that male nakedness has long represented "spiritual discipline, physical control, the vigorous appropriation of a religious identity, and undistracted pursuit of an athletic crown,"[5] female nakedness presents no spiritual element, but rather, women's inherent sinfulness. The representation of women in painting can have two results: first, the aestheticized and idealized depiction of the woman may de-eroticize, formalize, objectify, and generalize the female body, a tendency reflected in the painting of Ingres and David; or, the artist may realize on canvas the male erotic gaze, particularizing the body and making desire tangible enough for the viewer in turn to feel it.

These two seemingly contradictory modes of treatment both share the commodification of the female body, in the first case as a beautiful object to be possessed as one would possess a vase, and in the second, as the specific object of sexual desire. Commodification of desire arising from either of these treatments of the figure renders objects that can be bought, traded, sold, without their consent or consultation (as women in fact were in many countries).[6]

Pornography embodies the erotic power of complete possession. This is why the female figure is so frequently used to sell other objects offered for possession. The female form draped over the car for sale implies, by their contiguous display, that both are for sale; the pleasure of owning one implies the prospect of owning the other. The two objects merge into one image of desire. The object of the gaze lies at the end of the line of sight; through this distancing and objectification, the object of pornography experiences a death-like loss of the self.

Pornography's promise of possession underlies the simile of woman and doll. As men are socialized to become soldiers, so women are socialized to become dolls. Contrary to popular opinion, the playthings of each sex do not bespeak the stages of development, but rather the rigidification of gender roles. Mme. de Staël's heroine Corinne refers to herself during her stay in England as a "mechanized doll," and Isak Dinesen's story "The Invincible Slave-Owner" compares the doll-woman with the housekeeper, remarking how each depends upon the notion of possession. Susan Gubar, in "The Blank Page," also comments on the intimate association between woman and doll: "From Maggie Tulliver, who tortures her doll in the attic in *The Mill on The Floss*, to Pecola Breedlove in Toni Morrison's *The Bluest Eye*, who tortures herself because she cannot look like her doll, the heroines of women's fiction have played with dolls to define themselves."[7]

Further, I would say that playing with dolls is not merely rehearsal for the future role of maternity (the woman having her own dolls), but the preparation of women for their possession *as* dolls. "I am a plaster doll. . . I live in a doll's house," Anne Sexton writes in "Self in 1958," echoing Ibsen's Nora a hundred years earlier; Elizabeth Fenton likewise writes in "Masks," "I am the enormous doll / and you dive into me."[8] A startling example also occurs in Djuna Barnes' novel *Nightwood*, in which the two young girls smash their doll to the point of destruction. The doll's implicit daughterhood makes the girls' behavior seem more disturbing to the reader than that of, say, a young boy smashing his model train. We read this incident as symbolic infanticide, the ultimate refusal of motherhood.

Suzanne Valadon's oil painting, *The Abandoned Doll*, remarkably contains all these motifs. It depicts a nude adolescent girl sitting on her bed, her discarded doll on the floor, and a mirror—successor to the doll—in her hand. Her mother, presumably aiding the girl's rite of passage, brushes the daughter's hair, preparing her to be a doll herself. Thus there are two dolls, the abandoned one, and the one in process of becoming.

Aestheticizing, the first form of representation, distances the viewer from the object portrayed, thus idealizing the object. As Helena Michie points out: "Heroines throughout the nineteenth century in both Britain and America were constantly being compared to paintings, sculptures, books, or pieces of music."[9]

Revealingly, one of Whistler's portraits of a woman is entitled <u>Symphony</u> *in White* [emphasis added]. The women in the portraits become objects because we perceive them as *works*. Susan Gubar, in the essay cited above, concurs: "Woman is not simply an object, however. . . she is an art object, the ivory carving or mud replica, an icon or *doll*, [emphasis added] but she is not the sculptor."[10]

Such women are never autonomous but owe their existence to the artist—painter or writer—whose highest effect is to "*capture* a likeness." They are framed in text or gold leaf, in an imprisonment of the Beloved; reflections of the desires of others, they are reduced to ornamentation. Thus Gubar writes of Lily Bart in Edith Wharton's *House of Mirth*: "Because financially she cannot afford to maintain herself as a work of art without the money of a man, Lily's artful presentation resembles [Gwendolen Harleth's]. . . . She, too, must attract a husband. Furthermore, the only man in the novel who could possibly save her from becoming a commodity on the marriage market is himself incapable of viewing her as anything but a collectible in the aesthetic market."[11]

Similarly, Zenobia, heroine of *The Blithedale Romance*, despite the fact that she is perhaps Hawthorne's most complete character, is transformed into "a work of art" by Coverdale.[12] Lillian Robinson and Lise Vogel make the interesting observation that Vermeer's paintings immobilize women as "passive objects, part of the inventory" of the material household, an inventory to which the Dutch were singularly prone.[13] Christa Wolf, in her re-telling of Cassandra's tale, writes of this heroine: "Cassandra is one of the first women figures handed down to us whose fate prefigures what was to be the fate of women for three thousand years: to be turned into an object."[14]

In much the same way, Degas' ballerinas reflect a completely depersonalized idealization of the body. At once mobile and framed, the ballerina renders us, the viewers, voyeurs of perfect form or perfect fragments. Robinson and Vogel make their point by looking to Degas' notebook: "Of a dancer do either the arms or the legs or the back. Do the shoes—the hands . . . bare feet in dance action."[15] In a famous statement Degas explains that in his paintings of female bathers, "I show them deprived of their arts and affectations, reduced to the level of animals cleaning themselves."[16] Robinson and Vogel claim that a woman viewing these paintings identifies with "her own predecessors, women, who, like her, tended to be more *things* than *people* to the men who observed and lived with them."[17]

How, one might ask, does this "thingness' compare with the shapeless Breton laborer's shoes, the subjects of some of the early Van Gogh paintings? The difference is that while both toe shoe and boot tell us about work, the Van Gogh painting makes a class statement, the Degas a gender statement. Being the object of desire, however beautiful, expresses nothing of the desires of the woman herself, since an *objet d'art*, a *thing*, does not possess desires of its own. This holds as true for the aestheticization and idealization of the ice-skater as for that of the ballerina: her abbreviated costume is functional and decorative but does not express her sexuality.

The child-beauty, the always-potential perfect form that evokes pathos represents a different but related idealization. Charles Dickens and Lewis Carroll, for example, create such putative child-brides; their sexuality remains not only unexpressed but inexpressible because of cultural prohibition. In these cases, the gaze itself must substitute for the fulfillment of desire. The notoriety of Nabokov's *Lolita* shows the persistence of this prohibition against sexuality in young girls.

Implicit in the depiction of the female body is the message that although woman's essence is her sexuality, her desire is knowable only to the man who holds the phallic key to her secret. Hence, like Sleeping Beauty, she must await his seduction for her awakening. As an example, Susan Koppelman Cornillon cites Rona Jaffe's novel *Away From Home* as a story about a woman's "preternaturally extended state of unawakenedness. . . because the 'right' *man* hasn't come into Margie's life yet."[18] Similarly, in the opening poem of *Transformations*, "The Gold Key" (key implies a locked space, woman/space, and gold the treasure to be found there), Anne Sexton uses this symbol to foreground women's vulnerability. The poem asserts that only a goddess like Artemis or her counterparts in other mythologies may have the key as her symbol, implying her possession of the phallic power of opening. In addition to their specific sexual reference, the lock and key are, of course, symbols of women's subjection in general; men carry the key to women as the housekeeper carries the keys to the goods over which she maintains authorized control.

The lock and key are counterparts of the cage and the frame to which we have already referred. Women striving for subjectivity must also assuage the "ontological insecurity," to use R. D. Laing's phrase, produced by being transformed into an object, which in its extreme forms, produces fetishism and pornography. As Laing notes, our culture tends to objectify people, women especially. And women feel it beyond the general dis-ease which objectification induces, because it characterizes their most intimate societally approved relationships, specifically the male/female dyad.

Being objectified leads to a feeling of annihilation and worthlessness which the woman internalizes as an implicit judgment; there is something intrinsically bad about her, wrong with her, that elicits such treatment. Thus, unwittingly, the woman herself, by accepting this judgment, undermines her self-esteem and contributes to the anxiety of narcissism. We must bear all this in mind because the woman as body has never been more visible than today.

Jessica Benjamin believes that, despite this emphasis on physicality, "the representation of *women's* sexuality does not seem to have its own symbolic structures but rather seems to be incorporated into the system organized by phallic structures" (emphasis added). Therefore, she seeks for women an alternative means of representing desire since "the phallus as emblem of desire has represented the one-sided individuality of subject meeting object, a complementarity that idealizes one side and devalues the other."[19]

Because no account is taken of women's sexuality, no symbology of female desire has evolved, as many feminist critics or theorists such as Joan Rivière and Stephen Heath have noted. If masculine libido is the source of *all* sexuality, women lack their own signs.[20] Perhaps the final liberation from a cult of woman as aestheticized object will come with the development of a female symbology for the female gaze. In a culture that defines one sex as strong and the other as weak, owning the image is an important power. Toward this end, Olga Broumas in her book *Beginning With O* uses the circle as an alternative symbol to a phallic poetics; Monique Wittig, in her experimental novel, *Les Guérillères*, places on several pages a black circle alone on the page, symbol of feminine wholeness. James Joyce's archetypal female, Molly Bloom, conducts a monologue in which the repeated "O" sound vocalizes her sexuality.[21]

Moving from the first, the idealized, aestheticized representation of woman, to the second technique, that of painting onto the canvas or writing into the text the male erotic gaze, we find an excellent example in Degas' painting, *The Interior*. Critics of his time retitled his oil *The Rape*. Although the painting depicts no narrative action, the arrangement and treatment of the figures make such speculation about plot possible. A man, fully clothed, even hatted, stands with his back against the only door of the room; a woman, clothed only in her undergarments, kneels on the floor, her gaze averted from both the viewer and the man, and bends over an open trunk on the floor. Her *deshabillé*, especially taken in conjunction with the man's figure blocking the only door, underscores her defenselessness and unreadiness to escape from the room. The two figures are positioned at almost opposite margins of the canvas: he is in shadow; she, the direct object of his gaze, in light. The viewer senses acutely tense and forbidding control of the shaded masculine eye over the long space between the man and woman. Carol Armstrong finds the female figure in the painting "defeated";[22] certainly she is not the subject, the "I" (eye) of the work.

In the context of the definitions of Woman/Space we have been proposing, Degas' title for this picture, *The Interior*, assumes additional importance. The male and female figures are inside a bedroom; the trunk, mysterious half-opened container, echoes the compositional statement of the half-clad woman herself. Significantly, this painting subverts "the interior," a space customarily designated as belonging to women, from a place of security to one of danger in the same way that some of the novels we discussed in "Woman/Space" do. Indeed, the interior, far from exuding an aura of domestic safety, resembles that place of imprisonment in which so many literary heroines await rescue.

Sometimes the eroticization of the female figure and its simultaneous aestheticization are confusingly conflated. As examples, let us visualize some of the great portraits of women (the Women in White, as I call them) of Sargent, Monet, Degas, Homer, Whistler, Ruskin, and others. We remark first in these paintings the extensive use of the virginal emblem of whiteness in the garb of these women—bridal gown white, sheet white. But this virginal whiteness is contradicted by other elements in the paintings. While the Women in White are clothed, often lavishly, even cocooned, in layers of garments, they are, at the same time, frequently recumbent, stretched across beds or chaises, their sexuality covered but not transfigured into ethereality. Furthermore, most of these women appear alone and idle; conditions for intimacy are present.

Besides, as Anne Hollander argues in *Seeing Through Clothes*, fashions exist to produce erotic stimuli; the elaborate clothing tempts the eye to undress the guessed-at figure. Julia Kristeva's description of Céline's Molly as possessing "an aura of amorous idealization" aptly sums up the overall oxymoronic effect of the Women in White.[23]

I would suggest that although these portraits of women in white are of particular models, they belong to a convention which represents them in a way similar to that suggested by Hollander, one which has the effect of distancing them. Though Michel Foucault's idea of creating an aesthetic self may conceivably heighten individualism if it is *self*-creation, the aestheticization by male artists of the women in white accomplishes the reverse:

distancing. They remind one of the metaphor of woman as "The Blank Page," white waiting to be written upon.

The blank page, "invisibility," and the woman in white are all variations on the same theme: female lack of self-representation.[24] Even in portraits, they are creatures of male myth, not self-created people.[25] Kristeva observes in the same essay quoted above that Céline's Molly is endowed with "the enchanted existence of the *great white-draped priestesses* of ancient *Phallic* myths" [emphases added].[26] Therefore, new feminist notions of revision and of visibility must take into account the intimate relation between the male gaze upon the female object of desire, and epistemology (conveyed in the sense of the verb "to know," which means to have carnal knowledge of). Desire is representation, but representation is also desire.

Feminist film critics such as Laura Mulvey, Jacqueline Rose, and Teresa de Lauretis have paid close attention to the cultural phenomenon of the gaze, showing how the camera eye continues the painterly tradition of objectifying women. Mary Ann Doane's book, *The Desire to Desire: The Woman's Film of the 1940's*, tracks specific cinematic sub-groups from maternal melodrama to medical discourses seeking to 'cure' women's physical or psychological deficiencies, discussing a spectrum of films from *The Great Lie* to *Dark Victory*. As the film industry grew, women's identity depended upon the success of a particular, inherited, spatial arrangement in cinematic narrative. The male eye off-screen directed the camera as it had directed the brush, creating the image; the female image on-screen absorbing and deflecting the gaze. Mary Ann Doane speculates that the gaze of the camera is so closely associated with the male gaze that it is necessary to ask whether women *can* be represented in ways that avoid positioning them as mere spectacle.

Doane points to the extensive use of the staircase in films of the forties as the perfect vehicle for the specularization of the female body because it enables this body to become sculptural, literally viewed from all sides. (In her essay about becoming a Playboy Club Bunny, Gloria Steinem corroborates this, relating how she was instructed to descend the staircase in a particular manner so as to afford the male viewer below the optimal opportunity for such specularization). Moreover, this pose at the top of the stairs catches, separates, and isolates the moment of the female entrance into the onward-going, male, externalized narrative of the film.[26]

Creating a female gaze can only follow from a change from women as object viewed to women as subject viewer. We cannot guess the *range* of images women's gaze would choose because we do not have a sufficient body of recorded visual experience reflecting the woman's gaze. Sandra Lee Bartky, calling for the destruction of the categories "masculinity" and "femininity," admits that what she calls for is "a radical and as yet *unimagined* transformation of the female body" [28] (emphasis added). Only recently have women film directors such as Diane Kurys, Chantal Akerman, Sally Potter, Yvonne Rainer, and E. Ann Robinson, who present other views of the female body, reached a general audience. [29] We can conclude, from the evidence already presented, that the woman's gaze is more expansive, more inclusive, than the man's gaze—other viewers viewing different bodies. Robinson, for example, presents active, healthy female bodies that are nevertheless overweight by conventional contemporary aesthetic standards. [30]

In an effort to explore what might constitute a female gaze, what its potential objects and objectives are, I propose to look first at what is simplest to contrive fictively: some examples of role reversal, in which the female gaze directs itself erotically upon a male object (body) of desire. Second, I will discuss the changes in the dynamic of the gaze when the viewer and the viewed belong to the same sex. I also propose to examine in depth the figure of Medusa, first as an embodiment of male hysteria opposing redirection of the gaze, and then as a figure valorized by contemporary women poets.

Erica Jong's best selling novel, *Fear of Flying*, is an excellent example of straightforward erotic role reversal. The book's heroine, Isadora, gazes at men as sexual objects of desire and appropriates the tone and diction of male descriptions of desire. Three short but representative quotations will suffice:

> Even if you loved your husband, there came that inevitable year when fucking him turned as bland as Velveeta cheese: filling, fattening even, but no thrill to the taste buds, no bittersweet edge, no danger. And you longed for an overripe Camembert, a rare goat cheese: luscious, creamy, cloven-hoofed.

> Then the desires came and you were thrown into a panic of self-hatred. What an evil woman you were! How could you keep being infatuated with strange men? How could you study their bulging trousers like that? How could you sit at a meeting imagining how every man in the room would screw? How could you sit on a train fucking total strangers with your eyes? How could you *do* that to your husband? Did anyone ever tell you that maybe it had nothing whatever to do with your husband?

> He was so beautiful lying there and his body smelled so good. I thought of all those centuries in which men adored women for their bodies while they despised their minds. . . . now I understood it. Because that was how I so often felt about men. Their minds were hopelessly befuddled, but their bodies were so nice. [31]

Such a gaze inverts the male/subject—female/object relation, and by so doing, throws into relief the implications of the male gaze itself.

The female gaze destructs conventional barriers not just by inverting subject/object relations, but also by introducing other foci of sensuality. For example, in Lisa Alther's *Kinflicks*, the heroine's mother, critically ill in hospital and led by the graveness of her condition into new clarity, muses about her daughter Ginny:

> She forced herself not to study Ginny's braless breasts. Watching her children develop physically had never ceased to amaze her. . . . If *she* could have run things, she'd have arrested their development at around age five. She had adored their compact little bodies at that age. . . . And then the physical transformations—the boys' voices began cracking. . . . Ginny had begun menstruating, had developed hips and breasts. It was appalling really—because it meant that these creatures weren't a superior species after all. They would lust and hunger and burn, just as their parents had. And out of it would come children of their own, to whom *they* would look wistfully, hoping for more original things. . . .
>
> All Ginny's adult life Mrs Babcock had had to force herself not to think about who was doing what to this young female body that she simultaneously loved and loathed. Besides, it was ridiculous—her feeling of physical possessiveness. And yet after so many years of tending this body—bathing it, dressing it, feeding it, binding up its wounds—how could she be expected to feel otherwise?[32]

What is novel in this, it seems to me, is the insight about *physical* possessiveness shown to exist outside conventional Freudian Oedipal alignments. We find these sentiments, the physical attachment of the mother, say, to her daughter's body, in Anne Sexton's poem to her daughter, "Little Girl, My String Bean, My Lovely Woman," in which she repeatedly uses the possessive pronoun "my" when referring to her daughter's ripening body.[33]

The dynamic of the gaze is altered more significantly when lesbian experience replaces the male/female erotic dyad presumed to underlie romantic/erotic love poetry. I see this as an important shift, going beyond an expression of alternative sexual preference. For one thing, its same-sex dyad replaces dichotomy and opposition with familiarity and likeness. The female gaze, which in general tends to be a "both/and" rather than an "either/or" one, is particularly so here. And there are far-reaching implications for the non-lesbian woman as well; the lesbian experience valorizes connection and relatedness, rejecting the Freudian view based on a male model, that the mature individual is one who achieves separation and ego-centeredness.

Furthermore, if for women in general the expression of libido is a subversion of existing decorum, lesbian writing carries this one step further by positing a relationship that does not rest upon reproductive sexuality. Three contemporary novels by women, Lisa Alther's *Kinflicks*, Erica Jong's *Fear of Flying*, and Fay Weldon's *Life and Loves of a She-Devil*, challenge reproductive sexuality by introducing the theme of women's entrapment by their children. Motherhood as an institution is privileged in America, but inadequately supported by funding for day care, maternity leave, or child support. This paradox demonstrates both the power of the maternal myth and the actual subordination of women's role.

None of the three heroines in the novels named above is lesbian; there are other reasons for resisting the social pressure of female roles. Jong's protagonist, Isadora, expresses the social force dictating that "there is simply no dignified way for a woman to live alone. . . her husbandlessness, her childlessness—her *selfishness*, in short—is a reproach to the American way of life." [34] Carrying this further, feminist critic Monique Wittig presents male homosexuality and lesbianism as the only places from which the heterosexual, phallocentric culture (in which Isadora moves) can be effectively rejected. She takes issue with any revisionist philosophy that aims to combat from within everyday (heterosexual) portrayals of women this culture condones. [35]

Kinflicks, *Life and Loves of a She-Devil*, Rita Mae Brown's *Rubyfruit Jungle*, Audre Lorde's *Zami*, and the poems of Olga Broumas and Marilyn Hacker are but a few examples of how the female gaze operates. They describe women's bodies in terms that refute Bakhtin's and Céline's notions of the female body as grotesque, validating it instead as the particular object of the *female* gaze.

That the emergence of a female gaze has not been a more liberating strategy for all women, is the result of cultural anxiety. Gynephobia characterizes contemporary society in general; lesbian women arouse its most intense fear. Shown in frightening intensity in Alther's *Kinflicks*, this fear comprehends well that to change the gaze is to posit a major shift not only in aesthetics, but in power, particularly the heterosexual contract upon which social forms of organization are based. Possession is nine-tenths of the law; this precept extends to possession of the body as well. For this reason, Rita Mae Brown's novel *Rubyfruit Jungle*, published in 1973, marked a milestone because it offered a candid lesbian protagonist with whom lesbian readers could identify and who was not punished as a transgressor.

The lesbian gaze offers one way in which women can focus on the issue of female subjectivity, the larger reclamation of female subjecthood without which any construction of a heroine is impossible. Since the heterosexual contract concerning the female body relies on reproductive sexuality, i.e., motherhood, fiction by both lesbian and heterosexual women is re-examining the crucial maternal figure and her relation to sexuality, to the male and female gazes, while feminist theory is undertaking the same exploration in the effort to reclaim female subjectivity. A short overview of this disputed maternal territory follows.

Nancy Chodorow, in her landmark book *The Reproduction of Mothering*, locates the first sexual attachment in the pre-oedipal, pre-verbal stages as being that to the mother's body. This, she claims, holds equally true for both sexes. With this theory Chodorow challenges Freud's explanation of the pattern of childhood sexuality as centered in the father, substituting earlier important maternal influence. Moreover, Chodorow believes that the mother/daughter bond is based upon a recognition of likeness which is never totally ruptured by the daughter's necessity to develop a separate sexual role.[36] Therefore, she argues, women retain a sense of connectedness, of a fluidity of boundaries in their perceptions of relationships, whereas men develop a much stronger sense of "other."

Heretofore we have been concentrating on "otherness" as a boundary between male and female, but what is designated as "other" must always be understood not only as a function of gender, but also of race and class. Thus Toni Morrison, talking about the conception of Africanism in white American literature, charges that the American self knows itself as desirable because of its definition against Africanism, regardless of gender.

Feminists vary in their interpretations of the effects of the maternal body upon child development. Adrienne Rich emphasizes that whereas the separation of the male child from the female mother enables men to return finally to that body, to "gaze" at women, women are socialized to look at men and look away from women, thereby severing themselves from their earliest experiences of nurture, intimacy, and pleasure.

On the other hand, Dorothy Dinnerstein in *The Mermaid and the Minotaur* considers that this earliest relation remains experienced by *both* sexes as loss; that the mother reminds the adult child of helpless infancy when there was "unlimited access" to the maternal body. Rich and Dinnerstein agree on the importance of the ultimate proscription of the body of the mother for both sexes, and Chodorow and Dinnerstein agree that there are implicit dangers, as well as benefits in the mother/daughter identification: the daughter may unknowingly re-enact the mother's life, or the mother's unsuccessful attempts at alternative lives. Insofar as the cultural denigration of the mother takes place, the daughter, in her identification with the mother, will suffer also.

Complicating the role of the mother even further, Jacques Lacan writes that for either sex incest refers to the mother, not the father. Judith Butler suggests that the child's battle with the father revolves around his privileged place in culture, as the origin of meaning, speech, and thought.[37] And finally, for neo-Freudians who have shifted from an Oedipal to a pre-Oedipal focus in family relations, there remains a problem inherent in pre-Oedipal dependence upon the mother. Clearly, validating the maternal body as text remains problematic.

Such validation must contend with a further problem, the existing dichotomization of the maternal and the erotic female bodies, a legacy of the romantic heroine. Angela Carter's hero in *The Passion of New Eve* declares: "I'd dreamed of meeting Tristessa, she stark naked, tied, perhaps, to a tree in a midnight forest under the wheeling stars. To have encountered her on a suburban golf-course? Or Dido in the laundromat. Or Desdemona at the ante-natal clinic. Never!"[38]

We recall the remarks quoted earlier by the heroine of *The Life and Loves of a She-Devil*, who sadly muses, "A man cannot be expected to be faithful to a wonderful mother and a good wife—such concepts lack the compulsion of the erotic."[39] This polarity between the erotic and the maternal militates against the formation of a heroine independent of the romantic heroine who depends upon the male gaze for her heroinic role.

Beyond this, for the gaze of either male or female, hero or heroine, to be transformative, to truly create and project meaning, it must be validated by its audience.[40] Two interdependent questions then must be asked: How can the female gaze be constituted? And, will the female gaze be acknowledged as transformative by the male actor? Speculating about the development of a female gaze, let us start by looking where women supposedly do start—with the mirror, held to be the woman's clue to reality, and/or the clue to the woman's reality.

The Mirror and the Gaze

Only in mirrors is it well to look, for mirrors do but show us masks.
—Oscar Wilde

No more masks!
—Muriel Rukeyser

Women are not only commodified by becoming objects of the gaze, but are also castigated for their internalization of this objectification, which takes the form of vanity and narcissism. This view argues that women accept their beauty as the substance of their being, and that, in both literature and the visual arts, the mirror symbolizes this supposed complicity. Women are held to be accomplices in becoming "a sight." The tendency in Western art to depict the woman, even in the figuring of sexual passion, as supine and passive articulates this assumption. In the erotic art of India, by contrast, the sexes are equally active and participatory, as John Berger notes in *Ways of Seeing*. But the iconography using the mirror as the emblem of women's vanity is hypocritical. Rightly this image should feature a man standing behind the mirror, holding it up to the woman's face. That is, she is not truly viewing herself, but viewing herself as beheld, just as in the museum we are voyeurs beholding the artist beholding the woman.[41] Thus, we might speculate that anxiety (loss of identity) is the pathological extremity of the gaze's objectification of the individual.

I wish to pause here and discuss that anxiety rooted partly in the idea of Woman as Body, object of the gaze, and also in the concommitant narcissism this view induces that constitutes a common emotional disorder in women. There are many causes for the wide-spread incidence of anxiety disorders in women: women have less well-defined "ego boundaries" than men because, as Chodorow explained, they have not been forced in childhood themselves to sever from the mother in order to establish a different sexual identity; women are taught their subordinate position by texts of religion, law, medicine, and other standard-bearers of the culture; women are not yet accustomed to moving into and speaking from a public role; the social caretaking roles of women are not valued highly in the society and are most frequently unpaid; woman's sexuality frequently involves a commitment to motherhood, so that control over one's own body is compromised.

I wish here to single out the connection between anxiety disorders and the line of sight, between the loss of identification and the consequent anxiety that comes when the definition of woman is subsumed under Woman as Body. It is true that since the Women's Movement of the seventies women have been better informed and more confident to make choices concerned with athletic competition, dress codes, self-defense, and medical and psychiatric decisions. Such books as *Our Bodies Ourselves* and its successors, for example, helped women take responsibility for the welfare of their own bodies; but two decades are not sufficient to reverse the weight of conventions prevailing for centuries—for example, those governing employment in the building trades or the armed forces, and the harassment of women in these and other occupations.

Psychologists commenting on social phobias in women describe states of anxiety in which the patient is "oppressed by the sense of not being there," in which the patient feels "empty inside. . . feels her body as vaporous."

Among symptoms of panic disorders clinical psychology texts list "feelings of unreality (depersonalization, derealization)." Psychologists Linda Tschirhart Sanford and Mary Ellen Donovan report that "many women we interviewed complained of feelings of being outside themselves. . . this sort of self-consciousness often is accompanied by real self-doubt." [42]

We are not talking here about evidence of adolescent separation anxiety (anxiety over becoming independent, leaving the parental world), but anxiety as a condition among adult women. We can hardly fail to connect this pathology with the ways in which women's gender roles define them. To be looked at can be dangerous, yet at the same time, a mark of success. The social phobia which presents itself as "a persistent, irrational fear of, and compelling desire to avoid, situations in which the individual may be exposed to the scrutiny of others," obviously has a special acuteness for women because of the implicit threat of sexual harassment or rape (recall Degas' painting *The Interior*).

Yet, paradoxically, women work from the assumption that their power lies in their attractiveness. As Sanford and Donovan point out, this image-identification has increased with the advent of photography, film and other news media. Moreover, fears about being attractive are fostered by advertising which implants doubts in order to sell cosmetics, clothes, jewelry, hair care products. A woman must be constantly vigilant to maintain her attractiveness; a judgment proffered from the outside, it can be revoked at any time. Women's reality is shaped by what Naomi Wolf characterizes as "the beauty myth." Sanford and Donovan claim that there is always the underlying anxiety for girls, "Am I attractive?" which unhealthily replaces the question, "What do I desire?"

Narcissism, as it is manifested in obsession with appearance, does not represent vanity, but anxiety, and is most likely to be present in those women with low self-esteem since it attempts to build self-affirmation through self-negation. How can a woman develop her own self when she is occupied with developing a self, which is primarily a body, for men? "Flesh makes me visible. / Nothing I am can do that," writes Elizabeth Fenton in "Masks."[43]

Since paintings of nude women were painted by men for the consumption of men, neither in the painting nor in the mirror can the woman see the object of *her* desire, but only herself as the object *of* desire. The woman, then, cannot look to the mirror for a glimpse of the beloved, but only for reassurance that she is worth desiring. Think of Velásquez's Rokeby Venus; think of Rubens' Venus! Narcissism is an arrest in an early stage of sexual development; Freud traces it to infantile self-love, postulating that the erotic love which succeeds it finds another object for its focus. Narcissism (and how neglected, by the way, is the mythic origin of that self-eroticism in a male body) cannot bring joy because underneath it lies the self-hatred that reduction, objectification, and infantilism produce. Our understanding of narcissism remains inconclusive. Jacques Lacan, for one, develops a theory of a "mirror stage" of human development; he posits the maturation of a divided self, one part watching itself and the other aware of being watched. For women, however, the second part overwhelms the first.[44]

Furthermore, as Alicia Ostriker points out, Sylvia Plath sees in the mirror an ineluctable, therefore dreadful procession. In Plath's "All the Dead Dears," a mother, a grandmother, and a great-grandmother "reach out hag hands to haul me in." Similarly, Ostriker suggests, "Marilyn Hacker's mother-daughter poems fear that all women are 'beasts that repeat themselves' in a cycle of self-despisal;"[45] Sexton writes in "The Double Image" of a triple image—her mother, her daughter, herself. But this triad, the matriarchal triad of maid, mother, and crone, in Sexton's poem serves not to amplify power but to reiterate catastrophic familial legacies. In another poem Sexton portrays a Snow White who becomes, in the course of time, like her venal stepmother. Thus the mirror, for women, can open vistas of inescapable repetition, and cannot be, because of both this repetition and its mediated gaze, a *self*-portrait. What the mirror presents are not portraits but roles, gender roles. Part of the problem, then, of getting beyond narcissism is that the mirror, in its traditional function, confirms women's identity as objects, trapping them in their image. It also allows reflection of the male viewing the woman to interpose itself in the symbolic mirror.

Furthermore, the mirror serves to reflect not just the male's object of desire but in some sense, the male himself. Virginia Woolf: "Women have served all these centuries as looking glasses possessing the magic and delicious power of reflecting the figure of man at twice its natural size." Woolf argues that if women throughout history had held up a mirror which gave men a more realistic look at themselves, then their "fitness for life" would have been circumscribed.[46]

The assumption that woman's vanity and narcissism is endemic is clearly illustrated in the visual arts. In the paintings and graphic art of Hans Baldung in the early sixteenth century, we find, for instance, a drawing of a naked couple titled *Death and the Maiden*. Death, like an auctioneer, turns the maiden's naked body toward the viewer, while the maiden, preoccupied with looking at herself in the mirror, seems oblivious or indifferent to his actions. Even his proximity cannot deflect her gaze; we are clearly in the presence of someone irreligious who does not think, "Timor Mortis Conturbat Me." On the other hand, Death's gesture of intimacy, clasping the naked body of the maiden, conveys the close linkage between sexuality and death that symbolizes male fears and misogyny, as Margaret Miles' comments on Baldung's work inform us.[47] Bram Dijkstra's remarkable study *Idols of Perversity: Fantasies of Feminine Evil in Fin-de-Siècle Culture*, presents the same profound visual linkage of the female body and death occuring at the turn of the nineteenth century, three centuries after Baldung.

For women, the mirror also sights (sites) an image of beauty which is unattainable, yet posited as normative. Whatever each era dictates to be too fat or too thin, too short or too tall, the wrong color, is excluded from the beautiful; but, since beauty is supposedly the *raison d'être* of woman's existence, women easily feel they lack a reason for being. Ontological problems for women are intertwined with issues of desirability. Many contemporary poems by women, therefore, are redefinitions of the attractive body; for example, a poem by Kathleen Fraser begins:

> Legs!
> How we have suffered each other,
> never meeting the standard of magazines
> or official measurements.

The poem, however, is entitled, "Poem in Which My Legs Are Accepted." [48] In a similar vein, Sharon Barba's contemporary "A Cycle of Women" poems contain the following description of Venus:

> Until she rises as though from the sea
> not on the half-shell this time
> nothing to laugh at
> and not as delicate as he imagined her:
> a woman big-hipped, beautiful and fierce.[49]

Lucille Clifton similarly rejoices in her own ample proportions as "a city / of a woman," with a "geography" of her own, requiring a "map" for understanding.[50] The image of the big-hipped woman represents fecundity and childbearing; it is definitely not the slender, delicate woman's body of Botticelli's Venus, which today's models affect. Clifton's mature body defies not only current aesthetic codes, but codes which, as we saw in "Woman/Space," insist that women should *occupy* as little space as possible. Twiggy as the female role model of the 1970s has only her sex in common with Renoir's models. Gender definitions of desirability have markedly changed, but women are caught in whichever definition prevails in their day.

The protagonist of *The Life and Loves of a She-Devil*, Ruth, exclaims bitterly about aesthetic codes:

I am six feet two inches tall, which is fine for a man but not for a woman.
I am dark. . . and have one of those jutting jaws that tall, dark women
often have, and eyes sunk rather far back into my face, and a hooked
nose. My shoulders are broad and bony and my hips broad and fleshy,
and the muscles in my legs are well developed. My arms, I swear, are
too short for my body. My nature and my looks do not agree. I was
unlucky. . . in the great lottery that is woman's life. [51]

She paints herself as a grotesque, beyond the pale of romance, since
by common consent until now, a romantic (erotic) heroine must be beautiful. Again, our aesthetic criteria vary not only with the times, but with the
differences of race and class that provide their own powerful definitions of
beauty. The poetry and fiction of contemporary women's writing raise the
challenging question of what constitutes beauty, and whether a heroine *need*
be beautiful.

For either sex, the grotesque is whatever exceeds conventional laws
and limits or departs from the ideal form in which beauty is cast. The aesthetic view is exclusionary, since we use it to distinguish the beautiful from
the ugly, innocent from experienced, and so on. Those qualities judged inappropriate as objects of the gaze, by remaining unobserved, become invisible. One example of this is the destructive identification of women's beauty
(hence, of her visibility and power) with youth, a view that changes when
the viewer/speaker is a woman herself. When Ruth Fainlight in her poem,
"It Must," addresses her contemporaries who have "tenderness of the bruised
flesh / darkness under the eyes from held-back tears, / watery blisters on
frost-touched fruit already decaying," she asks:

Friends, tell me the truth. Do you also
sometimes feel a sudden jaunty indifference,
or even better, extraordinary moments
when you positively welcome the new
face that greets you from the mirror like
a mother—not your own mother, but that other
dream-figure of she-you-always-yearned-for. [52]

The feminist re-view of the mirror, then, allows new aesthetic definitions of desirability, both lesbian and heterosexual, that patriarchal culture
has disallowed.

The recurrent theme of women's invisibility in literature can be understood by means of the mirror, which implies but does not realize signification. Although women are in a literal sense invisible in many public roles,
there is also a profound private or psychological sense in which this invisibility obtains. If the mirrored image validates the woman's identity what
happens when the male hand holding the mirror up to [her] nature is re-

moved? Her identity is removed simultaneously. Poet Anne Darr writes that at the end of a love affair, "I look in the mirror, I see nothing." And Jane Cooper asserts in "The Knowledge That Comes Through Experience," that

> Feelings aside, I never know my face.
> I comb my hair and what I see is timeless,
> Not a face at all but (besides the hair)
> Lips and a pair of eyes, two hands, a body
> Pale as a fish imprisoned in the mirror.[53]

And in *Fear Of Flying*, Isadora says: "Obviously it was dangerous to stare at your eyes in mirrors too long. I stood back to examine my body. Where did my body end and the air around it begin?. . . It was a sensation I often had and I recognized it as a significant part of my panics. . . . I tried to examine my physical self, to take stock so that I could remember who I was—if indeed my body could be said to be me."[54]

Again, in Isak Dinesen's story "The Supper at Elsinore," two sisters, the protagonists, live in a dissociated state: "They stood in a strange, distorted relation to the world, as if it had been only their reflection in a mirror which they had been showing it, while in the background and the shadow the real woman remained a looker-on." The real woman observes: "Did she wish that the man would break the glass and the lovely creature within it, and turn around toward herself?"[55] In Angela Carter's words, woman's being is perceived by men as a "pane the sun shines through," whilst Cynthia Macdonald's "Stained Glass Woman" is "glowing, refractive, transparent, colorful. . . Trying to make light, as a stained glass woman should."[56]

Needless to say, contemporary women writers have been devising uses for the mirror other than the ones it traditionally has served, functions which will be enabling and constitutive for women. (A 1975 feminist conference on Goddesses convened under the title "Through the Looking Glass.") Praising Rita Mae Brown's poem "Feminist," Helena Michie remarks that Brown "seems to produce a woman who can look into a mirror and see reflected there a face and a body unmediated by male desire."[57] Toi Derricotte's *The Mirror Poems*, "The Other Side of the Mirror" by M.E. Coleridge, "Naked Girl and Mirror" by Judith Wright, and "The Mirror In Which Two Are Seen As One" by Adrienne Rich, though different from each other, all suggest alternative functions for the mirror, mirrors which the woman holds up to an unmediated gaze. For Rich, for example, the woman finally finds "the mother" in the mirror, the ancestral mother who is perceived as an ally, taking individual women past the trap of solipsism. Coleridge and Wright counter the idea of the mirror as the tool of vanity by suggesting that it reflects not only the image of the body, but of the soul. In Isak

Dinesen's story "The Roads Round Pisa," the husband expects his wife to be a mirror for *his* soul. Men have no mirrors of their own, asserts Denise Levertov in "Abel's Bride," but as for the woman, "When she goes out / she looks in the glass, she remembers / herself." [58]

Sandra Gilbert and Susan Gubar suggest: "The persistent feminist metaphor of revision, along with the recurrent appearance in female au-thored writing of mirrors in which two are seen as one and one is seen as two [i.e., everywoman] suggests that women's enterprise in patriarchal cul-ture might be precisely the excavation and confrontation of the uncanny, i.e., themselves." [59]

Here, Gilbert and Gubar take issue, as did feminist theorists like Luce Irigaray, with the Freudian contention that "women's sexuality is no doubt the most basic form of *unheimlich*, the 'uncanny.'" Obviously, if *women* are doing the viewing and the defining, then their sexuality is no longer "other," and losing its "otherness," no longer uncanny. (Ironically, Freud's culture assumed women to be the providers of *heimlichkeit*, or domesticity, at the same time as they were being labelled *unheimlich* or "uncanny.")

The mirror may become for women, as it does for many Isak Dinesen protagonists, a locus of epiphany, the place where they confront the "mask." "I am she!" exclaims the woman in Coleridge's "The Other Side of the Mirror," and Anne Sexton's "The Double Image" asks: How many are seen? Who is seen? Who is seeing? "She eyes me from that face, / that stony head of death / I had outgrown." [60] In this Sexton poem the mirror may present a self divided or conflicted, or show aspects (witch-like, for instance) usu-ally suppressed by the mirror's demands for equilibrium and equipoise. Thus, women recognize the "other;" it offers the shock of recognition that "The Monster in the Mirror," the Medusa or stony head of death, the Terrible Mother, the witch, is one self among selves. The mirror becomes the lamp; the woman moves from narcissism to self-scrutiny (Lacanian self-regard), and finally, as we'll see in the next chapter, to comedy. So, if for the man the Dark Lady and the Bitch-Goddess encode unspeakable dread, for the woman these figures are part of self-recognition. The mirror may aid women in developing an ontological sense, not merely an iconological one. Further, the mirror is a central image to object-relations theory, the tool of the self-in-relation.

As with the larger category of the gaze under which the mirror is sub-sumed, the feminist project of re-viewing the mirror is expansive, taking in, besides the unpropped self, mothers, sisters, everywoman. The mirror of-fers not merely a self-portrait, but a group portrait; it seems to me that the difference between this group portrait and the familial ones noted earlier, which were rejected as destructive by Plath, Sexton, and others, is that the portraits here become instruments of self-understanding and contextualization. These feminist writers propose the restoration of women's history, and they use the mirror as one agent in this project. They use it not as a record of defeat or oppression, but as a means of providing women with a past of their own, female figures with whom to bond. The new re-visioning, shedding the old masks and replacing them, produces a radical re-disposition of social relations between the sexes.

Beauty, then, has meant power, as women's preoccupation with their appearance testifies; furthermore, it is one of the few powers men have not denied them, as Kate Millet observed in *Sexual Politics* almost three decades ago. But if women choose to mirror each other, for example, and the father loses this power, then the Oedipal triangle is broken. If women choose to mirror the mother and not the lover, the object/subject erotic relation is changed. The mirror has the potential to reflect many relations, social images, and through them, social issues. We may finally be able to transcend the female anxiety which Snow White's stepmother personifies, and which Carolyn Kizer applies to women in general:

> Our masks, always in peril of smearing or cracking.
> In need of continuous check in the mirror or silverware,
> Keeps us in thrall to ourselves, concerned with our surfaces.[61]

This indeed does become the anxiety of Snow White herself, who finally grows up to become the (mirror-) image of her stepmother:

> rolling her china-blue doll eyes open and shut
> and sometimes referring to her mirror
> as women do.[62]

Medusa and the gaze

Like some galactic vision the Medusa comes in
on the waves to startle your quiet gaze

—Nicolai Kantchev

A discussion of the Medusa figure follows since she is one important embodiment of male apprehension of female power, particularly sexual power. Culturally received opinion asserts that Medusa's returning or originating the gaze will change the object of that gaze into stone. This projected narrative shows the consequences of contravening the dictum that women should not direct anything, especially a gaze, or a voice.

The proscription of the female-directed gaze is patently clear in the injunction that women shouldn't make spectacles of themselves because this involves a change from being specular object to spectacular actress. The spectacle is performative, projective, considered excessive and tending toward erotic ecstasy, or *jouissance* as French feminists term it, which women are not permitted to express.[63]

The male gaze upon the woman as specular object is, to the contrary, circumscriptive. The gaze returned, however, the woman subject *directing* the gaze in literature or the visual arts, has the potential to represent woman, but it is an image fraught with difficulty. The entrenched tradition of woman as object of the male gaze constrains women themselves from being gazers by ancient dictates about female modesty; the maiden or nun whose eyes are lowered to the ground, the yasmak and the bridal veil, attest to a "natural" lust in men that women should not provoke. Proscriptions around the gaze are, importantly, indicative of women's entire role, for powerful as the cultural injunction to sexual modesty is for women, there exists a more encompassing injunction to a generalized womanly decorum of obedience and submission.

The Medusa, however, is a focus of resistance to the male gaze. I will look at some of the apprehension aroused by such resistance. Bulfinch's *The Age of Fable*, chosen because it is most familiar to the reader, supplies the well-known tale:

> When Perseus was grown up, Polydectes sent him to attempt the conquest of Medusa, a terrible monster who had laid waste the country. She was once a beautiful maiden whose hair was her chief glory, but as she dared to vie in beauty with Minerva, the goddess deprived her of her charms and changed her beautiful ringlets into hissing serpents. She became a cruel monster of so frightful an aspect that no living thing could behold her without being turned into stone. All around the cavern where she dwelt might be seen the stony figures of men and animals which had chanced to catch a glimpse of her and been petrified with the sight. Perseus, favored by Minerva and Mercury, the former of whom lent him her shield and the latter his winged shoes, approached Medusa while she slept, and taking care not to look directly at her, but guided by her image reflected in the bright shield which he bore, he cut off her head and gave it to Minerva, who fixed it in the middle of her Aegis.[64]

Both omissions and commissions in this account deserve attention. We note first that Medusa's original impulse to flaunt her beauty was the expression of an erotic self which challenged the chaste Minerva, a contrast employed later by Milton in *Comus*, his masque of revelry. For the average reader, it comes as something of a shock to think of Medusa as young and beautiful at all! Her hair, singled out for special notice, is itself a sexual symbol, as the custom of shearing off or concealing the hair of nuns and orthodox Jewesses attests.[65] The snakes that replace Medusa's own locks are likewise a sexual symbol, and her sexuality is emphasized in Nicolai Kantchev's epigraph to this section on Medusa by the image of her rising from the sea like a Botticellian Venus, goddess of love. Indeed, it is precisely this union of eroticism and destruction, fused in Medusa's visage, that is particularly associated with *feminine* evil, as we saw earlier in the work of Hans Baldung, and the art of the *fin de siècle*.

Bram Dijkstra includes in his study *Idols of Perversity* representations of Medusa by *fin-de-siècle* artists including, but by no means limited to, Gabriel Ferrier, Kenyon Cox, Fernand Khnopff, Carlos Schwabe, Joseph Mullner, and Franz von Lenbach. In these visual representations, as well as in literary texts, Medusa becomes a monster, with her hissing head of snakes and wild staring eyes. Her transmogrification is the evidence of her "unnatural," "monstrous" nature, both lustful and destructive, of which the telltale sign is the usurpation of the male function of directing the gaze. We might compare, in passing, the use of the Medusa head as a common apotropaic device in Greek, Coptic, and Roman art; it was frequently placed in the center of a mosaic floor, while the herm or phallus, a pillar, usually was set outside the house. Both were devices employed to fend off evil. Though the herm was more explicitly sexual, curiously it did not, as did Medusa, represent evil (evil sexuality), only the power to repel evil.

We notice, too, that the myth as Bulfinch relates it locates Medusa in a cavern; we have already discussed in the essay on Woman/Space the fear of the underground and how this fear is projected onto woman generally. It is fear of mysterious, recurrent, absorptive, chthonic power. Thus Eric Neumann believes: "The Terrible Mother may be associated with a tendency toward the transformative character. . . . Her appearance may introduce a positive development in which the ego is driven toward masculinization and the fight with the dragon, i.e., positive development and transformation. . . . Perseus must kill the Terrible Mother before he can win Andromeda."[66]

What is neglected not only in Bulfinch's account, but in subsequent accounts based upon this story, is that Medusa gives birth to a pair of twins as she is being decapitated by Perseus. Medusa represents generative energy, not merely destructive energy, but the last part of the tale, revealing her generative powers, is little known and rarely promulgated. Although in the Medusa figure the horrific and the erotic are intertwined, the horrific suppresses the erotic.

George Napier, tracing parallels between Greek and Hindu art and mythology, insists on the close relation between eroticism and the horrific. Napier observes that the three-pointed mark of the Hindu deities "is so much connected with both the horrific and the erotic that the ideas of death and parturition are, as they are with the Gorgon [i.e., the Medusa] central to it." He continues, "that the erotic and the horrific are part of the same iconographic structure proves better than any single testimony that ambivalence is at the basis of the Gorgon." [67]

We have lost the idea of that "ambi-valence," or double-valenced power. Whereas in earlier times, goddesses like Kali and Ishtar combined the erotic and the horrific, the powers of birth and death, such figures as these have been reduced to solely destructive functions. [68] For example, the Medusa is analagous to certain Hindu deities who possess, as she does, snake-entwined heads. Yet these Hindu deities also have a third eye, which is the inner eye of enlightenment and which, in our iconography, Medusa lacks. As a horrific figure, her gaze tantamount to death, she has no such *in*sight. [69]

When we know what has been suppressed about her, we may speculate that the overriding image of Medusa as a destructive agent may be no more than a male response to female self-formulation, self-scrutiny, in/sight. The view which perhaps most supports this speculation that the Medusa is one visual correlative of male fear of female power, especially sexual power (a view which in itself seems to have petrified thinking about Medusa!), is the castration theory set forth by Freud in his 1922 note on "Medusa's Head:"

> We have not often attempted to interpret individual mythological themes, but an interpretation suggests itself easily in the case of the horrifying decapitated head of Medusa. To decapitate is to castrate. The terror of Medusa is thus a terror of castration that is linked to the sight of something. Numerous analyses have made us familiar with the occasion for this: it occurs when a boy, who has hitherto been unwilling to believe the threat of castration, catches sight of the female genitals, probably those of an adult, surrounded by hair, and essentially those of his mother. [70]

Freud's view that the Medusa's head takes the place of a representation of the female genitals finds substantiation in the *fin-de-siècle* paintings collected and analyzed by Bram Dijkstra. Such interpretation seems very close to Céline's identification in his vision of childbirth with total degradation. "He makes," as Kristeva points out, "amply clear which fantasy is involved: something *horrible to see* at the impossible doors of the invisible—the mother's body." [71] Displaying the genitals functions in other contexts besides that of childbirth as an apotropaic act; Freud, in the essay cited above, recounts that "we read in Rabelais of how the Devil took to flight when the woman showed him her vulva." The practice of women revolutionaries during the French Revolution lifting their skirts in defiance of firing squads so that the soldiers' rifles would have to take aim at the exposed site of prior erotic pleasure, the naked female body, provides another startling example of this apotropaic act linking the horrific and the erotic.

In our day we can find similar gestures—for example, the sculpture by Nancy Spero of Sheela-na-Gig, Celtic goddess of fertility *and* destruction, displaying her enormous vagina, and facing the spectator with a grin upon her face. A notably similar figure appears in Fleur Adcock's poem, "Kilpeck":

> The Victorians broke some of these figures
> as being too obscene for a church;
> but they missed the Whore of Kilpeck.
> She leans out under the roof
> holding her pink stony cleft agape
> with her ancient little hands.
> There was always witchcraft here, you say.[72]

Additionally, I would refer to Hélène Cixous's essay "The Laugh of the Medusa," which reminds us that Medusa was not a monster but young and beautiful; the laugh to which Cixous' title refers indicates Medusa's knowledge that she embodies what for men are the two unrepresentables, unspeakables: death and the feminine sex. Perseus' heroic deed is to destroy the terrible mother. The misogynistic representation of women that Rider Haggard offers in his novel *She* is kin to the Hollywood femme fatale or "vamp," short for vampire or blood sucker; the "femme fatale," as we know from the *silent* movies, kills with a glance. If looks could kill, they did.[73] The profound association of the feminine sex with death may, as Freud suggests, be founded on fear of castration (obviously, the fear of castration is irrelevant in a lesbian dyad), but in any event, death, like the feminine, belongs outside the male symbolic order.

Cixous shares her re-focused interest in the Medusa figure with May Sarton, Louise Bogan, Ann Stamford, Rachel Blau du Plessis, Sheryl St. Germain, Amy Clampitt, and Karen Lindsey, all of whom have written poems about Medusa. Allowing for individual differences, the burden of these poems has been the identification with, and general reclamation of, the Gorgon. Women writers are dismantling received images of patriarchal anxiety, recognizing that figures of female evil simply may be women embodying power who can usefully be centralized in a new mythology, who may even provide some attributes for constituting the heroine. In this light, Medusa, the lamia, Circe, the siren, figures who are the many guises of evil displaced onto women, share a disobedience, a refusal to be passive or silent and objectified. They should not be suppressed because they reveal capabilities women have been schooled to disown; rather, these figures should be reinterpreted as symbols of female power.

To re-evaluate the Medusa figure we need not say dismissively, "Those snakes are a figment of male hysteria and a libel" or "Let's ignore that sinister image." We may insist more positively that the snake, though a Christian symbol of evil, particularly sexual evil and therefore often depicted in Christian art as having the head of a woman, was, to the contrary, for the Greeks the sacred symbol of the mysteries at Eleusis, rituals performed by women at a site reserved for them.[74]

We can recall the legendary Tiresias, unwitting voyeur, who, because he saw snakes mating, saw a female mystery not meant for men to behold. For this trespass the gods turned him into half-man, half-woman, with a long grey beard and drooping breasts. He becomes androgynous, but this transformation makes him not less but more; embodying the wisdom of both sexes, he becomes a seer. We may also see the snake representing the sacred in the Minoan Snake Goddess of ancient Crete, a symbol of female power but one who is beneficent, a protector of the house. Similarly, the phython at Delphi was sacred to Earth and her prophetess, Gaea, before Apollo slew the snake and claimed the sanctuary for himself.

The snake is a powerful symbol of creation: it sloughs its skin and emerges from a dead husk, thus embodying reincarnation; it is chthonic; it can wrap its tail in its teeth, forming a complete circle, an image of perfection and unity. It is also a symbol for the feminine, immortalized by Cleopatra, *serpent* of the Nile who, in her complete femininity, chose a snake as the instrument of her death. The snake is, too, the symbol of Aesculapius, Greek god of healing; priests at the grave of Aesculapius bred the special snakes sacred to him. Since the snake is a female symbol, the myth implies that Aesculapius took over the art of healing from women.

Part of the recent reclamation of the Medusa figure represents a return to these repressed or neglected interpretations of her crown of serpents. Examples range from Isak Dinesen's description of her heroine in "Copenhagen Season" as possessing a "serpent's head" and "serpentine curls," to Sheryl St. Germain's poem, "Medusa Explains Herself," in which the Gorgon asserts that those who find themselves perching petrified on top of her TV are not her victims, but victims of their own lack of self-scrutiny. And here is a rich example, taken from Monique Wittig's novel *Les Guérillères*, which changes negative imaging to positive:

> . . . an orchard planted with trees of every color. A naked woman walks therein. Her beautiful body is black and shining. Her hair consists of slender mobile snakes which produce music at her every movement. This is the hortative head of hair. It is so called because it communicates by the mouths of its hundred thousand snakes with the woman

wearing the headdress. Orpheus, the favorite snake of the woman who walks in the garden, keeps advising her to eat the fruit of the tree in the center of the garden. The woman tastes the fruit of each tree asking Orpheus the snake how to recognize that which is good. The answer given is that it sparkles, that merely to look at it rejoices the heart. Or else the answer given is that, as soon as she has eaten the fruit, she will become taller, she will grow, her feet will not leave the ground though her forehead will touch the stars. And he Orpheus and the hundred thousand snakes of her headdress will extend from one side of her face to the other, they will afford her a brilliant crown, her eyes will become as pale as moons, she will acquire knowledge.[75]

Wittig's remarkable book not only transforms the snake into an agent of the good and the beautiful, but also an agent of creativity.

Perhaps the most valuable reinterpretation of Medusa for our purposes can be found in May Sarton's "The Muse as Medusa." The title by itself indicates the profundity of change from destructive to creative power. I quote the poem in full:

> I saw you once, Medusa; we were alone
> I looked you straight in the cold eye, cold.
> I was not punished, was not turned to stone—
> How to believe the legends I am told?
>
> I came as naked as any little fish,
> Prepared to be hooked, gutted, caught;
> But I saw you, Medusa, made my wish,
> And when I left you I was clothed in thought. . .
>
> Being allowed, perhaps, to swim my way
> Through the great deep and on the rising tide,
> Flashing wild streams, as free and rich as they,
> Though you had power marshaled on your side.
>
> The fish escaped to many a magic reef;
> The fish explored many a dangerous sea—
> The fish, Medusa, did not come to grief,
> But swims still in a fluid mystery.
>
> Forget the image: your silence is my ocean,
> And even now it teems with life. You chose
> To abdicate by total lack of motion,
> But did it work, for nothing really froze?
>
> It is all fluid still, that world of feeling
> Where thoughts, those fishes, silent, feed and rove;
> And, fluid, it is also full of healing,
> For love is healing, even rootless love.
>
> I turn your face around! It is my face.

That frozen rage is what I must explore—
Oh secret, self-enclosed, and ravaged place!
This is the gift I thank Medusa for.[76]

This poem is a veritable repository of feminist themes; in stanza one ("I was not punished, was not turned to stone— / How to believe the legends I am told?"), we are sharply reminded of Rich's declaration that "nothing that was written was true for us." (Karen Lindsey's Medusa poem has a strikingly similar line: "But the legends are wrong, / it is those who do not look / who turn to stone." [77]) In Sarton's second stanza we find the maternal image (the muse as a mother clothing a naked child) which, when we remember that Medusa in fact bore twins, makes Medusa/Muse more plausible.

The third stanza presents the Medusa as both procreator and artistic creator, that particularly potent conjunction of powers. Sarton augments Medusa's power here by referring to the "healing" effect of her love, indicating the full extent of the Gorgon's creative powers. The fourth stanza projects a persona who can swim in a "fluid mystery," a medium identified with feminine flux. And finally, in the last stanza, we have the poet's cry of recognition, the epiphany we have already met in the mirror, "I am she!" The face in the mirror is the speaker's, frozen not by the Medusa, but by her own suppressed rage that needs to be scrutinized. The face in the mirror becomes now for Sarton the subject of self-analysis, as it had gone on to become for Rich, Plath, and Sexton.

For all these reasons, the Medusa emerges not as a monster, but as a liberator, a mother, a goddess of love. Grotesquerie, which fashioned the image of Medusa, reveals itself to be a function of repression, of the skewed vision that fear and marginalization produce. Once we understand that gender decides the reception of the image as well as its creation, women can actually incorporate images of themselves as "grotesques" in their quest to become image makers, subject of the gaze.[78]

4

Woman/Speech

A woman in the shape of a monster
a monster in the shape of a woman
the skies are full of them.

—"Planetarium," Adrienne Rich

What would happen if one woman told the truth about her life?
—Muriel Rukeyser

The witch parallels Medusa in certain ways: first, as a locus of misogyny, of male epistemic and sexual anxieties; and second, as an empowered female figure with characteristics being reclaimed by feminist writers. The witch adds a unique capacity to the powerful but silent Medusa, for the witch, in addition to other powers, traditionally functions also as *speaker*. All the current feminist efforts to validate 'relatedness' and 'connectedness' as female contributions undervalued by society, important as such correctives are, can distract us from the primacy of the word. My contention is that it is the power of speech which ultimately transforms the witch and dooms her in male thinking to evil caricature.

What figure does the word 'witch' conjure up in the imagination? A crone, a hag, bent and misshapen, with fangs for teeth and horny hands? A 'weird sister?' For such an image, we need think back no further than John

Updike's 1987 novel, *The Witches of Eastwick*, prefigured almost exactly a century earlier in Rider Haggard's *She*, about an old, uncanny (Freud's *unheimlich*), potent woman, who, like Medusa, men must seek out and destroy. The profound fear of witches may be traced to the fact that they are transpositions of the Fates, of the Furies, all held to be women capable (according to the OED) first of controlling destiny, and, later in time, of forecasting events. Their supernatural power of prognostication, one of the most familiar of their attributes, is in fact a residuum of this original identity as Fates or Furies, monstrous women who also avenge wrongdoing in Greek mythology. Thus the human fear of the future and the fear of women who control or foresee that future coalesce in one monstrous or weird female shape.

The witch figure is ancient, far antedating Christianity, reaching back to our earliest mythologies: Demeter/Kore, Ishtar/Tammus, the Celtic Grail legends, Hecuba/Hecate. She is part of an early matriarchal trinity of daughter, mother, crone, equal aspects of the same persona. Annis Pratt believes that witches belong to female archetypes, with "ladies of the lake, fairy queens, elf maidens. . . expressing the repression of powerful women."[1] Thus, St. Augustine called Cybele, the Great Mother Goddess, a "monster," an anathema to Church Fathers, an inheritance from pagan Rome where the Great Mother had been worshipped from the second century before Christ. Conversely, the possession of power by a woman may have been enough to elicit the tag "witch." In Fay Weldon's recent novel, *The Life and Loves of a She-Devil*, the central character, Ruth, muses, "it is not a matter of male or female, after all; it never was: merely of power."[2] But as Ruth finds to her misfortune during the course of the story, power *is* precisely a matter of "male or female."

Through analysis of the powers attributed to the witch, we gain understanding of what society sees as suspect in women which therefore must to be repressed. Conversely, this helps us see where women may find strengths to facilitate the difficult process of empowerment.[3] These powers are, first, that of female sexuality; second, that of female bonding; third, that of female entry into discourse. I will discuss these powers in turn as they bear upon an understanding of the witch. One arresting fact is that none of these powers involves magic. The imputation of the supernatural stems from the irrationality of fear.

There is no better place to begin our consideration of the witch than fairy tales, the place, for many readers, of initial encounter with that character. Bruno Bettelheim, Maria Tatar, and Jack Zipes, among others, have undertaken new textual narrations or revisionary readings of traditional fairy tales. In the process of re-reading the originals through their eyes, we un-

derstand that the traditional tales are not only repositories of cultural images and characters, as rich a resource for self-knowledge as mythology, but
also that our early reading of them polarizes male and female readers through
rigid division of tasks, experience, codes of decorum. Ruth Bottigheimer's
Grimms' Bold Boys and Bad Girls, mentioned earlier, reflects the prevailing
decorum in its choice of titular adjectives. How does this operate?

Fairy tales and romances characteristically embed danger to women
as a strong plot element; their sub-text is violence. That violence may take
the form of physical or psychological abuse heaped upon the helpless, illus-
trating, for example, the dangers of economic dependence (Cinderella) and
narrative passivity (Sleeping Beauty). But most commonly the violence is
sexual, implicit in the woman's position as object of desire. The awareness
of multifarious perils encoded in the false promises the fairy tale holds out
for women leads many contemporary women writers to subvert its conventionally happy ending; "and the Fairy Tales / rose-colored off-colored / have
never had any ever after," maintains Marjorie Agosin.[4] In "Snow White and
the Seven Dwarfs," Sexton describes the dwarfs as "little hot dogs."[5] No
Walt Disney helpers they! Rather, Sexton makes the same conjunctions
among unbridled sexuality, animals and "the little men" that we saw male
painters and writers make among unbridled sexuality, animals and women.
Marjorie Agosin strikes this same note of sexual hazard in her "Fairy Tales
and Something More," as she wonders "And who knows / how she ended
her nights / in a room with seven precocious fellows?"[6]

That sexual violence committed against women is built into gender
roles and encapsulated in fairy tales is demonstrated clearly by a mixture of
sensuality and morbidity in Angela Carter's *The Bloody Chamber and Other
Stories*. Similarly, in a graphic metaphor, Simone de Beauvoir claims in *The
Second Sex* that in order to fulfill their female roles, women make themselves
not only into objects but into *prey*, a term transposed from the male vocabulary about the conquest of blood sports to sexual conquest, predation.[7]

One of the tasks of works like Carter's and Sexton's is to reappraise
characters who are shunned or deemed evil because they have departed from
customary female roles, and to inscribe them in new texts as heroines. For
instance, upon the witch's wisdom depends the success of many a quest, for
the witch's narrative function in many fairy tales is to be a helper figure,
similar to the animal/helper. Witches in fairy tales do bestow valuable gifts,
not just poison apples. Again, like the animal, the witch may also embody
an important lesson about the benefits to be derived from acknowledging
and respecting difference.[8] The quester, after all, must penetrate the witch's
old/ugly/humble appearance before he or she can trust the wisdom of her

words. The interaction of plot and the character of the witch in fairy tales suggests that a shunned character is perceived as evil, rather than an evil one being shunned.[9]

Witches and sexuality, like the Gorgon (Medusa) and sexuality, have been closely associated from time immemorial. This is one reason witches are excoriated and feared. The familiar virgin/whore polarity also appears as virgin/*witch*; "witch" functions, then, in this dichotomization as a designation of unregenerate sexuality, like whore.

Furthermore, as historian Margaret Miles has noted, witch-hunting manuals such as the *Malleus Maleficarum*, disseminated in Europe between 1486-1520, purveyed the idea that *all* women are naturally prone to evil through their weak will and insatiable lust; all women, it follows, are therefore equally susceptible to the sin of witchcraft. Witches were by no means exclusively imaged as crones; as we have previously remarked, sixteenth century artist Hans Baldung, for instance, by painting young and old, exotic nudes and naked crones as witch-like, created visual substantiation for the connection between women's sexuality in general and witchcraft.[10] By creating witches who appear young and desirable, Baldung was also able to invoke subliminally the image of Eve in the Garden, thereby intensifying the connection between female nudity and evil sexuality. In Goya's etching, "The Witches' Sabbath" (1789), the painter positions Bacchus in the center of a group of revelling witches of indeterminate age, thereby representing this same idea that women's unbridled lust gives rise to witchcraft at *every* age.

History tells us that many of the women hanged as witches in Salem were young maidens and young matrons; we know too, as Ruth Bottigheimer has emphasized in her study of Grimms' *Fairy Tales*, that many *young* maidens in fairy tales possess the magic, witch-like ability to cast spells. Records demonstrate that between the fourteenth and the eighteenth centuries, approximately nine million individuals in the Western world were murdered as witches, including girls of ten and eleven and pregnant women, as well as sterile or senile old women.

In sum, there was a generic association of woman with temptation, with sexual power, *bewitching* power, visually symbolized in the image of the woman-headed serpent. (Goethe, that enlightened humanist, asserted that female sexual bodies meant witches' bodies!) Moreover it was believed that although evil might originate in sexual power, witches extended it to other powers, such as curses, predictions, black magic. For instance, witches were frequently held responsible for the plague in Europe.

Linking women's bodies and evil sexuality is based in part upon the ages-old association of women and animals, an association indicating re-vulsion from excess, grossness, something unbridled, and out of nature. Examples abound. As far back as the *Oresteia* of Aeschylus, woman was seen as a sexual monster: the chorus comments: "And then, / worst of all, / the inordinate desire, / the lust of the woman." [11] We cannot help but remember Lear's taunt: "Down from the waist they are centaurs, / Though women all above."[12]

More recently, fin-de-siècle art and literature, and that of the period immediately following, repeatedly connect women to animality, and not just Medusa's snakes—think of Egon Schiele, think of Gustave Klimt, think of Paul Klee, who, in 1904, painted *Woman and Animal* about which he wrote: "The beast in man pursues the woman, who is not entirely insensible to it. Affinities of the lady with the bestial. Unveiling a bit of the feminine psyche. Recognition of a truth one likes to mask."[13] This view prompted the depiction of women disporting themselves with animals, holding them, caressing them, intertwined with them. Bacchantes and nymphs, the counterparts of witches, entertained satyrs and centaurs. The modern Swiss painter Balthus has a painting, oddly disturbing in its suggestion of sexual play, of a nude girl frolicking on the floor with her cat. Through the ages the common thread is the power of evil incarnate in women.[14]

Women bring out the beast in men; it is no coincidence that Circe, the witch, turns Ulysses' sailors into animals. Bram Djikstra documents a startling number of visual representations of women in sensual poses with animals; the implication is inescapable. Women resemble animals in their sensuality, the body is all there is to women; their nature, imbalanced and soulless, frees men to "fantasies of evil" and justifies a treatment of women that accords with their bestiality. Djikstra explains that the title of his own book derives from the belief current at the turn of the century that "as a result of her instinctual affinity with the animals, women had truly become 'the idol of perversity.'"[15] Two different cautions to men are buried in this last phrase: first, the commandment not to worship idols; secondly, the identification of woman with something perverse, unnatural, monstrous, both larger than life and animalistic, like the idol of the Golden Calf itself.

The denigratory association between woman and animal is still an *idée fixe*. Thus the female narrator of Angela Carter's *The Passion of New Eve* remarks that the women the master Zero keeps in captivity through sexual thralldom tell her Zero believes "women were fashioned of a different soul substance from men, a more primitive, animal stuff, and so did not need the paraphernalia of civilized society, such as cutlery, meat, soap, shoes, etc., though, of course, he did."[16] Carter's nomenclature supplies a special irony, since the macho master, Zero, keeper of a desert harem, is himself a nothing, zero not even a true acronym of eros.

In 1989 a new perfume, Animale, was introduced in America, launched by an advertisement with the caption "The new fragrance. Unleash it!" Above the slogan appeared a picture of the head and upper torso of a sultry female, unclothed, but decorated with green, purple and black stripes in the marking pattern of a tiger. The profound identification of woman and animal surfaces in a line from Randall Jarrell's poem "In Nature There Is Neither Right nor Left nor Wrong:" men "suck childhood, beasthood, from a mother's breasts."[17] This animal nature is not mediated by a moral sense; like Nature itself in the poem's title, the mother is at best unaware. This reflects one of the oldest charges against women, another female lack, the lack of a *moral* signifier.

The generic association of woman with animality, with lust, going back as far as the satire of Simonides, held true most particularly for the witch; her unbridled sexual power was part of what made her monstrous. Her excess of appetite was doubly to be condemned because it did not serve reproductive ends. Non-reproductive sexuality, traditionally censured by the church and often for political or economic reasons by civil states, remains the target of pro-life protest today. Such protest, however, is not limited to those speaking from religious beliefs. Non-maternal feelings, the argument runs, which the witch is held to personify, open women to any degree of perversity; in Jim Henson's film *Witches*, the witch leaders devise a scheme to turn all children into mice! In a national magazine Norman Podhoretz argued that the woman not possessed by a man is guilty of a refusal to accept responsibility for her female nature, i.e., motherhood, returning women to the biological imperative. Opponents of non-reproductive sexuality share, predictably, a generally conservative outlook about women's claims to broader roles in society.

Until recently, sexual freedom for women entailed the risk of pregnancy; the witch, however, was perceived as sexually autonomous. The familiar image of the witch astride her broomstick riding through the sky actually fuses two crucial images of transcendence: the first is an image of freedom, manifest in the witch's ability to "rise above" human limitations and fly (we contrast this power immediately with Erica Jong's *Fear of Flying*, a metaphor for the fettered feminine psyche); the second image relates specifically to the witch's sexual autonomy. Astride the broomstick, a phallic extension, she is autoerotic. Just so, Angela Carter's hero confronting the hundred-breasted underground goddess (Astarte) in *The Passion of New Eve*, responds, "I was appalled by the spectacle of the goddess. She was a sacred *monster*. She was personified and *self-fulfilling* fertility" (emphasis added).[18] In fact, this motif of self-impregnation is very old, and its veiled threat is the self-sufficiency of the androgynous figure, Carter's goddess/ woman who can procreate without men.

Although men experience the tension between eroticism and aging desire ("That is no country for old men. The young / In one another's arms"), ageism, because of the "beauty myth," is particularly punishing for women.[19] Louise Bogan expresses this self-consuming pain of desire in age, particularly in the metaphor of the last line of "The Crows." The whole poem is made all the more poignant for its predominantly monosyllabic words and matter-of-fact tone:

> The woman who has grown old
> And knows desire must die,
> Yet turns to love again,
> Hears the crows' cry.
> She is a stem long hardened,
>
> A weed that no scythe mows,
> The heart's laughter will be to her
> The crying of the crows,
>
> Who slide in the air with the same voice
> Over what yields not, and what yields,
> Alike in spring, and when there is only bitter
> Winter-burning in the fields.[20]

But witches of *all* ages were held to be sexually potent, overturning the common assumption that age vitiates both desire and desirability. The Kerch terracotta *senile pregnant* hags in which Bakhtin finds his embodiment of the grotesque I would clearly identify as witches, precisely for their continued fertility and sexuality.[21] Sara Stambaugh notes in her study of witches and goddesses in Dinesen's work that her *old* women are quintessentially feminine; the feminine does not end with child-bearing. A feminist interpretation can perceive witches as an inhering traditional part of the daughter / mother / crone triad. They are not monsters but rather a temporal part of the familiar. They follow the ancient idea of a natural temporal progression such as we find in the phases of the moon, itself a symbol of the feminine. Like the waning moon, the witch or crone is able to effect rebirth; thus, a favorite poetic image is the old moon with the new moon in her arms. The maiden, mother, crone trinity is circular, as is the moon.

The witch may serve, then, as a rare figure who restores sexual autonomy and sexual subjectivity to women. She contrasts sharply with the romantic heroine of the nineteenth century, who either dies for love or is passively swept away by it toward the harbor of marriage. But a new view of women's sexuality, mediated here through the witch, is not the only reason, albeit an important and worthwile one, that leads feminist writers to recuperate this figure, so marginalized and problematized in mainstream culture. And clearly a revisionist reading and writing of the witch *is* taking place: in contemporary poetry Susan Sutheim, Jean Tepperman, Gwendolyn Brooks, Julia Randall, Lucille Clifton, Margaret Walker, and many more, have employed this persona. They rush to recognize kinship: "I have been her kind," affirms Anne Sexton, and, again, the same poet in "The Gold Key" explains, "the speaker in this case / is a middle-aged witch / me."[22] Mary Coleridge exclaims "I am she!" restoring the witch to what many affirm is her true nature, now a palimpsest. Why do women fantasize that they are witches? What besides the significant issue of female sexuality is at stake here?

We come to the second power ascribed to witches. Annis Pratt sees in the witch a female archetype who not only desires "erotic autonomy," but also "meaningful social roles" and correlatively, the "celebration of femininity."[23] The meaningful social roles that the witch filled were, historically, those of midwife, abortionist, healer, botanist, herbalist. The female goddess Isis, for instance, represents the healing power of the feminine: she takes her murdered husband, the dismembered Osiris, and puts him back together again. Rosemary Dinnage points out that witches used charms, spells, and herbal remedies for *curing* illness, as well as inflicting it, and they were often summoned to the bedside in advance of male practioners. In *Seven Ages*, Eva Figes develops this very theme. In her multi-generational novel, women healers provide remedies unknown to the cunning of the novel's male physicians, who, in turn, scoff at women's skills as "old wives' tales." But the "old wives" in this tale belong to the witch archetype. In *Seven Ages'* early centuries the female practioners are shunned as witches; later in time, they remain outcasts in the male medical world, fighting for the right to abortion and the legalization of midwifery. Like Figes, other women writers today are portraying the witch as Isis's descendant, dispensing white, not black, magic.[24]

Moreover, witches as healers were associated with the female reproductive cycle not only in their function as midwives, but also as descendants of mythic fertility goddesses. Anne Sexton, in her book *Transformations*, hints to the reader that her witch is such a mother-goddess; similarly, the Lapp witches found in Dinesen's *Seven Gothic Tales* are connected to fertility rites. These witch figures of Sexton and Dinesen fulfill Pratt's requirement that they play a "significant social role" by serving, both practically and symbolically, as links to matriarchal culture, storehouses of feminine lore and wisdom. But because witches concerned themselves not only with female secrets and lore, but were in attendance at the rites of birth and death involving both sexes, they were able to lay claim to special knowledge which provoked male anxiety. The familiar witches' cauldron is a curious and revealing example of how such anxiety evolved iconographically: this stewpot into which evil crones throw loathsome ingredients served the original therapeutic purpose of holding a supply of hot water with herbs which midwives used during delivery!

Pratt's "celebration of femininity" (discounting for now the fervid debate over the term "feminine") was evident in women's ways of healing, and also in their communal life together: witches gathered in colleges, or covens, a word now connoting a place of evil plotting, but which literally denotes a convent. Exclusivity and self-sufficiency in these women's communities gave rise to fears of conspiracy, and indeed one could speculate that a coven, originally consisting of thirteen witches, may have contributed to the superstition that thirteen is an unlucky number. Once again, Monique Wittig's *Les Guérillères* provides a useful commentary, this time a summary of many themes relating to the witch:

> They speak together of the threat they have constituted towards authority, they tell how they were burned on pyres to prevent them from assembling in future. They were able to command tempests, to sink fleets, to destroy armies. They have been mistresses of poisons, of the winds, of the wills. They were able to exercise their powers at will and to transform all kinds of persons into mere animals, geese pigs birds turtles. They have ruled over life and death. Their conjoint power has menaced hierarchies systems of government authorities. Their knowledge has competed successfully with the official knowledge to which they had no access, it has challenged it, found it wanting, threatened it, made it appear inefficacious. No police were powerful enough to track them down, no paid informer so opportunist, no torture so brutal, no army so overwhelming as to attack them one by one and destroy them. Then they chant the famous song that begins, Despite all the evils they wished to crush me with / I remain as steady as the three-legged cauldron.[25]

These women "*speak*" of the threat, they "*sing*."

For women there have been thousands of years of silencing. The speech-act itself is a rebellion against stifling social norms which call for women's silence; witches claim a voice, their third important power. This explains the significant place witches occupy in the feminist redemption of "evil" female figures. Just as women lack visual representation of their own and are viewed mainly as objects of the male gaze, objects of desire, so do they lack verbal representation, including the verbal representation of female desire. Cultural control over the female body, codified in writing, is a male prerogative—now, in issues of reproductive rights, health care, and research; earlier, in dicta about chastity. Thus, "the entire history of the idea of virginity," writes Sonya Rudikoff, "its advocates and interpreters, its theology and ideology, the holy acts and martyrdom of the virgins"—all of it is reported by witnesses other than the virgins themselves. "No women's voices," she observes, "speak here, no women's experiences are recorded."[26]

Women's silencing extended and extends far beyond expressions of sexuality. The seer Cassandra, scorned for her prophecies in the time of Aeschylus, represented a true depiction of woman's place. At the height of Athenian civilization, no woman *had* a public voice in the theater or other civic institution. (It is a matter of scholarly dispute whether women were even permitted inside a theater!) Women were not qualified to be Athenian citizens—how could they have a voice? This silencing is lifting only by slow degrees. How many churches ordain women bishops, how many synagogues invest women rabbis? What about women's voices raised in protest within the Catholic Church because of their exclusion from the higher ranks of the religious hierarchy? We must either return to figures of remote history, when women were goddesses at shrines male gods later usurped, or look forward to a feminist utopian vision such as Doris Lessing's *The Marriages Between Zones Three, Four, and Five*, to find female figures of authoritative utterance validated by their communities.

My emphasis upon the witch as *speaker* (though she is a resource of other powers for women, as we have seen) is proportional to the central and suffocating place silence occupies in women's lives. Social strictures against authorship and even against speech become part of women's psychological makeup, to their great detriment.

Women's silence has many contributive elements: fear of provoking the wrath of those upon whom one is emotionally or economically dependent; existence outside public authority and its commanding discourses, and its converse, the fear women have that their speech will be judged trivial, chatty, discursive, lacking in disciplined reason; the feeling of moral responsibility for "keeping the peace" within group situations, avoiding overt conflict by "not speaking up," the silence that results from separation from the written culture.[27] Carol Gilligan's *Meeting at the Crossroads* discusses how adolescent girls learn to say "I don't know." When gender roles become firmly fixed is when silence begins, according to Gilligan. In recognition of the profound silence which engulfs women, and the need to alter it, a book such as *Women's Ways of Knowing* constructs a new pedagogical paradigm for women, one that would proceed from the "initial stage of silence" which the authors observed in their data to a final stage in which women could construct their own epistemology. The idea that female experience needs its own language, "parler-femme" as Luce Irigaray calls it, has been widely explored by feminist scholars, particularly Irigaray and Julia Kristeva who see it as a way of expressing and establishing difference of sex and gender, of women being an "other" that goes beyond lack or absence. Whether women require a special tongue or not, whether that discourse arises from the body, as some feminists suggest, they must enter some discourse for their own health.

The phenomenon of women's muteness, what Sandra Gilbert and Susan Gubar term the "speechless woe" of the heroine of Charlotte Perkins Gilman's story "The Yellow Wallpaper," has a pathological counterpart, depression, of which silence and withdrawal are diagnostic symptoms. Women are more vulnerable than men to depression "to an almost staggering degree."[28] This pathology, rooted in the socialized habit of women's silence, shows why we need to valorize the witch as word-monger.

Current psychopharmacology teaches us that depression may be the manifestation of a chemical imbalance in the body. Or, it may be an exogenous reaction to loss, such as the death of a family member. And certainly many men experience depression. Nevertheless, it is noteworthy that depression among women has reached almost epidemic proportions in the past few decades. It is now axiomatic that women's social situation in middle-class western culture—isolation, lack of financial reward, and lack of respect accorded the homemaking role—dispose women to depression, though this is a class-bound finding and depression is not. Phyllis Chesler in *Women and Madness* finds two major contributants to widespread depression among women: women's inferior social status and their socially informed helplessness, which Freud, for one, viewed as a hallmark of feminine identity. Maggie Scarf probes further: "Is it possible that those personality traits and characteristics associated with 'being feminine' are, in themselves, depress-ogenic?"[29] In other words, are traits considered "healthy" for women, but immature for men (submission, dependence, lack of competition, excitability, emotionality, lack of objectivity) unhealthy for *both* sexes? Answering in the affirmative, Chesler believes that the high incidence of treatment for Dependent and Histrionic Personality Disorders among women reflects the fact that women overconform to accepted, even prescribed, gender stereotypes.

These "depressogenic" social definitions are profoundly rooted in our western traditions. Elaine Showalter, in *The Female Malady: Women, Madness and English Culture 1830-1980*, explains the linkage between women, speech and clinical disorder:

> the tradition of English psychiatric medicine during the nineteenth century has also tended to silence the female patient, to make her the object of techniques of moral management. . . In England, psychiatrists believed that their therapeutic authority depended on domination over the patient's language. "If a patient. . . interrupts the speaker," Robert

Carter admonished his fellow doctors, "she must be told to keep silence and to listen; and must be told, moreover. . . in such a manner as to convey the speaker's full conviction that the command will be immediately obeyed."[30]

Thus submission and silence become synonymous, equally desirable ends. Given these proscriptions against will and speech, it is small wonder that women used their *bodies* as the means of assertion and attention-getting. As Diane Wood Middlebrook observes in her recent psychobiography of Anne Sexton, hysteria *is* body-*language*; Luce Irigaray also maintains that the hysteric body is *speaking*. It seems clear that the purpose of exhibitionism is a *statement* of presence, an attack upon annihilation.

Classic hysteria, a woman's emotional disease described by doctors in the early nineteenth century, had among its many symptoms the sensation of choking. At that time physicians, at a loss to understand this symptom, interpreted it as "the rising of the womb," the *globus hystericus*, attributable to unsatisfied sexual and maternal feelings. Showalter ventures the alternative explanation that the *globus hystericus* was a physical manifestation of "choked-off speech." In a contemporary case study discussed by Maggie Scarf, speech is the measure of emotional improvement, silence of the pathology:

> Her bedroom door was unlocked, and Bette silent. So she'd remained, in her bed, curled in a fetal position. The weekend had slid by. . . . She'd simply remained there, silent and blank-eyed, staring at the narrow vertical design of her yellow wallpaper.
>
> She had been like that, as much as she could be, during her first days on the ward. . . . But just recently, as had been noted with satisfaction at the early-morning ward rounds, she'd been becoming progessively more communicative. She was, though still relatively silent, growing 'more approachable,' according to all reports. She was answering questions with a full phrase, or even a sentence, rather than a grudging monosyllable.[31]

The silence of women, whether self-imposed as a strategy of resistance or societally imposed as a tool of subordination, is a classic clinical symptom of depressive illness. Since depression is disproportionately present in women, the strong connection between gender roles that enjoin silence for women and depressive illness in women indicates that prevailing norms and traditional definitions of what is "feminine" are harmful to women, and need to be changed.

Even the identification of woman or the feminine with Nature, which may seem enabling, or even ennobling, is weakened because Nature is *mute* Nature; rather, it is the mind, the male mind, from which speech springs and codifies authority. Retaining the first line intact, Adrienne Rich gives a seventeeth century lyric by Herrick a wry twist in the second line: "When to her lute Corinna sings / *neither words nor music are her own*" (emphasis added).[32]

If the language of the subordinated is in things, things of the hand, the garden, the quilt, surely the language of the equal must be lexical.[33] Historically, the quilt and the garden are anonymous and impermanent creations, reflecting the fact that history is male history; women's economic, political, and educational disadvantage leads directly to their omission from the written record. For this reason Simone de Beauvoir, unlike Kristeva and Irigaray, rejects the discourse of the maternal because her goal was to enter the symbolic order, the law of the father, to enter language and discourse.

Though we may honor the unspoken language of things as Alice Walker does in *In Search of Our Mothers' Gardens*, as silent expressions they still require an interpreter; only to the initiated do they "speak for themselves." Writing about Adrienne Rich, Catharine Stimpson notes that "lesbian/feminism has rooted female experience less in language than in things, objects, inarticulate by pregnant silences."[34] But the word is respected, even feared, as possessing its own autonomous power; that is, the act of speaking something magically bestows a reality upon it. Why else did Adam name the animals?

Now witches' magic is embedded in language, as is shamanistic language. In the Bible, Saul consults the Witch of Endor before battle, to hear her prophecy. In *Macbeth* the witches predict Macbeth's fate; that predictive power is sufficient to cast them as witches, old, ugly, targets of opprobrium. They are reviled, but, as we have seen, so was the young Cassandra reviled, reminding us that witches can be young as well as old. In short, women who transgress gender injunctions to silence are transmogrified into witches, grotesques. Conversely, we can infer that the reclamation of the speech/act confers authority upon women.

In "To William Wordsworth from Virginia" Julia Randall makes an explicit connection between witch and word, and the connection is power:

> I stand beside barberry and dream
> Wisdom to babes, and health to beggar men,
> And help to David hunting in the hills,
> The Appalachian fox. By words, I might.[35]

The linguistic power of the witch may be prophecy, may be curse. Strikingly, Fay Weldon structures her novel *The Life and Loves of a She-Devil* not only episodically but paragraphically, shaped to a pattern of short, exclamatory curses characteristic of the witch, enunciated here by Ruth: "Mary Fisher, I hope such a wind arises tonight that the plate-glass windows of the tower crack [the Fisher Princess lives in a glass tower] and the storm surges in, and you die drowning and weeping and in terror."[36]

Interestingly, Caliban, himself an outcast and son of a hag (witch), defies Prospero: "You taught me language, and my profit on't / Is, I know how to curse!"[37] Language is a powerful tool.

Though it is in their destructive capacities alone that Medusa, the witch, the siren, and other figures of female power survive to us, originally there had been creative power inhering in them. It is on this note of authorial creativity that contemporary Chilean poet Marjorie Agosin's witch poem concludes:

> And if I'm a witch
> come to me
> to light the candles
> rumple my hair
> and dance
> in a benign orgy
> dance
> and write
> alastfirstpoem.[38]

Here Agosin recuperates the witch as a viable heroine, casting her in a role which is not only benign and erotic, but creative—a poet, a word-maker—as well. Moreover, Agosin manages, in the final line, by attaching "last" and "first" typographically, as well as by placing "first" last, to suggest the endless circle of the snake, a female generative symbol, a doubled creativity.

Elizabeth Bishop's poem to her colleague and mentor Marianne Moore describes the older poet with unmistakably witchy trademarks; she invites her to come flying with her "pointed toe of each black shoe," a "black capeful of butterfly wings and bon-mots," and with angels riding on the "broad black brim of [her] hat." Identifying her mentor as a witch clearly intends a compliment to Moore's power. Bishop begs Moore to grant her the pleasure of a visit; the refrain of the poem is "please come flying." Further, Bishop imagines Moore flying to her in a cloud of glory: "like a daytime comet / with a long unnebulous train of words." These two women, being poets, can play at words together, "play at a game of constantly being wrong / with a priceless set of vocabularies."[39] Language is priceless, and with it they can practice together the witchcraft of their art.

In sum, the witch holds power which is intimately tied to the word, so that the metaphor "Marianne Moore is a witch" refers less to the witch-like features of her costume than to her craft of words, signified by flight. With the power of speech/act in mind, I would suggest that the antithetical figure to the witch emerges as the mythological Philomena, whose tongue was cut out so that she would be unable to testify against her rapist. This myth is the key to a pathology of women's silence which underscores the importance of the witch/speaker. Not for nothing does Jacques Lacan maintain that lack of language is a symbol of castration. An authentic voice is a voice of self-differentiation. This vital connection between self-definition and speech has not escaped Christa Wolf, who asks, "How quickly does lack of speech turn into lack of identity?"[40]

Speechlessness is powerlessness, the power to tell your own story and retell that of your ancestors, which is ultimately one important way we relate ourselves to the world. This is why the unearthing of so much buried writing by women is so important. It confers upon women a way to relate to history, their own history. Further, we have the medical hypothesis that failure to be the speaking subject of narrative is an important component of clinical depression.

As long as women remain silent, history will be a recital of male patronymics. How can anyone, male or female, decide whose version of experience, of culture, is authoritative, significant, true, normative, when we possess but one account? We have Freud's account of Dora; we lack Dora's own account of herself (or of Freud). Yet such an account, showing Freud's to be a *version* of the circumstances, incomplete and therefore misleading or misguided, could offer a corrective to what was previously accepted as unimpeachable. One such corrective is offered in Hannah Decker's *Freud, Dora, and Vienna, 1900* which, by providing the cultural context for Freud's theories, reveals him as a product of his times. Another, a recent feminist film, questions Freud's objectivity, his claim to approximate a scientific viewpoint: *Sigmund Freud's Dora*, directed by Jane Weinstock (1988) challenges psychoanalytic emphasis on women's sexual deficiency and its denial of women's voice.

To the extent that women, for historical, social and biological reasons, experience a different reality from men's they complete an incomplete story. Women writers, for instance, are able to describe *from their own knowledge* a different role for the mother, a role apart from Freud's Oedipal romance. Women's writing is a directive toward autonomy, presenting faithfully what the reader's sense of experience tells her is true.

For much of history, women were virtually excluded from becoming practitioners of the written word by being denied the education which prepared men for some career of public service. (Even today it is not standard practice for women, no matter what their means, to attend university in Great Britain, for example.) As a consequence, women's relation to words was largely oral, demotic, and unrecorded. As art historian Leo Steinberg points out, with the exception of religious reading, women for the most part were not imaged in the visual arts even as *readers*, and certainly not as writers.[41] Rather, erotic or at least decorative poses of women predominate. The presence of a gazer as the reader of the *woman's* own text (body) is always implied.

In the poem "Katia Reading" based upon the Balthus painting of the same name, Stephen Dobyns imagines the liberation of this adolescent girl, sprawled on the floor, her face in a book:

> Perhaps you would have laid aside your book,
> but so completely was the world lifted out of
> its daily banality that you kept on reading.
> What had your world been until then? First you
> ate something, then you bought something, then you
> went bowling; a world where men passed their lives
> peering under the hoods of cars. And like the girl
> in the painting you must have turned your head
> slightly as if from a loud noise; and you too became
> like someone who has left on a journey, someone who
> has become the answer to his own impossible riddle:
> who condemned to his room is at last free of the room.[42]

The girl breaks out of the confinement of what I term "woman's space" through the instrumentality of reading; she becomes, suddenly and unexpectedly in the final two lines, identified with a traditionally male protagonist, the voyager. Through the enablement of the word, a world is uncovered that seems to promise male performative powers, answers, freedom.

A special issue of the journal *Critical Inquiry* devoted to "Writing and Sexual Difference" explores the idea that writing is in itself a determinant of sexual difference. Jane Gallop, in a later essay, uses the journal's own front and back cover illustrations to substantiate the point:

> Together they [the front and back cover] compose a particularly well-articulated illustration of 'writing and sexual difference.' The woman is writing a letter, the man a book. Women write letters—personal, intimate, in relation; men write books—universal, public, in general circulation. The man in the picture is in fact Erasmus, father of our humanist tradition; the woman without a name. In the man's background:books. The woman sits against floral wallpaper.[43]

The contemporary Polish poet Zbigniew Herbert makes the same observation of Dutch painting: "In Dutch painting the theme of the letter was extremely popular. Formally it is simply a portrait, always of a female, a girl or woman who puts down the letter or else reads from a piece of paper . . . As a rule the women represented in these paintings are reading love letters."[44]

The relation of the woman to the written word is, most commonly in western art, an intimate, private, not intellectual or creative relation.

So when Sexton says of herself in "The Gold Key," "My face in a book," her gaze is being seduced by a self-directed and self-contained pleasure. As she goes on to say in the poem, she is at once reader and author, "ready to tell you a story or two." Both in her self-reflexiveness and in her defiant readiness to speak out, Sexton flouts sexual stereotyping about women and words. It comes as no surprise, therefore, to find her calling herself a "witch" in this poem.[45]

Incontrovertibly, the large issue of female subjectivity is reflected in this relation of authorship to authority. For women's subjective event, be it desire or discourse, is seen as at worst inimical and at best incidental to the main project. The pitting of male *author*ity against female *author*ity within the arena of the logos is the central conflict of Margaret Atwood's "Circe/ Mud Poems" which show the power of this particular witch or enchantress to reside, as Estella Lauter comments, in "gathering syllables from the earth," literally laying her head to the ground to do so, and making those fragments into "healing *words*" (emphasis added). By this creative act of remembering, she immediately connects herself to nature as well as nurture, to Mother Earth and the maternal earth goddesses. But it is the words that have the power, not the earth alone. Lauter also notes that "Circe's part in it [the battle between herself and Odysseus] is *largely verbal* [emphasis added]; she openly berates Odysseus for his lies, his passivity, his greed, and his delusions of power." Ultimately, Lauter asserts, "this Circe seems to emerge from centuries in the unconscious to complete the cleansing acts of telling off the hero."[46] She is, in fact, a paradigmatic heroine—at once earth-mother and poet, the Creatrix.

W. B. Yeats' "Crazy Jane" poems introduce a female figure who embodies many significant characteristics of the witch. Foremost among them she proclaims her truth aloud, shaming not the Devil in this case, but the Bishop. Despite the Bishop's reproof that she and her lover live like "beast and beast," she speaks frankly of her sexual passion, dismissing the Bishop. In part this is because the clergyman banished her lover, but also because he is physically repellent: his skin is "wrinkled like the foot of a goose," and he has "a heron's hunch upon his back." She gives verbal representation to her subjective desire. In "Crazy Jane Reproved" Jane is equally outspoken: "Great Europa played the fool / That changed a lover for a bull." And finally, in "Crazy Jane on the Day of Judgment," Jane herself grounds her persona in verbal agility:

> Take the sour
> If you take me,
> I can scoff and lour
> And scold for an hour.[47]

Although witch and mad woman are not identical personae, Crazy Jane and the witch share an emphasis on voice. Moreover, the kind of voice each turns out to be characterizes them. The "Crazy Jane" poems, belonging to the late phase of Yeats' own stylistic development (the 1930s), may also be read, in the light of their central female persona, as belonging to a women's style derived from the vernacular: full of life's minutiae, pleasure, and practicality.

To devastating effect, I believe, both Freud and Lacan situate woman outside language, and feminist theorists such as Irigaray and Kristeva respond by locating a new discourse in the body. The witch provides a helpful circumvention, for the utterance of the witch, female and powerful, may and can depart from conventional linguistic usage. Language can speak some hidden verity, in much the same way that fools give kings advice. And as the fool's language is often riddling and fragmented, so is the witch's; here is a verse from the Witches' Multiplication Table in Goethe's *Faust*:

> See, thus it's done!
> Make ten of one,
> and let two be,
> Make even three,
> And rich thou'lt be.[48]

We learn that words are mysteries, language a mysterious force.

The witch's language is often pre-verbal communication: groans, exclamations, *sotto voce* hisses.[49] Kristeva mentions both the "echolalia" of infants and the "glossalia" of psychotics as belonging in this realm. In *Beloved*, Toni Morrison relates such speech to a lost mother tongue (African) which she recalls from her maternal relations, one apart from the logos and the law of the father: "In the beginning there was no word. There was sound." This pre-verbal expression is the weird talk of a weird sister; a wyrd-woman was a witch-woman. Thus, commenting on a recent study of witchcraft in contemporary Britain, Rosemary Dinnage reminds us "words themselves, within magic, have a status beyond that of a mere signifier; that is the essence of a spell. . . . There is also what [anthropologists] called 'the co-efficient of weirdness,' the use of vague language to arouse awe."[50]

In "The Crazy Woman," Gwendolyn Brooks has *her* madwoman threaten "I'll go out in the frosty dark / And sing most terribly."[51] Margaret Walker's protagonist in "Molly Means" sings a similarly awesome song:

> You can hear her holler and whine and cry.
> Her voice is thin and her moan is high,
> And her cackling laugh or her barking cold
> Bring terror to the young and old.[52]

This different wisdom, like the fool's, is one that derives from second sight, or in-sight (symbolized in the Gorgon by a third eye), a truth disguised or left unspoken by other characters. Here is a female character who breaks silence. Here is a precedent. What has hampered the reclamation of so many of these female figures of power—Medusa (as we've just seen), the witch, the Terrible Mother—is the separation of functions which allows such female figures to be marginalized. Such rendering (rending) reduces power as it reduces function. Thus for D. H. Lawrence, Aphrodite, the goddess of love, is "the goddess of destruction, her white cold fire consumes and does not create."[53] This description ignores Aphrodite in her embodiment as the goddess, through love, of birth—a creative goddess, who, legend says, used lilies and myrtle, flowers sacred to her as herbal magic to assist at childbirth. The process of reclamation requires the restoration of the full duality of powers.

Lucille Clifton, in "the coming of Kali" restores this completeness to the ancestral figure of the goddess in her song:

> it is the black God, Kali,
> a woman God and terrible
> with her skulls and breasts.
> i am one side of your skin,
> she sings, softness is the other,
> you know you know me well, she sings,
> you know you know me well.[54]

The importance of language in which to couch women's experience and heal their anger is the subscript of Doris Lessing's compelling novel, *The Diaries of Jane Somers*. The narrator, Jane, a woman who works for a slick fashion magazine, meets, quite by chance in a neighborhood shop, the crone of the story, Maudie. Maudie strikes Jane immediately:

> I saw an old witch. I was staring at this old creature and thought, a witch . . . here she was, beside me, in the chemist's. A tiny bent-over woman, with a nose nearly meeting her chin, in black heavy dusty clothes, and something not far off a bonnet. She saw me looking at her and thrust at me a prescription and said, "What is this? You get it for me." Fierce blue eyes, under grey craggy brows, but there was something wonderfully sweet in them. I liked her, for some reason, from that moment.[55]

In fact one might say that Jane, who has earlier confessed to the reader a chronic failure of compassion, is "bewitched" by Maudie on the spot. Jane, almost incomprehensibly to herself and to the reader, "for some reason," is emotionally pulled out of her usual guardedness to the extent that she assumes full care of Maudie, performing exhausting and intimate tasks—bath-

ing her, dressing her, grocery shopping for her, cleaning her apartment, in-
tervening on her behalf with the housing authorities. Maudie moves into
the center of Jane's life—as teacher, as liberator, as an incarnation of female
endurance, female independence.

Importantly, though much of Jane's effort is directed toward Maudie's
body (her food, her warmth, her cleanliness), the relationship between
Maudie and Jane develops into friendship through the telling of stories: Jane
listens, Maudie relates. Jane finds Maudie, quite literally, spellbinding.
Through Maudie's recitals, Jane comes to understand not only this old
woman, but times gone by, the hardships being a woman entailed for Maudie:
abandonment, poverty, losing custody of her child. Yet, as we see from the
storytelling, Maudie has remained the author of her own narrative. To come
into subjectivity is to come into speech, as Kristeva tells us. Jane also begins
to understand the condition of being old and she takes on the care of some
of Maudie's *cronies*. Maudie leads Jane to understand difference, to penetrate
otherness, as fairy tale witches do. One learns by seeing beyond appearance. Knowing Maudie, hearing the continuum of her life through stories,
the younger woman can no longer isolate crone from maiden and mother.
She recognizes the cycle/circle of generation, death, regeneration.

Ursula Le Guin captures the full import of this. If women do not shun
the crone, but welcome her, she may bring the birth of a new and freer self:
"Loss of fertility does not mean loss of desire and fulfillment. But it does
entail a change, a change involving matters even more important. . . than
sex. The woman who is willing to make that change must become pregnant
with herself, at last. She must bear herself, her third self, her old age, with
travail and alone."[56]

Yet the title of the book from which this quotation is taken, *Dancing at
the Edge of the World*, emphasizes the glee of the crone, not her travail. In
this new autonomy "there are things the Old Woman can do, say, and think
that the Woman cannot do, say and think."[57] Broadly, as women we can
look to the witch for independence, boldness, and incisiveness. More particularly, telling is the gift she brings.[58]

5

Spirit, Sorority, Sense

Feme/Sole:
> —Words derived from the Old French, signifying
> "woman alone" for legal purposes, such as taxation

At least I have the flowers of myself,
and my thoughts, no god
can take that;
I have the fervour of myself for a presence
and my own spirit for light

"Eurydice," H.D.

In response to such voicelessness and invisibility as we have been exploring, feminism has assumed the task of facilitating new selfhood for women. Three foci have emerged from these efforts to project female authenticity and self-transcendence: the renewed emphasis on women's spirituality; the rhetoric of unity within feminism; and the use of the female body as the privileged metaphor for women's existence, self-articulation, and definition. How effective are these foci—spirit, sorority, and sense —in developing narrative authority for women? My contention is that each provides a partial but incomplete strategy for advancing women who are subjects-in-the-making.

As to the first strategy, there are two compelling reasons for the advent of the women's spirituality movement within feminism. The first was and is to counteract male forces of aggression and war which have not been sufficiently tempered by patriarchal religion. Feminist leaders and many women writers are working to change radically the material, oppositional, and exploitative values which dominate our society and are promulgated by powerful institutions, religious and secular. The second reason for the rise of the women's spirituality movement was dissatisfaction with traditional Christian and Jewish theological themes, images, and practices concerning women.

For example, one such theme embedded in western patriarchal religion, whether Jewish or Christian, that has proven especially deleterious for women is the high value attached to the passive will, i.e., submission to the will of God as the way to self-control and self-discipline. This is a lesson which women, already constrained to passivity by secular cultural mores, can only internalize at great cost.

As for religious imagery: Carol Christ, Starhawk, Rosemary Radford Ruether, Naomi Goldenberg, and Mary Daly, among many others, have pointed to the almost exclusively male imagery and male vocabulary of the Judeo-Christian tradition.[1] Ultimately, images of female monotheism in this tradition are hard to locate. Where are women to find figures less androcentric than God the *Father* or God's *Son* through whom they may channel transcendent impulses? This problem has important linguistic corollaries, addressed by Mary Daly in *Beyond God The Father*, in which she shows how strongly the idea of a Godhead is identified with masculine nouns and pronouns. There is no vocabulary, as there is no iconographical tradition, for making the woman's body transcendent in the Judeo-Christian west. Although as we have seen earlier, *libido*-as-masculine is a universal principle, in the west, paradoxically, it is also men who are the bearers of a transcendent body. And if we reject this assumption? The Virgin Mary in her singularity can inspire cults but cannot show women the way to a nascent divinity because she illustrates the complete divorce between spirituality and eroticism which still underlies much of western religious thinking about women.[2] Women remain with an unintegrated image. This is a fundamental problem which dogs many approaches to female subjectivity. For this reason Ann McCoy, painter, sculptor, and Jungian feminist, said in a recent interview, "We need to think of the entire range of feminine possibilities . . . as forces in the psychic lives of both sexes as of a psychic wholeness . . . . Mary is too limited. We need Artemis, the animal goddess, the Gorgon."[3]

There are, of course, within the existing record, feminine *principles* so significant that they may offer direction and instruction: surely the "feminine" principle of nurturance finds one of its great expressions in the Twenty-Third Psalm's extended metaphor of the shepherd. Similarly, though the Holy

Ghost is a male figure in Christian theology, the image of a spirit brooding over the waters may suggest a female bird brooding over the nest; the Gnostics, in fact, did refer to the Holy Spirit as "a divine mother." Though such latent femininity is insufficient for women to identify with existing theological imagery, it indicates that theological imagery cannot satisfactorily be expressed by male principles alone. At the present time, however, western religion is discriminatory toward women; women are equal neither in its teachings and texts nor in representation in its ministry, and the aims of feminist spirituality leaders are reactive to this prevailing condition.

Some feminist theologians have referred women to the more embracing imagery of Taoism and Tantric Buddhism in which both sexes have participatory roles. Others have attempted to reinstate matriarchal goddesses and matriarchal religious mythologies which some feminists claim were only overlaid and lost by a historical change to patriarchy and the subsequent development of the heroic mode. Provision of a spiritual mother, ancestress/deity, represents, then, a response to a felt lack and may prove a salutary correction to the dominantly patriarchal historical record.

What are some of the broad implications of the women's spirituality movement? Its first aim—emphasizing unaggressive, unmaterialistic values, and urging human reconnection with the natural world—is a crucial one, and any success feminists meet in this area must be applauded. My caveat has not to do with the aim, but with the potential risk incurred. Feminist theology in the west needs to be alert to the danger that this aim may return us to that moral idealization of women as spiritual caretakers of the world, "naturally" good because "naturally" less appetitive, more sensitive, finer, all of which virtually denies them a corporeal self. Tennyson's lines from "Guinevere" exemplify this:

> Of no more subtle master under heaven
> Than is the maiden passion for a maid,
> Not only to keep down the base in man
> But teach high thought, and amiable words
> And courtliness, and the desire of fame,
> And love of truth, and all that makes a man.[4]

This attitude that woman is the moral custodian and inspiriter of men does not, in fact, empower women but rather penalizes them. Reconfirming a vision of gender-segregated tasks, it makes women shoulder responsibility for what should be the combined spiritual quest of both sexes. Thus, in our own times Gillian Clarke moves from a consideration of the domestic responsibilities of women in the first stanza to the unequal *moral* responsibilities they bear in the second:

If we go hunting along with the men,
Who will light the fires and bake bread then?
Who'll catch the nightmares and ride them away
If we put to sea and we sail away?

Will the men grow tender and the children strong?
Who will teach the Mam iaith and sing them songs?
If we adventure more than a day
Who will do the loving while we're away?[5]

We move from viewing women as the conservators of the social fabric to a view of women responsible for instilling humane values into the whole society.

If we look at current issues which reflect this genderization of roles, we note that it is an organization of *mothers* who are fighting against pervasive violence on the television screen, though presumably children also have fathers who could speak for their welfare. And though peace may be women's primary issue, we will not achieve it until it is the first priority of both sexes. In 1991 the American polls that measured support for the Iraqi war still demonstrated a sizeable gender gap. If as many men as women had indicated non-support for this aggression, the Gulf War might never have happened.

This is not to say that women's voluntary involvement in both local and national issues is to be taken lightly. Engaged in this way, women play an active rather than a passive role and they work for causes which remove them from victimization. They demonstrate capability and are effective workers, thus conferring benefit upon the society as well as themselves. My reservation is that their *moral* stewardship tends toward a perpetuation of separation of powers: women responsible for the moral realm, men for the economic. But these concerns impinge upon each other. War is a moral issue but also an economic and political one. Moreover, moral superiority often goes hand-in-hand with economic oppression because our society as a whole does not reward moral values, however much lip service it pays. Even when the women are not working as unpaid volunteers, but in competitive jobs and careers, they are disadvantaged economically.

Regarding the second aim, the women's spirituality movement has and is endeavoring to create an equal place for women within a theology: the problem is one of sources and resources. Certainly women today feel the lack of a strong female historical identity, and of their own spiritual heritage. Francine du Plessix Gray remarks, for instance, that the interest in women's religious quest is now so strong that it has generated a new genre, the woman's religious quest novel. Marija Gimbutas, a feminist archeologist and mythologist, has become a beacon for women who wish for their own spiritual tradition, attached to a matriarchal goddess who fosters peace, cooperation, and classlessness. In over twenty books, Gimbutas brings evidence of the existence of agricultural matriarchal societies, closely tilled, which she defines as emblematic of peaceful existence.

Nonetheless, I would question whether equality can be achieved by connections to images of matriarchal cultures which have been interrupted, discontinuous in the narratives of our historical patriarchal society. According to Marija Gimbutas and other archeologists studying ancient matriarchal societies, the last temples of the Goddess were destroyed in Rome, Athens, and Ephesus in the fourth or fifth centuries of the Common Era of the Hebrew calendar. How closely can contemporary women identify with or put on the strength of those invoked so self-consciously after millennia, with little recorded history of their own, whose very sway is a matter of debate?[6]

The effort on the part of some feminist theologians to be post-Christian, post-Jewish, or, one might say, pre-Christian and pre-Jewish, is not merely ahistorical. It also seems to ignore issues of ontology as they apply to women. Even if we wish to do so, can we put aside powerful Judeo-Christian legacies at will, extirpate them from our consciousness, disseminated as they are in music, the visual arts, poetry, architecture, as well as chronicle? Can we gain present equality by authenticating societies such as the Minoan in which women served as priests, or in which the succession was matrilinear? It is true that wherever the deepest shafts are dug, images of fertility goddesses are discovered. But does our right to public roles for active, educated women, for spiritual leadership, rest upon this evidence?

We need to remember that we are exploring ways to advance toward female subjectivity, not only to correct the historical record, a worthwhile, but not identical goal.[7] Certainly, as most subordinate, emergent groups are insisting today, knowing one's history contributes to self-esteem. And many women today find new access to a spiritual life through goddess mythology. Yet I agree with Christa Wolf who asks "doesn't this harking back to an irretrievable past reveal more clearly than anything else the desperate plight in which women see themselves today?"[8] In other words, for some feminists this cultural archeology reflects deprivation more than it provides an alternative spiritual tradition.

Naomi Scheman sounds an additional, political, warning about the project of unearthing a female past: "It is, in general, a risky business for feminists to identify images of women's power in some long lost time and place as authentically female, since such images are often, as much as anything else, misogynist creations used to justify the allegedly liberating nature of male power, as in the *Oresteia*."[9]

Finally, given the misogynistic belief that all women who aren't Marys are Eves (the tediously familiar split of mother and whore), the foregrounding of women's spirituality may inadvertently perpetuate the dualism which Mary and Mary Magdalene personify, and into which women's nature traditionally has been separated.

As we have noted, women lack an integrated image of body and spirit. This is partly because a strong historical bias toward separation of powers seems to operate. Artemis or Diana, goddess of the moon, of hunting, and protector of women, was also once *mother* goddess of Nature. Yet by the time we meet her in classical mythology, she has become the converse, a deity of chastity. In this case, the division is between the spiritual and physical powers of female deities. But the deity that feminist spirituality leaders wish to reinstate is a spiritual goddess who also integrates generative powers, an Earth-Goddess whose arts include "healing, writing, the giving of just law." She has proven elusive because an Earth-Mother is too identified with the sole function of fecundity (just as Mary's spirituality isolates *that* condition). The Mother Goddess, her healing powers ignored, is, unfortunately, a victim of cultural essentialism, the same reductionism that made the witch a figure of unadulterated evil.

The question then, is whether the women's spirituality movement is the advance of the guard, which will succeed in establishing an integrated figure, or a movement which will remain marginalized because of the overriding western identification of women only as female bodies, and fecundity specifically. This "mismeasure of women," as Carol Tavris phrases it, which links, through menstruation and pregnancy, women to Nature and therefore to Life with a capital L, denies woman access to spiritual transcendence. The problem for the women's spirituality movement is to overcome this diminished definition, which also proves to be the limitation of the third strategy, the use of the female body as the prevailing metaphor for women's experience.

The obvious problem remains: from what source *can* spiritual or transcendent power for women be derived? One hopeful sign is a line of creative descent. Artistic mothers who offer transcendence of a creative kind to their daughters figure importantly and productively in the consciousness of many women artists: thus Adrienne Rich pays homage to Emily Dickinson and Paula Mödersohn-Becker, Elizabeth Bishop to Marianne Moore, Muriel Rukeyser to Käthe Kollwitz, Jane Cooper to Rosa Luxembourg, Alice Walker to Zora Neale Hurston.[10] These women write about creative mothers, creative sisters, as a resource and example. The belief that artistic mothers bring spiritual empowerment is very attractive, especially in the light of Harold Bloom's theory that literary fathers engender Oedipal anxiety in their male literary offspring. Rather than committing Oedipal patricide, female writers celebrate their literary foremothers, imaging themselves standing on maternal shoulders, inventing metaphors of continuity which enable them to transcend themselves.

Having glanced thus briefly at the growing emphasis upon women's spirituality as an empowering influence, I next raise the issues which inhere in feminism's second strategy for achieving female subjectivity, the injunction to collectivity, or what Nancy Cott observes functions as a "rhetoric of unity." The purpose of rhetoric is always persuasion, and the "rhetoric of unity" aims not so much to persuade the opposite sex as to bond through rhetoric all members of the female sex, including those too disadvantaged or too intimidated to speak for themselves.

Feminism, in its theory, its activism, and its literary practice stemmed from a sense of injustice, and addressed the struggle for equality between the sexes, as the name women's "liberation" movement indicates. The issues are wide-ranging: the prevention and punishment of rape, of the battering of women, of child molestation; the right to abortion, to professional equality of status, to equal opportunity and equal remuneration. Originally, the issues were perceived as being essentially the same for all women, and the notion of a rhetoric of unity expressed that perception.

Such expression of commonality falls outside both the tone and substance of male narrative. As Nina Baym has pointed out, literary canon formation has been spread in modern times by male critics such as F. O. Matthiessen, Perry Miller, Henry Nash Smith, Lionel Trilling, and Leslie Fiedler, who all, to varying degrees, invoke a male ideology of *individual* heroism.

Contrariwise, what we find in the fiction and poetry of feminism of the 1960s is an emphasis on sorority, on bonding with all women and becoming spokeswomen for the inarticulate, for the poor, the disenfranchised, and minority women. White middle-class women provided the strongest impetus for this renewed feminist energy, women fortunate enough not to have race and class as significant deterrents. Although later to be challenged, their belief at that time was that a rhetoric of unity ultimately espouses unconventional and pluralistic values for a heroine, values which directly conflict with the dominant male ideal of individual heroism. Sandra Gilbert points out that female discourse, in contradistinction to male discourse, projects "an ideology which defines excellence as the inscription of communal, conventional, conventionally female virtues like maternal nurturance, sisterly supportiveness, pious purity and emotional expressiveness."[11]

Both in Adrienne Rich's poem, "Phantasia for Elvira Shatayev," about women alpinists who perished taking care of a sick member of the expedition in a storm on Lenin Peak in 1974, and in the prose testament of Irina Ratushinskaya, *Grey Is the Color of Hope*, about women political prisoners in a Russian camp, loving, even undergoing punishment for each other, singing and celebrating each other's birthdays, we have non-masculinist valorizations of community effort and tending. Psychologist Jessica Benjamin finds that women's sense of personal attachment challenges the male idealization of personal independence and the heroic presumption of the primacy of independence for the quest. Women's experiential narratives run counter to male heroic values of separation and ego-centeredness, and contain characters who do not have referents in the literature of action which values the plot of victory over enemies, but in female books of relation such as the biblical story of Naomi and her daughter-in-law Ruth ("Whither thou goest, there go I").[12] New values may enter society in this way. For example, the quest for signification need not begin in personal detachment as both ancient mythology and modern Freudian psychology posit.[13]

One of the major accomplishments of the consciousness-raising groups of the 1960s was the phenomenon of female bonding. The literary expression of female bonding is a highly important development because it presents women with a vision beyond the near-exclusive focus on romantic attachment which had defined their roles. Moreover, it exposes the truth that competition among women is in part a by-product of competition for male favors, both sexual and economic, and that women create strong ties with each other when they operate outside the romantic plot. Thus in Maxine Hong Kingston's *The Woman Warrior*, mother and daughter form a tie which results in the daughter carrying the mother's oral tradition into written expression. Or, as the character Isadora in Jong's *Fear of Flying* wryly admits, "we were attracted to men, but when it came to understanding and good talk, we needed each other."[14] By initiating plots which afford women representation, literary sorority compensates for the virtual exclusion of women from the male heroic plot.

Adrienne Rich writes of ordinary women whom she deems extraordinary: women who have changed patriarchal values to preserve life in a violent society. Her poetry validates the common woman and sees power in community:

> I have to cast my lot with those
> who age after age, perversely,
>
> with no extraordinary power,
> reconstitute the world.[15]

For many women writers today, then, the emphasis is neither on praising nor becoming a superior individual; they see speaking for the inarticulate or the invisible group as an obligation. This is admittedly a controversial concept. But in any event, the feminist project probes that middle distance between the extraordinary and the ordinary, and considers how to make an aesthetic of it. So May Sarton, after extended references in "My Sisters, O My Sisters" to her "sisters" who are named writers—Dorothy Wordsworth, Emily Dickinson, Sappho, George Sand, Christina Rossetti, and others—still offers the plea for commonality: "To be through what we make more simply human, / To come to the deep place where poet becomes woman." [16]

One of the most successful examples of yoking the one and the many, the individual and the group, is Monique Wittig's inimitable "novel," *Les Guérillères*, based on the myth of Penthesilia. The author is not present as actor or even narrator; she is a transmitter of other voices. Though individuals are sometimes named within the fable, Wittig inserts, on special divider pages between sections, full-page *lists* of women's names in capital letters. (Interestingly, these names derive from Edmund Spenser's *The Faerie Queene*, whose Amazonian women make his epic a slyly appropriate source for Wittig.) Wittig's device emblematizes the fact that a collectivity, not an individual, relates the narrative; the collective pronoun "we" or the collective noun "the women" occurs at the beginning of most paragraphs. As a collective voice, "the women," emphasizes community, as does the injunction they utter: "Beware of dispersal. Remain united like the characters in a book. Do not abandon the collectivity." [17] The literature and the life are inseparable.

The impulses toward community, the "being nobody together" as Alicia Ostriker, harking back to Emily Dickinson's "I'm Nobody—Who are You?" calls it, is reflected in other similar titles such as Judy Grahn's "The Common Woman" and Maxine Hong Kingston's "No Name Woman." Anne Sexton's "In Celebration of My Uterus," a poem prompted by an impending hysterectomy, reaches toward a manic if not Whitmanic identification with multitudes. Here is a representative stanza:

> Each cell has a life,
> There is enough here to please a nation
> It is enough that the populace own these goods.
> Any person, any commonwealth would say of it,
> "It is good this year that we may plant again,
> and think forward to a harvest."
> A blight has been forecast and has been cast out.
> Many women together are singing of this:
> one is in a shoe factory cursing the machine,

one is at the aquarium tending a seal,
one is dull at the wheel of her Ford,
one is at the toll gate collecting,
one is tying the cord of a calf in Arizona,
one is straddling a cello in Russia,
one is shifting pots on the stove in Egypt,
one is painting her bedroom walls moon color,
one is dying but remembering a breakfast,
one is stretching on her mat in Thailand,
one is wiping the ass of her child,
one is staring out the window of a train
in the middle of Wyoming and one is
anywhere and some are everywhere and all
seem to be singing, although some can not
sing a note.[18]

Through the use of taxonomy which simultaneously indicates inclusiveness and diversity, through the incantatory repetition of the phrase "*one is*" which has the effect of insisting on the symbolic nature of the individuated image, this poem affirms that the experience of women is marked by commonality more than difference. The female fertility which provides the starting point of the poem extends hyberbolically to the fertility of earth and "harvest." Speaking, or almost singing, "seeming to be singing" (Whitman's "I hear America singing" transposed to a different context), the individual identity is subsumed into a vast collective female identity. And in the last three lines with their abstract nouns "anywhere" and "everywhere," the embracing "all" and the anthem-like "singing," the poem stretches beyond authentication toward a kind of self-transcendence, though rooted in the immanent.

Lessing's *The Diaries of Jane Somers* also elevates to dignity and importance the "ordinary women," women seen here as holding the world together:

And now the bus. By now the office workers have ebbed from this area, and the bus is full of women. The freemasonry of women, who sit at their ease, shopping baskets and bags all over them, enjoying a nice sit-down and the pleasant day. A bus at half past ten in the morning is a different world: nothing in common with the rush-hour buses.

These women who keep things together, who underpin our important engagements with big events by multifarious activities so humble that, asked at the end of the day what they did, they might, and often do, reply, Oh, nothing much.

They are off to a shop three stages away to buy knitting wool for a jersey for a grandchild, buttons for a dress or a shirt, or a reel of white cotton, for one should always have some about. They are going to the supermarket, or to pay the electricity bill, or to get their pensions. The Home Helps are on their way to get prescriptions made up for Eliza Bates, Annie Reeves, Mrs. Coles, Mrs. Brent, Mr. Hodges. Someone is off to the stationer's to buy birthday cards for all the family separately to send to Uncle Bertie, aged sixty-four. A parcel is being sent to Cape Town, to an emigrated niece and her family, for she has asked for a certain make of vests you cannot, it seems, get in South Africa. Or a parcel containing homemade biscuits to Wales, for a cousin. Some are off down to Oxford Street, on a weekly or monthly jaunt, regarded as a holiday, a rest, and will spend hours trying on dresses and keeping a sharp eye open for clothes that might be suitable for mothers, daughters, husbands, sons. They come home from several hours' hard labour around the shops with a petticoat, two pairs of nylons, and a little purse. All of which they could have bought in the High Street, but it's not so much fun. They will later go to visit housebound relatives, taking with them all kinds of specially needed commodities, like tooth powder, or a certain brand of throat lozenges; they will go to the hospital and sit for hours with a granny; they drop in to have a cup of tea with a daughter or take a grandchild to the park. They are at it all day, these good women, and the good nature that is the result of their competence at what they do overflows and splashes about the inside of the bus, so that smiles get exchanged, people remark on the weather—in other words, offer each other consolation or encouragement—and comment humorously on life through events glimpsed on the pavement.[19]

In a different medium, the same intention is manifest. Visual artist May Stevens depicts in a collage the life of political activist Rosa Luxembourg, comparing this famous "extraordinary" woman with her own unsung mother whom she valorizes as equally significant and tragic. As these examples show, the feminist world is questioning what constitutes a "significant social role" and seeking to extend it to humbler practice within the scope of each individual. From such reconceptualization, ordinary heroines may spring.

Yet hints of problems arise in the wake of the rhetoric of unity. If we look back on Lessing's encomium quoted above on the commonplace, even trivial round of activities of ordinary women, we see she interjects a note of ambivalence by including herself (and by implication the addressed reader), among those enjoying larger duties and responsibilities than the women she is praising. When she writes of these women that they "underpin our important engagements with big events" it is unclear how to interpret the pronoun "our" and the adjectives "big" and "important;" are they ironic, is the author mocking her professional self, her creative self? She describes the activities of these "good women" lyrically, even sentimentally, yet she is *not* of them, nor can she realistically wish to belong to their world of self-definition through abnegation and service, or she would cease to write. As in the Sexton poem, what happens in the homage is a deliberate blurring of boundaries between ordinary and extra-ordinary.

These "good women" raise questions pertaining not only to personal definition or selfhood; there is also the highly important matter of influence or lack of it. The diffused goodness they exemplify, like *all* theories of benevolence, regardless of gender, rests upon the continuation of the status quo. Beyond maintaining their close family ties, the good works these women do supplies comfort and aid to those society neglects; they evince no interest in changing that world. In this, they resemble closely the benevolent heroines discussed in Chapter 1, and contrast sharply with the heroines in Chapter 7 who also emphasize community, but one within a vastly different world.

For much the same reason, I find troubling the following lines of Adrienne Rich:

> Sometimes, gliding at night
> in a plane over New York City
> I have felt like some messenger
> called to enter, called to engage
> this field of light and darkness.
> A grandiose idea, born of flying.[20]

There can be no question that women writers deflating notions of artistic pride, as Rich does here, serve a useful purpose for both sexes. The danger is that there may be nothing between Erica Jong's *Fear of Flying* (a metaphor for feminine phobic incapacities in general) and Rich's dismissal of her sense of mission "born of flying" as "grandiose," i.e., heroically male and self-aggrandizing. Her lines enunciate the conflict, stated before, that arises between the necessary will to representation, to individuation, and feminist values which stress humility and commonality. Located within the shift toward matriarchy, Adrienne Rich's poetry nevertheless displays the tensions implicit in the rhetoric of unity: the role of the extraordinary woman, the role of the ordinary woman, and the poet's wishful and deliberate erasure of the boundary between the two. The theme of connection among women, daughters to mothers, mothers to their mothers, very strong in many feminist writers, is a preoccupation of Rich; "she longs then," says Catharine Stimpson, "for wholeness, for touch, a desire the hand signifies. The hand. It holds the pen, clasps the child, finds the lover, sews the quilt, cleans the pot, dusts the house."[21]

Thus, one important part of the problem of developing a new heroine is the unresolved pull between egoism and feminism. Finding an appropri-

ate relation among difference, self, and individual is as much a feminist issue as a Lacanian one. "*The* hand," despite the definite article, is everywoman's hand, an unnamed hand. Rich's most recent poetry is her most
expansive poetry, but even her poems about individual heroines, e.g., Harriet
Tubman, Jane Addams, Sojourner Truth, emphasize a sororal, non-com-
petitive spirit. These were extraordinary women who nonetheless achieved
broad social commitment, and serve her as models.

Beyond doubt, the rhetoric of unity has created an opening for a new
paradigm of the heroine. On the other hand, the rhetoric of unity can have
the effect of discouraging individuation and individuality in general as secondary, even indulgent, goals for women. Perhaps a collective voice must
precede an individuated one. As with the women's spirituality movement,
hidden dangers in these emancipatory strategies arise from their evocation
of highly gendered roles. For the women's spirituality movement, the risk
is an unequal share of the moral responsibility for society, or a split between
physical and spiritual. For the rhetoric of unity, the hazard is the erasure of
hard-won representation.

Tatyana Mamonova, in her study of sexism in Russia, encourages
women to see themselves as *extraordinary*, as superior: "Imagine an athlete
or scientist who says 'I'm not a bit better than any one else.' Will he be able
to break a record or make a discovery? Will a person be of any general benefit if he patterns his behavior on the negative or the mediocre?"[22]

Women, feeling a group identity rooted in their common experience
of oppression, are reluctant to separate themselves out, or to overtake.
Charges of elitism and privilege hang in the air like a bad odor. The problem of finding a voice is not unique to women; the point at which the
ordinary intersects with the extraordinary is a problem for every underclass
or group.

George Orwell, laboring saint and saint of Labor, was an extraordinary
man who shouldered the task of speaking for the common man. Perhaps
Orwell's great triumph was that he became not only a common man, but an
archetype, *the* representative man. That is, he functions simultaneously on
two levels: as author, as creator, he functions as the uncommon man; in the
role he chooses to valorize in fiction, he becomes the representative man.

In a sense, this is what Adrienne Rich and other women authors are
striving toward, but with this significant difference: she and they are writing in a tradition which emphasizes silence for women, invisibility for
women, women's non-representation. In other words, feminists cannot ignore Freud's insight that real fathers want real sons to inherit and admininster
their laws. To surrender representation is to surrender power, and the vex-

ing problem remains as to whether the representation of anonymity can effect change. So what is always risky becomes for feminist writing politically risky as well, leading away from representation.[23]

We need a conscious strategy for *self*-representation, announcement and naming. So the Muslim poet Furūgh Farrokhzād, who died in a car accident in 1967, voices her conviction of her own artistic immortality in a poem aptly titled "It Is Only the Voice That Remains," and poet Brenda Marie Osbey writes, "i plant words / and bring up myself." The oppositional pull of a unifying voice and an individuating one brings us to the most serious objection to the rhetoric of unity.

If women's sense of collective grievance was a starting point of organization which served well to rally women and to "raise consciousness," in time it became evident that differences of class, race, and culture were being obscured by this stress on collectivity. This has been a growing complaint among Third World feminists like Gayatri Chakravorty Spivak who wish to distinguish their needs, experience, and situations from those of white middle class women who presume to speak for them. Audre Lorde writes of the need for racial identity as well as female identity in "From the House of Yemanjá," calling upon her black mother:

> I bear two women upon my back
> one dark and rich and hidden
> in the ivory hungers of the other
> mother...
>
> Mother I need
> mother I need
> mother I need your blackness now
> as the august earth needs rain.
> I am
> the sun and moon and forever hungry
> the sharpened edge
> where day and night shall meet
> and not be
> one.[24]

Here, opposites are not reconciled; differentiation insists upon itself. The category "woman" is not, after all, unitary. Race, class, and gender are all formative components of any particular woman. In fact, Judith Butler advises feminists to think of the pronoun "we" as a suspect word.

Ultimately, speaking on behalf of all women seems to me to contain the seeds of arrogance, though its intention (to provide representation for all, a kind of level inclusiveness) is surely the reverse. The problem raised in the preceding chapter about a "mother tongue" which is outside the law of the father must be asked in the context of a unity of rhetoric. Can we find "a mother tongue" that will not distort the multifarious reality of the speechless? Unity is not a prerequisite for representation, whether visual or literary. Patriarchy is not unitary and is being represented (although the range of representation, predominantly white male, has also become a source of rancour). The emphasis on women's "difference" has so long referred to biological difference and how far that creates gender difference, that it has tended to divert attention from the issues of "difference" *among* women. Can we be authentic for others? Judith Stacey proposes, instead, and I concur, the acceptance of the "polyphony of diversity." In sum, what I discern in the rhetoric of unity, as in the women's spirituality movement, is a strategy that is partially successful, a signpost or the way toward missing female subjectivity.

Finally, I wish to discuss the strategy I regard as the most successful and important of the three for strengthening women's sense of self: the use of the body as the prevailing metaphor for experience. This strategy has achieved two aims: it has delivered the gaze back to the female subject, and, as a consequence, it has brought about the direct expression of female eroticism, one of the striking changes in women's writing in the last few decades.

What has been repressed is the theme of Balthus' paintings of adolescent girls and Stephen Dobyns' poems based upon these same paintings, fascinating examples of *male* representation of unexpressed female desire. What the viewer feels as shocking in the Balthus paintings, many of them with innocuous titles such as *Patience* and *Getting By*, is an incipient violence the frame can barely contain. The threat arises from the tension between the intensity of awakening, adolescent eroticism and the captivity of the domestic interiors in which these young girls wait to enact their roles. In his poem about Balthus' picture *Patience*, Dobyns' pellmell rush of rhetorical questions, coupled with descriptions of the young girl's physically extreme behaviour of one sort or another, "What if she ran shouting from the house? What if she / pursued their aged terrier and bit him unmercifully?" suggests that violence proceeds from impatient feminine sexuality. But it would be more precise to state that both in Balthus' oils and Dobyns' *Balthus Poems*, there is a field force created of suppressed rage at diffused and objectless sexuality, which, remaining unexpressed, is unlikely to find resolution.[25]

Interestingly, the banked fires of women's sexuality are directly linked to a motif of arson by women characters in novels such as Marilynne Robinson's *Housekeeping*, Fay Weldon's *The Life and Loves of a She-Devil*, Jean Rhys' *The Wide Sargasso Sea*, Charlotte Brontë's *Jane Eyre*, and many others. The image of fire is linked to "unappeased" sexuality in the fourth part of May Sarton's "My Sisters, O My Sisters," a paean to the love of women:

> We think of all the women hunting for themselves,
> Turning and turning to each other with a driving
> Need to learn to understand, to live in charity,
> And above all to be used fully, to be giving
> From wholeness, wholeness back to love's deep clarity.
>
> O, all the burning hearts of women unappeased
> Shine like great stars, like flowers of fire,
> As the sun goes and darkness opens all desire—
> And we are with a fierce compassion seized.[26]

To provide representation of women's desire and will, heterosexual or lesbian, is the project of poets such as Sharon Barba, Lucille Clifton, Helen Cooper, Ellen Bass, and Judy Grahn. How profound a difficulty they face we discussed with relation to the male gaze in Woman/Sight. For maleness is seen not only as creating the authoritative institutions of culture but as creating female *desire*. As film critic Naomi Scheman phrases it, "the right man is the one who, because of *his* desire for *her*, has a claim on her."[27] That is, her desire does not claim an object, it has no prior and distinct existence. Her subjective desire is assumed to be aroused only by being herself an object of desire, a contradiction in terms.

If feminist theorists such as Kristeva, Hélène Cixous, and Michèle Montrelay see the body as a way of interpreting, even narrating female being, thereby risking essentialism, it is in direct response to the possessive male gaze which heretofore was assumed to bestow sexual identity. These feminists feel, as do others like Naomi Scheman and Carole Vance, that the acknowledgment of woman's desire, and of woman as an author of desire, is what makes the female protagonist equal.

Carole Vance, author of *Pleasure and Danger*, (her title is in itself a rough approximation of *jouissance*, that untranslatable word which may imperfectly be conveyed as "bliss" or "ecstasy") exhorts women in general to make sexuality one of their subjects, that to do so is a political position because the absence of a female discourse for the expression of female desire has in fact been misconstrued as an indication that no independent female desire exists.[28] "Feminism must insist that women are sexual subjects, sexual actors, sexual agents . . . that our experience is not a blank nor a mere repetition of what has been said about us, and that the pleasure we have experienced is as much a guide to future action as the brutality," writes Vance.[29] Sandra Gilbert notes that the work of feminist critics like Irigaray and Cixous "is marked by its persistent references to the erotic, to *jouissance*."

A larger claim can be made: for women to release the sexual libido is an insurrectionary act insofar as it alters gender stereotypes (male/subject, female/object). Moreover, the expression of a female libido alters aesthetic criteria as well, and offers grounds for authenticating women's experience. Thus poet Olga Broumas challenges Homeric truth as the paradigm of aesthetic and sexual authenticity for both sexes: "What *if* one memorized the *Iliad* in school? / Stubborn and generous / about our pleasure let us be." [30] *Our* pleasure here is lesbian eroticism. Wittig's *Les Guérillères* makes this identical point: "Is the finest thing on the dark earth really a group of horsemen whose horses go at a trot or a troop of infantry stamping the ground? Is the finest thing really a squadron of ships side by side? Anactoria Kypris Save have a bearing grace a radiant brightness of countenance that are pleasanter to see than all the chariots of the Lydians and their warriors charging in their armour." [31]

Both Broumas and Wittig draw here on Sappho:

> Some say cavalry and others claim
> infantry or a fleet of long oars
> is the supreme sight on the black earth.
>   I say it is
>
> the one you love . . .
> So Anaktoria, although you are
> far, do not forget your loving friends.
>   And I for one
>
> would rather listen to your soft step
> and see your radiant face—than watch
> all the dazzling chariots and armored
>   hoplites of Lydia. [32]

Nevertheless, the emancipatory strategy that uses women's bodies as the primary source of female subjectivity provokes the question: Who's the viewer? That is, what women may experience as emancipatory may evoke a different response in men. Female bodies have been both targets of opprobrium and magnets for praise. Any view of female power rooted in the physicality of existence brings to the fore, a highly charged *doubling* of power. If women have the power of creation, may they not also possess the power of destruction? In fact the original Earth-Mothers were beneficent, active and aggressive; they did possess both powers. As we have remarked, the Indian goddess Kali and the Celtic goddess Sheila-Na-Gig *are* creation and destruction, linking intimately in their person the erotic and the horrific. [33]

Such integrated figures, representing natural, cyclical forces and imaged in the rounded contours of Aphrodite and Demeter, goddesses who teach about the relation of love to death, arouse male fear by this very link-age of eroticism and destruction. In Céline's words they are "women who can wreck the infinite," while Harold Bloom maintains that Vergil's Juno embodies the "male dread that origin and end [creation and destruction in our terms] will turn out to be one and the same."[34]

Of the duality of the feminine erotic and horrific, Wendy Lesser suggests in her study *The Life Below The Ground: A Study of the Subterranean in Literature and History* that ". . . at the root of men's feelings about women in general [lies] the fear of being lost in a 'dark tunnel', of losing one's bearings, of [s]mothering (of falling down a 'manhole,' so to speak)."[35]

Part of our common cultural reference to the underground, with all the frightening connotations of the subterranean, is its connotation as a female place. Gilbert and Gubar speak of the male poet's "fear of feminization or an engulfment by the [literally] unfathomable forces of the feminine."[36] The subterranean is frightening because it is female; the female is frightening because she represents the subterranean.

In *Faust* Goethe writes:

Faust: The Mothers! Mothers—sound with wonder haunted.

Mephisto: True, Goddesses unknown to mortal mind,
            And named indeed with dread among our kind.
            To reach them, delve below earth's deepest floors.[37]

If the underground is the place from which the seed springs, the mother, it is also the place to which the body returns and crumbles to dust. Lesser explains further the male fear of the underground as deriving in part from the fear of "risking one's hard-won sense of adult separation from the mother's body."[38] In the same vein, Anne Sexton writes in "Housewife," "Men enter by force, drawn back like Jonah / into their fleshy mothers."[39] Fear of Woman/Space in this traditional visualization recalls the origin of the word "grotesque" in the root, *grotto*, a subterranean cave, and in fact the caves in Greece were known as the womb of Gaea, the earth goddess.[40] For women, the cave is not a threatening image, since it is feminine.

Perhaps the most extreme visualization of this fear of woman's space as castrating is the Freudian interpretation of Medusa, which we discussed. But Freud did not invent castration fear. The image of the castrating woman may actually date all the way back to myths about the German fertility goddess, Holda, who, when enraged, turns into a hag with huge teeth. Imaging castration fear as tooth-like projections was prevalent in *fin-de-siècle* costume and decor, for example in the work of Aubrey Beardsley.[41] In our time, Norman Mailer has returned to the myth of the *vagina dentata*, nor is he

1. *Charcot Lecturing on Hysteria at the Salpêtrière*, anonymous: etching, after a painting by André Brouillet.

2. *Interior*, oil on canvas, 1868–69, by Edgar Degas.

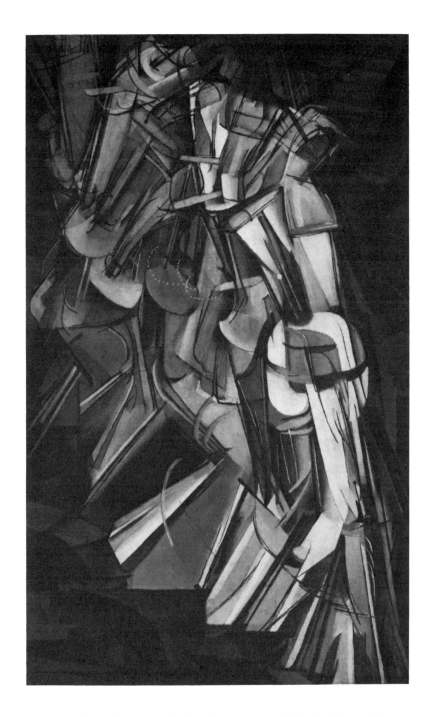

3. *Nude Descending a Staircase, No. 2*, oil on canvas, 1912, by Marcel Duchamp.

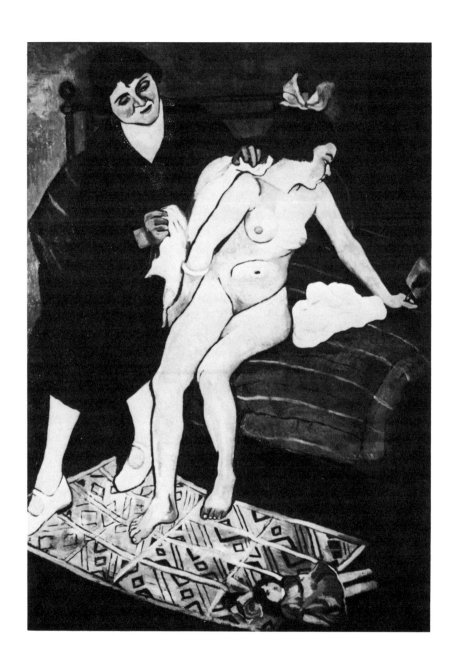

4. *The Abandoned Doll*, 1921, oil on canvas, 51″ × 32″ by Suzanne
Valadon, French (1865–1938). The National Museum of Women
in the Arts. Gift of Wallace and Wilhelmina Holladay.

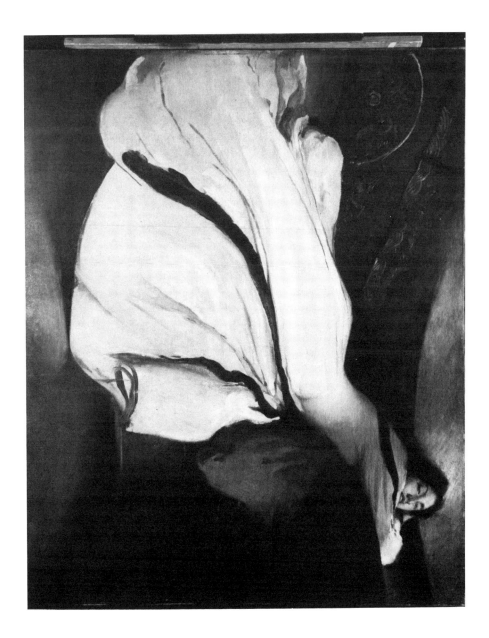

5. *Repose*, oil on canvas, 1895, by John White Alexander.

6. *The Wyndham Sisters*, oil on canvas, 1899, by John Singer Sargent.

7. Gloria Steinem. Reproduced by Special Permission of *Playboy* magazine. Copyright © 1973 by *Playboy*. Photo by Frank Eck.

8. *Toilet of Venus* ("Rokeby Venus") by Diego Velázquez. Reproduced by courtesy of the Trustees, The National Gallery, London.

9. *Death and the Maiden*, 1510–11, by Hans Baldung.

10. *Mosaic Floor with Head of Medusa in Center*, anonymous.

11. *Snake Goddess*, Minoan from Crete, ca. 1600–1500 B.C., gold and
    ivory, h. 6 ½".

12. *Lucas van Uffele*, oil, by
Sir Anthony Van Dyck.

13. *The Witches' Sabbath*,
oil, 1797–98, by
Francisco Goya.

14. *Mistress and Maid*, oil, by Johannes Vermeer.

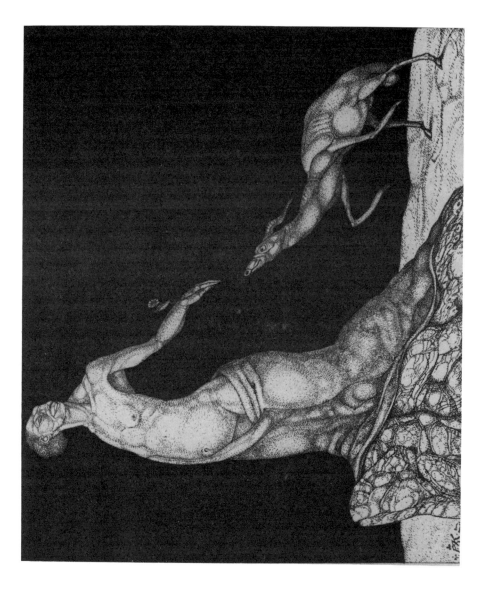

15. *Woman and Animal*, 1904, etching by Paul Klee.

16. *The Peacock Skirt*, black ink on white paper, 1894, by Aubrey Beardsley.

17. *Hydria*, Meikirch/BE, Grächwil, bronze, sixth century B.C.

unique in this reversion to male panic. Psychologist Miriam Greenspan assures us that "this male terror of the 'Vagina with Teeth' is one of the most deeply entrenched myths of patriarchal culture." [42] Angela Carter also sees contemporary male hysteria producing that image; her apocalyptic vision of New York City during a fantasized war of the sexes includes graffiti of "the female circle . . . with, inside it, a set of bared teeth." [43]

Finally, Cynthia Macdonald, in a stunning fusion of the conventions of woman as *objet d'art* and woman as castrator, parodies both stereotypes; the first is inverted, so that the *male* becomes the *objet d'art*, while the second stereotype of the woman castrator is raised to a professional level.

> When I was seventeen, a man in the Dakar Station
> Men's Room (I couldn't read the signs) said to me:
> You're a real ball cutter. I thought about that
> For months and finally decided
> He was right. Once I knew that was my thing,
> Or whatever we would have said in those days,
> I began to perfect my methods. Until then
> I had never thought of trophies. Preservation
> Was at first a problem: pickling worked
> But was a lot of trouble. Freezing
> Proved to be the answer. I had to buy
> A second freezer just last year; the first
> Was filled with rows and rows of
> Pink and purple lumps encased in Saran wrap.
>
> I have more subjects than I can handle,
> But only volunteers. It is an art like hypnosis
> Which cannot be imposed on the unwilling victim.
> If you desire further information about the process and
> The benefits, please drop in any night from nine to twelve.
> My place is east of Third on Fifty-sixth.
> You'll know it by the three gold ones over the door.[44]

The business-like tone borrowed from male corporate diction and instruction manuals, coupled with the author's deadpan delivery, stand gender stereotypes on their heads. Similarly, Diane Ackerman creates an eponymous heroine named Lady Faustus, thereby positioning a woman squarely in what had originally been a male plot of hubristic daring. One section of Ackerman's long poem about this character refers specifically to Andrew Marvell's seventeenth century ode "To His Coy Mistress." Ackerman even appropriates as her title, "A Fine, A Private Place," which echoes Marvell's lines: "The grave's a fine and private place / But none I think, do there embrace." In Ackerman, though, it is no longer the male lover who is importunate, as it was in Marvell's original ("Had we but world enough, and time, / This coyness, Lady, were no crime,") but the lady, her hips rolling "like a Spanish galleon." [45] Enhancing the tongue-in-cheek diction of Ackerman's poem, humor reverses gender stereotypes—the impatient male becomes backward, the reticent female, forthcoming; Ackerman's poem celebrates *female* sexuality.

Whereas for men the female body is equivocal because it is perceived as potentially destructive, for women the female body is an agent of autonomy and subjectivity. In fact, Alicia Ostriker observes that its usage by women poets is now so ubiquitous that "as women relocate spirituality within the body and especially within the body's despised sexuality, we find certain radical redefinitions of art." [46]

Women poets like Toi Derricotte, Ai, and Gwendolyn Brooks deliberately turn to female experiences of birth, nursing, menstruation, menopause, penetration, lesbian love-making, abortion, and bodily care of others, because such subject matter has previously been excluded from the canon. We have but to think, on the other hand, of the exhaustive literary record of male experience with both Mars and Eros to realize how much *both* sexes know about the physical experiences of men. The new look at female bodies, middle-aged and old, sick and well, comely and homely, performing intimate bodily functions which have been taboo as literary subject matter, has been a preoccupation, even an obsessional recuperation of the sex as a whole by women (critics such as Hélène Cixous, poets such as Lucille Clifton, novelists such as Rita Mae Brown leap to mind). Representation of women by women is entering women's consciousness, and, much more slowly, the literary canon.

The force of reaction against such an enterprise indicates the necessity for undertaking it; Carolyn Heilbrun reminds us that as late as 1963 James Dickey complained that Anne Sexton dwelled on the "pathetic and disturbing aspects of bodily experience," [47] though one might reasonably object that Dickey's own description of violent acts performed by male bodies in his novel *Deliverance* (1971) is no less "disturbing."

A strong attempt, then, is being made to universalize images of female power by means of the valorization of the female body. This brings new literary innovations, of which role reversals such as the examples quoted, are the most obvious. And "Lady Faustus," and other wryly humorous poems, manage yet another twist. The ode, originally a lyric of lofty and elevated feeling, elaborate in style, becomes, in the hands of poets like Lucille Clifton ("Homage to My Hips") and Anne Sexton ("In Celebration of My Uterus"), humorous, colloquial, personal.

The traditional *blazon*, a catalogue of praise of the beloved woman's body, and a staple ingredient of the traditional love lyric, is also put to comic effect when women poets describe their *own* bodies, or those of other women. Indeed, since comedy in general arises from a critical glance at society, I take as a hopeful indication of textual if not sexual equality, the fact that women poets like Diane Ackerman as well as Diane Wakoski and Sharon Olds have incorporated humor in their love poetry, as John Donne, Shakespeare, and Marvell did in theirs.

Further, restoring the autonomy of the female body to the female sex allows the expression of a broader range of female sensuality. As we saw in "Woman/Sight" (Chapter 3), as women become the subject, not the object of the gaze, the gaze broadens. For example, Diane Wakoski's "Belly Dancer" delights in her green silk costume: "Surely any woman wearing such fabrics / would move her body just to feel them touching every part of her." [48] Whereas T. S. Eliot's Prufrock can only ponder, "Do I dare to eat a peach?", Lady Faustus not only dares to do so but does so with relish: "sinking her teeth / into the cleft / of a voluptuous peach." Similarly, in another poem, "Cave Diving in the Tropics," Diane Ackerman speaks of the sensuous caresses of the ocean on her body.

We have also seen that the use of the body as prevailing metaphor for women's experience has meant the important inclusion of the lesbian body in erotic poetry with the result that the romantic dyad which underlies most love poetry is now re-defined. Both Monique Wittig and Luce Irigaray explore the potential of lesbianism in this connection. Taken together with heterosexual *and* lesbian women's refusal to accept the "perfect" body marketed by the media, *aesthetic* criteria of desirability are less rigid and less uniform when women look at their own and other women's bodies.

Why, then, given all these important advances, should there be *any* problems for women attached to this new representation of a range of female bodily experience as the prevailing metaphor for women? After all, as Harold Bloom points out in a very different context, what Falstaff teaches us is that the ego is always a *bodily* ego. (But look how articulate Falstaff is— that windbag is pregnant with words!) The problem is that the feminist choice of body is based upon a converse assumption that is troubling. That is, language is perceived by many feminist writers as being evasive, patriarchal, missing for them. As a result, they adopt an adversarial or dismissive stance toward it.

Thus, with the overwhelmingly male canon in mind, Tillie Olsen asserts that "the mother tongue" is the language of emotion that doesn't derive from book-learning. Poet Kathleen Fraser writes , "It is difficult, even at this moment, to assert my / language in the powerful field of your reality."[49] And Monique Wittig, connecting the revolutionary social change brought about by the female warriors with a concommitant change in language, reports:

> In speaking of their genitals the women do not employ hyperboles metaphors, they do not proceed sequentially or by gradation. They do not recite long litanies, whose refrain is an unending imprecation. They do not strive to multiply the intervals so that in sum they signify a deliberate lapse. They say that all these forms denote an outworn language. They say everything must begin over again. They say that a great wind is sweeping the earth. They say that the sun is about to rise.[50]

In Wittig's Utopia the women, "the integrity of the body their first principle, advance marching together into another world."[51] And Adrienne Rich writes in "Images for Godard" of language and women:

> When all conversation
> becomes an interview
> under duress
>
> when we come to the limits
> of the city
>
> my face must have a meaning.[52]

and again, in "I Am in Danger—Sir—," Rich, a celebrant of the female body, arrives at the conclusion that language is masculine territory and false to women's experience:

> Gardening the day-lily,
> wiping the wine-glass stems,
> your thought pulsed on behind
> a forehead battered paper-thin,
>
> you, woman, masculine
> in single-mindedness,
> for whom the word was more
> than a symptom—
>
> a condition of being.
> Till the air buzzing with spoiled language
> sang in your ears
> of Perjury
>
> and in your half-cracked way you chose
> silence for entertainment,
> chose to have it out at last
> on your own premises.[53]

Contrasting the "perjury" of Rich's patriarchal "spoiled language" with the truth of physical experience, Anne Sexton informs her daughter, "What I want to say, Linda, / is that there is nothing in your body that lies."[54] That is, the body becomes the new female language, because it is seen as participating in common female experience, as being the common denominator of difference. The emphasis on the female body may lead women to choose "silence for entertainment," as Rich remarks—or resistance.

But a female discourse still needs to be forged, not only because the body's experience varies with class, race, culture much more significantly than was generally conceded at the outset of the women's liberation movement, but also because female experience is not limited to the body any more than is male experience. To gain admittance for the body and to use it as women's governing metaphor say very different things about how we conceptualize ourselves. Thus, although there are poems such as Audre Lorde's "Now That I Am Forever With Child," Toi Derricotte's "Natural Birth," and Sexton's "Somewhere in Africa," which suggest the transcendence of the immanent experience, commonly the metaphor of the female body establishes authenticity in immanence. Thus Denise Levertov writes of "The Goddess" who

> came upon me where I lay in Lie Castle!
>
> she who plucked me from the close rooms,
> without whom nothing
> flowers, fruits, sleeps in season,
> without whom nothing
> speaks in its own tongue, but returns
> lie for lie![55]

Lines about lies—Sexton's "your body, Linda, does not lie"; Rich's denunciation of language for women as "perjury"; and the lies of Levertov's "Lie Castle" above—suggest that in all these cases, what is found is authenticity; the message true to one's own experience is the *bodily* voice. The same truth emerges in Levertov's invocation on the Babylonian goddess of love and fertility, "Song for Ishtar."

> The moon is a sow
> and grunts in my throat
> Her great shining shines through me
>
> so the mud of my hollow gleams
> and breaks in silver bubbles
>
> She is a sow
> and I a pig and a poet
>
> When she opens her white

lips to devour me I bite back
and laughter rocks the moon

In the black of desire
we rock and grunt, grunt and
shine.[56]

This poem, by the use of the words "shining," and the phrase "and a poet," and especially in the odd coupling of "grunt and / shine" hints at transcendence. But the impact of the poem and of the goddess come from its description of physical desire. Now transcendent experience may or may not be impossible to express in images other than the immanent, but here the spiritual seems to be actually repressed by the overwhelming physicality of the terms describing the Goddess.

We have mentioned earlier with regard to the women's spirituality movement the cultural propensity to perceive men's bodies, but not women's, as capable of transcendence. So, a significant objection to this third strategy is that the female body and the female language that is an extension of that body are dangerously close to the essentialist view of woman as existing in a state of nature, an animal creature culture would only corrupt. The belief of some historians such as Margaret Murray that fertility goddesses and a fertility religion lie behind Christianity only strengthens the Goddess's primary identification with fecundity to the neglect of her spiritual powers. For instance, one of the most familiar images of the Goddess, the ancient Venus of Willendorf, depicts a female figure exaggerated in her proportions for the purpose of representing fertility. She has no facial features at all, she is the highly stylized representation of Nature, of abundance.

If we do proceed for the sake of argument with the dominant metaphor of the body despite this reductionism, another objection arises. Which female body is being validated? In Woman/Sight, we have already raised the problem of the deep cultural split between the erotic body and the maternal body. The mother is perceived in our culture as a figure whose very children testify to her prior possession and attachment; hence she cannot be viewed simultaneously as the erotic object of male desire, disembodied and prepared for framing. She has already, in every sense of the word, been "framed." For Freud, there was no imaging of the mother in her sexuality.

In literature, as in life, the figure of the mother is weakened further by her divided loyalties. In Shakespeare, for example, as others have noticed, mothers frequently take the part of their children in opposition to their husbands, placing the extent of their own authority in question and in jeopardy. The mother is so problematized by relation to her children, by the necessity to be "good," that she is severely limited. Freud's materialism, which led him to derogate the affective ties of the domestic sphere and replace them with the competitive skills necessary for the workplace, legitimated the devaluation of the mother.[57]

Therefore, the enterprise of reaching subjectivity by means of that female body which links us to mothers and maternal figures from times past is undermined on many counts: first, by the schism between the erotic and the maternal; then, by the divided loyalties of the mother; finally, but not least, by the contemporary cultural image of the mother as powerless, suffering, sacrificial, and, when past fertility, useless, and certainly past desire.[58] Where have all the mothers gone?

Mary O'Brien draws our attention to the fact that Aeschlyus' *Oresteia* gives us the motherlessness of Athena, Clytemnestra as an unnatural mother, and the female Furies banished. The absence of mothers in opera is also noteworthy, and Robert Donington speculates about the reasons, finding in his study, *Opera and its Symbols: The Unity of Words, Music, and Staging*, either the presence of monster-mothers like Mozart's Queen of the Night in *The Magic Flute*, or mothers safely dispatched, as in *Parsifal* and *Siegfried*.

Why is Hedda Gabler's most influential relation that with her father while, without explanation, her mother never appears at all? One might speculate whether Hedda Gabler would have had to kill herself when she discovered she was pregnant if her own mother had not been missing. Marianne Hirsch notes that Victorian heroines are either submissive victims of the paternal system, or if rebellious, then squelched by it. Their relation to the mother remains an insignificant part of the story because the fathers hold power. This debased, or rather, effaced, role of mothers holds true also for cinema; cinematic heroines have usually been presented as if they were the result of spontaneous generation, without mothers, as Naomi Scheman documents in her survey of cinematic heroines, "Missing Mothers/Desiring Daughters." If mothers cannot be heroines, and heroines can't be mothers, it seems as if heroines can't *have* mothers either.

Because mothers are part of a system which diminishes *all* women, daughters receive the message that mothers do not have sufficient power to be effective agents for empowering them. Yet many psychiatrists believe mothers provide the best models for nurture our society has produced. Faced with this paradox, the question that arises here is why the capacity for nurture is *not* regarded as influential and powerful. The fact is the mother cannot empower herself and therefore cannot be the agent to empower her daughter; her role has been described by such diverse observers as Julia Kristeva and Sigmund Freud as conducive to melancholy.

Despite all this, providing the missing mother figure is desirable and important insofar as it frees women from the necessity to identify with males, whether they be actors in the actual society or heroes in narrative and film. This has been a common viewer/reader response, as women report their experience. For this reason many feminists (Rich, Colette Inez, Diane Di Prima, and Kristeva) talk about re-membering, whether it be re-membering, reconstituting, the individual secular mother or the universal Great Mother goddesses of feminist archetypal criticism and theology. For these feminists, the female body receives additional validation as the missing link in a chain connecting women to a lost matriarchal mythology of goddesses—Goddesses of Animals, Goddesses of Snakes, Goddesses of Birds, all of whom are intimately tied to the creativity and energy of the natural world.[59]

But this annexing of the powers of Mother Earth *still* may not ensure an effectual transference of power from the mother. First of all, when women are seen as Nature, as Mother Earth, as in Diane Di Prima's poem, "Prayer to the Mothers," are they not exchanging individual vulnerability for a larger, broader vulnerability? Isn't "Mother Nature" now an object of control and exploitation? Don't we speak metaphorically about the "rape of Nature" despite her encompassing powers? In her poem "she is dreaming," Lucille Clifton links women both to Nature ("landscape") and to rape ("blood"):

> sometimes
> the whole world of women
> seems a landscape of
> red blood and things
> that need healing.[60]

Furthermore, aren't we nowadays more frightened of our own nuclear potential for destruction than of a Nature we once felt to be supremely awesome? Nature itself is not the empowering identification it appears at first glance. The ozone layer too can be penetrated.

Second, the notion of woman as Nature, as Earth Goddess, has given rise to a destructive opposition of energies—if woman is Nature, man is Culture—a conception which overlong has situated woman exclusively in the body. Although Nature and Culture may at first glance appear interdependent, complementary terms, they are, in fact, hierarchical. Culture includes language and therefore the ability to transcend the bodily self.

That is, if man is Culture, then though he possesses a body, he also possesses the means to transcend it, to transcend himself. If woman as Nature, on the other hand, is the *embodiment* of flesh for both sexes, then she is deprived of the possibility of transcendence. She remains in the body. Moreover, as we observed in the last chapter, Nature herself is mute, standing in opposition to mind, which speaks, and is male. Nature listens; Culture speaks. But we have seen in preceding chapters that silence inflicts severe damage upon women in every realm—spiritual, economic, social, and even sexual.

Another argument against the desirability of identifying woman with Nature is that this classification supports a binary system, borrowed from cultural anthropology and particularly from the work of Claude Lévi-Strauss, that opens the way to exclusion and hierarchy: nature/culture, moral/intellectual, physical/spiritual, instinct/intellect. These are not neutral pairings; presented as scientifically accurate, disinterested observation, they actually contain judgements of failure and success, and lend the very principle of binarism spurious authority.

Through Angela Carter's reaction to this gendered division, we see the essentialism which underlies it: "On this most insulting mythic redefinition of myself, that of occult priestess, I am indeed allowed to speak but only of things that male society does not take *seriously*. I can hint at dreams, I can even personify the imagination; but that is only because I am not rational enough to cope with reality."[61]

We have pointed out multiple ways in which the agency of the mother's body is undermined, including the split between the maternal body and the erotic body.

Yet—and this is a paradox—the very term *Mother* Earth privileges the maternal body over the erotic body, even equates it with creativity in general, certainly with the essence of femaleness, so that non-reproductive female sexuality becomes commensurately less important. If the maternal body is perceived to be *the* honored symbol of woman, (though this symbolism is shaky), what happens to female eroticism outside motherhood? What happens to lesbian eroticism? Moreover, what about this sanctification of motherhood? As we've noted before, women's experience tells them the institution of maternity is unsupported. Lip service is paid to motherhood, but few social services exist for the mother's benefit. The power of the maternal body for the society in general lies in its idealization.

This poses a last and difficult hurdle for the heroine to overleap if the female body is to be an enabling metaphor for women's experience. Having repudiated the abstractions which cluster around the male hero—glory, honor, derring-do—she confronts the male abstraction about maternity which halts the emergent heroine in a permanent condition of being, not doing.

As particularly limiting as the Nature/Culture polarity is for women, it has important consequences for the whole society. This kind of specious division and distribution between the sexes of what are common *human* capacities has had many detrimental outcomes: one is the danger that women will overthrow, in anger and despite, the best of rational thought because it has not solicited, or even allowed, the contribution of women. This is, in fact, one respected position of feminism, one held by influential critics like Luce Irigaray. Yet the romanticizing of an anti-rationalist but supposedly matriarchal state brings its own attendant risks. One, as Christa Wolf warns, is the glorification of primitivism. Moreover, though we may well connect the materialistic, aggressive values of our dominantly masculinist society with current crises in international peace and environmental security, we cannot hope to achieve humanistic solutions by jettisoning discourse, including the discourse of law.

So, though the body may now be the female body presented by *women* authors activating women agents, it is still, if taken by itself, a reductive and divisive strategy of reclamation. It struggles first with patriarchal identification of women as a sexual threat and source of anxiety. Further, it reinforces the vulnerability of that body to male violence. Last, it leaves out a crucial part of women's experience. As Francine du Plessix Gray remarks, there is a liberation *of* the body, but also *from* the body. In short, the body has narrative authority it can bestow upon us, but it cannot be the *prevailing* metaphor for narrating women's experience. Both immanent and transcendent experience require discourse for their truths to be expressed.

Directly tying the absence of a female discourse, as well as the more familiar objectified female body, to pornography, Kaja Silverman explains: *"Histoire d' O* is more than O's story. It is the history . . . of the territorialization and inscription of a body. . . . That history will never read otherwise until the female subject alters her relation to discourse—until she succeeds not only in exercising discursive power, but in exercising it differently."[62]

Monique Wittig also ties the absence of female discourse directly to female oppression: "He has made of you that which is not which does not speak which does not possess which does not write. . . . He has gagged abused betrayed you. . . . He has invented your history."[63]

Just as the female body has been defined by Freudians in terms of lack, so the blank page designates the absence of a female discourse, the surface waiting for inscription of the text. In this condition there is no signification for the woman without the male signifier, of which the pen(is) is the symbol.

If we remain with the body as the primary or *ad feminam* locus for our experience, the feminist project of constituting female subjectivity may be presently expansive but ultimately restrictive, perilously close to sexual stereotyping and the biological imperative.

In sum, these three strategies—the woman's spirituality movement, the unity of rhetoric, and the use of the body as the privileged metaphor for women's experience—are qualified successes. In the movement toward female subjectivity, assessing what women can do, each initiates a progress; each complies with Kristeva's view of women as subjects-in-the-making, their own making. To regard women as subjects in the making is to throw into relief the negative effects of the allegorization of Woman, which is static, leaving no room for development and change. Further, it opens immediately the issue of essentialism and its total disregard for race and class: Which woman is Woman?

Most significantly, no one of these strategies succeeds completely because not one of them engages the question: Where is the intellect? Neither in the women's spirituality movement, nor in the unity of rhetoric, nor in the body as metaphor, is this crucial question asked. We must remember that "mind" is not and has never been a *sine qua non* for the hero's selection. A striking omission, with dire consequences. If we are to go beyond heroic definition, surely *each* woman needs what the goddess of wisdom, Minerva, in Julia Budenz' epic of female growth calls for:

> A central self,
> A mind,
> Is my desire.[64]

In-the-making suggests a future still to be enacted. Where can we find female subjectivity as a central self with a mind? And will we then find heroines, too?

6

Gender and Genre:
The New Romance and the Crime Novel

What next, what else? What's left
but a scale model of our world rising
infinitesimally to meet our falling steps
            —Alice Fulton, "Roman de la Rose"

Women have gravitated to novel-reading and novel-writing since the beginning of the genre, in some measure because its anti-heroic realism affords them an organic function within it—that of being social observers. More specifically, realism makes the novel an appropriate vehicle for registering societal change as it occurs. And there are contemporary works, such as Penelope Lively's *Moon Tiger* and Janet Kaufman's *Obscene Gestures for Women: Stories*, which go beyond this function, introducing heroines who have more than a choric role—who can be comedic, who can stand solitary and unpartnered, who are larger than life or the covers of the novel can contain.

Despite this encouraging development in mainstream fiction, three literary sub-genres—the "new" romance, the crime novel, and science fiction—reward our attention most if we ask: what roles does each afford women? What *can* their women do, to revert to our opening question? These "entertainments" are worth examining because sub-genres of fiction are more likely to be bellwethers of innovation: both reader and writer hold different expectations of them than they do of mainstream fiction. More-over, postmodernism itself has attempted the fusion of pop culture and high art, and therefore attention to sub-genres has become a serious subject of "cultural studies."

Specifically, I want to trace the connections of the romance and the crime novel back to their origins in social realism and see how this connection ulti-mately becomes a condition of limit. Then I will look at greater length at science fiction as a particularly congenial vehicle for a feminist vision.

Based on a lowbrow-highbrow system of classification, these three types of fiction are frequently dismissed by the general public and reviewers as trivial entertainment, yet all three are important to gender study because feminists are consciously using them to subvert female stereotypes. Each of the three types draws upon energy created by the women's movement of the 1970s, which still propels women authors and their enabled characters. The businesswoman of the "new" romance and the woman detective of the crime novel represent fresh images of success for women; these protago-nists are, to some degree, contemporary heroines. Science fiction does even more: it presents not only female protagonists now empowered in tradi-tionally male roles but a vision of a humanistic society in which feminist values prevail. A new psychology of women, partially evident in the other two fictions, advances, in science fiction, prospects of a new female destiny.

The first sub-genre, the romance, used to be a novel about female lack of development and the consequent event of rescue by an outside male agent: the heroine waited; the hero arrived and swept her up. The rules for the heroine were strict, but the reward was the happy conclusion of the Love Plot. In fact, some critics, such as Shulamith Firestone, have argued that the love story began as a demand for a place of female experience. What's new about the "new" romance is that the plot does not require for its reso-lution that the woman relinquish anything; the governing assumption is that the plot can/will work out, as life can and will for women.

If opera enacts the "undoing of women," as Catherine Clément ob-serves, these fictions represent the *doing* of women.[1] The new romance treats the reader to fictions of women who "have it all" yet are not punished. In these novels, the heroines attain both sexual expression and positions of public power; this is treated as fact, not fantasy, and entails, at least within the work, an important breakdown of female stereotypical roles—the suc-cessful bitch or the self-abnegating angel. A female winner is now common enough in romance novels that a letter to the *New York Times* Book Review rebuked a reviewer as naive for *not* knowing that "many of the romance novels—both contemporary and historical—published in the last few years present powerful, independent female characters."[2] The choice which had always dealt women a losing hand, the choice between a personal and a professional life, is no longer evidenced in the novels: the personal and professional meld, even if they do not marry.

In contradistinction to the older or "bodice-ripper" romance, these contemporary romances, as part of their gender revision, discard approved sexual roles for women: maidenly chastity followed by marital submission. Rather, woman's erotic desires, her own sexuality, are a controlling part of the "new" romance scenario, one means by which she gains subjectivity. Her eroticism helps drive the plot much as did that of her male counterparts in earlier "bodice-rippers."

Additionally, in romances such as Anne Tolstoi Wallach's *Women's Work* (the "work" ironically that of empire building, not domesticity) and Judith Krantz's *I'll Take Manhattan* (its endearing titular graspingness scotches feminine self-denial), women achieve money and power, not only the expression of sexuality; they are tycoonesses, not secretaries taking dictation from tycoons. Importantly, these two novels do not assume self-denial to be either part of woman's essential "nature" or the foundation of her best relation to the community, as the older romances did. Hence, the heroine of *Women's Work* is named Domina and the heroine of *I'll Take Manhattan*, Maxi. Goodbye to the *little* woman forever. For these corporation presidents, a feminine nature does not preclude making shrewd business decisions, but neither does it render them conniving, cold careerists like the caricatured woman executive in the film *Working Girl*.

Power corrupts these magnates no more and no less than it does their male counterparts. For example, Maxi, in Krantz's Manhattan novel, takes on a corporate battle for worthy personal reasons: "I'm doing it for my [dead] father. . . . I'm doing it because I loved him more than anyone in the world and this is the one way I can show how much he meant—how much he *means*—to me."[3] Maxi's filial sentiment not only rejects the age-old public/private split, but also reassures readers that women's feminine nature is not threatened by the attainment of a public role.

Hearteningly, Krantz is mindful of the social roles that women *in general* are co-opted to play. When Maxi founds a magazine, she storms that she is not going to publish

> all those damn service books: *Good Housekeeping, Family Circle, Woman's Day, Redbook, McCall's*, and anything else that digs, digs, and digs some more at every woman's guilt. . . . It's only September, and they've got '101 Christmas Gifts To Make,' and 'All-Time Favorite Cookie Recipes' on the cover and Doctor Art Ulene's book on *How To Stop Family*

Problems Before They Start. . . . What if you don't bake, what if you *buy* your presents and don't want to know more about your family problems at Christmastime than you do already? How *guilty* will this cover make you feel?[4]

To the extent that these best-selling romances (and there are literally hundreds of them, six or eight Danielle Steels simultaneously revolving on racks in the newstands) reflect only the experience of a few women, they are futuristic, but their roots, nevertheless, are in the novel's social realism. To put it differently, these romances seize upon elements of the world-as-it-is, here the corporate world, and insert women C.E.O.'s into it. Since we all know of the barriers women face in the business professions, the "glass ceiling" that keeps them from getting to the top, this gender equality may be risky prediction. But the "new" romance is a sort of "Horatia" Alger story, and perhaps no more misleading than the original about the facts of opportunity.

But there is an issue deeper than false encouragement, and it bears on the reason these heroines are not, finally, acceptable paradigms for a contemporary heroine. Liberated these entrepeneurs may be, but equality is not the only goal of feminism. Though women enjoy leading roles in these novels of corporate life, a drama of power, betrayal, materialism, egotism, and ruthless ambition unfolds on their stage. These women executives provide vicarious satisfaction, even images of freedom for their less empowered sisters, but they are hardly transformative messengers. Like Erica Jong's characters in *Fear of Flying*, they adopt the role of their male counterparts but in all other ways leave society as they find it.

Maxi's daughter Angelica in Krantz's *I'll Take Manhattan*, for example, fills the role customarily allotted to the business executive's wife in corporate patriarchy, both in life and in the novel. Angelica is truly a ministering *angel*, assuming responsibility for the well-being of her mother, acting with forebearance and out of a steadfast devotion to her mother's career. Executive heroines like Maxi take the self-sacrifice of others for granted; they have been co-opted into the world of patriarchal competition that requires this arrogance for success. In short, gender hierarchy has changed to gender equality; traditional roles have been discarded. But beyond that, the informing social vision has remained the same.

Does the same hold true for the mystery novel? Although women writers assayed the detective novel as early as the 1860s, not until the advent of the women's movement in the 1970s was there a concerted and telling effort to change crime fiction's gendered role for women as either villain or victim. This lag of a century results from what were prevailing gender definitions, specifically the contradiction between those qualities necessary to a detective and those which social roles defined for women: active/passive, solitary/relational, adventurous/timid. Consequently, in early examples of the genre female protagonists were either imperfect women or imperfect detectives. Sexist conventions were thus incorporated into the formulaic cast of the crime novel. This formula, moreover, as Dennis Porter remarks, bases the male detective on the heroic model of a lone superior figure—and the heroic model, as we know, wherever it appears, traditionally excludes women.[5]

The male hero of the crime novel appeared as the detective, eliciting hero worship from the reader and/or from other protagonists. Even in novels employing a male/female sleuthing partnership, the dominance of the male was evident from the relative positions of the partners, e.g., father-daughter, mentor-pupil. For instance, though the reader remembers Harriet Vane as a most independent spirit, it is Lord Peter who actually solves the crimes they jointly investigate in Dorothy L. Sayers' classic mysteries. In Dashiell Hammett's beloved Thin Man series Nick and Nora Charles both engage in sleuthing, but Nick is the problem-solver, Nora the foil. Nick and Nora, though equals in wit, poise, and sophistication, are not so in function. In fact, Nick often sends Nora on a shopping spree when he's working on a case. Because they're rich, childless, urbane, we think of Nora as a "liberated woman;" in fact she retains qualities of "the little woman."

The partnerships of Elizabeth George's female detective Sergeant Havers and the male detective, Inspector Lynley, for whom she works, and Lucille Kallen's Maggie Rome and C. B. Greenfield (both are amateurs, but Greenfield is Rome's boss), illustrate pupil-teacher inequities. Such teams are no longer the rule. Rather, balanced sleuthing partnerships such as those between Susan Kelly's Liz Connors and Lieutenant Jack Lingeman, Charlotte MacLeod's Sarah Kelling and Max Bittersohn, and P. M. Carlson's Maggie Ryan and Nick O'Connor, are replacing the older model of professionally subordinate women. Power relations have shifted.

The last few decades have seen women occupy, to an unparalleled degree, center stage as independent, unpartnered sleuths. Today, newspaper columns carry round-up reviews of books starring women sleuths; bookstores designate shelves for the special display of mysteries with women leads. Women mystery authors have formed a writers' league of their own called Sisters in Crime, and anthologies of crime stories by women have been collected under the same title. So marked has been the increase in women sleuths that they are now the subject of gender studies: *Sisters in Crime: Feminism and the Crime Novel* by Maureen T. Reddy and *The Woman Detective: Gender and Crime* by Kathleen Gregory Klein are two examples.

What can these women detectives do in their expanded roles? Despite their sex, female "private eyes" may confront physical danger, i.e., "walk down mean streets," in Raymond Chandler's phrase. They can control their own sexual roles: they are gazers, private *eyes*, not objects of the (male) gaze. They can employ logic, be cerebral in their puzzle-solving, unlike, say, Christie's earlier Miss Marple, who, though in fact quite logical, was made to seem to rely on gossip and feminine intuition about character gained from long experience of village life. Contemporary sleuth Kate Fansler, despite her bookish allusions, depends heavily on feminine intuition in Amanda Cross's novels, an interesting holdover from the Golden Age.[6]

Contemporary women detectives initiate action; and perhaps most strikingly, as we have said, many operate alone, not in a relational mode, in their professional capacity. Certainly some of the most independent female protagonists around in fiction are investigators: Kate Fansler, V. I. Warshawski, Kinsey Milhone, Claire Conrad and Maggie Hill, Carlotta Carlyle. Detecting is no longer *An Unsuitable Job for a Woman*, as P. D. James's own detective Cordelia Grey proves in a novel by that title.

So what women can do in the detective fiction of today is to be liberated; as Kathleen Klein summarizes it, these women detectives are strong and competent, they do not allow men to tell them how to act or to make fools of them; they do not depend upon men to rescue them from danger. Without doubt, we have progressed beyond Sleeping Beauty, Cinderella, or "wifey" who must scheme in covert ways. This last type, represented by Lucy of the television sitcom *I Love Lucy*, wins phenomenal popular support—not "I" but everyone loves Lucy—because she outwits her husband, thereby enlisting admiration for the trickster and sympathy with the underdog. At the same time, however, she acquiesces in the dominant status of the male within the heterosexual marriage contract, so that she actually undermines no one (except women who take her for a model). Lucy, like any trickster, acts complicitously, since traditionally the trickster, male or female, speaks with the voice of marginalization.

In Lucy's place have come women sleuths who can take center stage themselves rather than operating from the wings. Moreover, of those female detectives who are amateurs, many lead professional lives, only sidelining as detectives: Kate Fansler in the Amanda Cross series is a professor of English; Nina Fischman in Marissa Piesman's series, a social worker; Loretta Lawson in Joan Smith's *A Masculine Ending* and *Why Aren't They Screaming?*, a professor of linguistics; Lia Matera's Willa Jansson, a lawyer; and Kathryn Lasky Knight's Calista Jacobs, a book illustrator. The burgeoning of women crime novelists has meant, in the words of one of them, Nancy

Pickard, "we are creating the sort of heroines we couldn't find and creating the books we wanted to read."[7] The result is that women are authenticated in the two most important detective types—either the genteel amateur, à la Kate Fansler, or the hard-boiled sleuth, à la V. I. Warshawski.

Still, even the "tough" women detectives face sexist bias. In *Burn Marks*, Sara Paretsky's serial sleuth, V. I. Warshawski, finds out indirectly that her beloved father figure, Lt. Bobby Mallory, best friend of her dead father, would rather halt her investigations than believe her evidence proving his godson to be a "bent" cop. The Lieutenant's mistrust of her abilities and her conclusions, and his overt preference for the surrogate son over the surrogate daughter (herself), wound her psychologically as well as placing her physically at risk. The woman sleuth has entered the arena, but the arena is still a male club. Mallory constantly tries to persuade V. I. to abandon her sleuthing; *he* still feels it is, as P. D. James's title puts it, "an unsuitable job for a woman." This is the old question: even if women speak, will male audiences accept their representations of reality?

There is another frustration the reader and the woman detective face. Rooted in social realism, the crime novel still features heroines who are largely outsiders in the world of crime detection, particularly in its official investigations. As Lillian O'Donnell's Norah Mulcahaney of the New York City Police Department discovers in the course of her duties, the higher echelons of law enforcement officers are almost exclusively male and, as a result, sexism pervades the department. Even an official as high on the ladder as Lynda La Plante's Detective Chief Inspector Jane Tennison of Scotland Yard in the book and TV series *Prime Suspect*, finds her position as a woman in the department so indefensible that she resigns. Tennison doesn't "play ball"; she isn't humble; she conducts her private life as she wishes, but pays for that; and, unforgivably in the eyes of her superiors, she doesn't cover up departmental snafus. These women investigators may step into the gumshoes of the male detective (*G Is for Gumshoe* is the title of one of Sue Grafton's novels starring Kinsey Milhone), but the world in which they function still supports male hegemony, and solving its crimes does no more than return that society to its prior state of existence.

The traditionally conservative outlook of the crime novel explains the seeming inconsistency in this statistic: although ninety-one out of one hundred and twenty respondents to a questionnaire for a Sisters in Crime/National Project Survey called themselves feminists, more than fifty per cent described their heroines as protectors of traditional values.[8] In other words, it appears that the detective, like other heroes, is a conservator, not a subverter, and his *or* her social mandate is quite circumscribed. Indeed, this restorative function supports Porter's claim that the detective is based on a heroic model, for the hero does return the society to its pre-endangered condition.

What predisposes many heroines of mystery fiction to be conservative is that their stories stand in a line of descent from the Golden Age of mystery fiction. It is perhaps easier to incorporate a female detective into the world of the English village, so prominent a setting for Golden Age mysteries—the world of Margery Allingham, Ngaio Marsh, Dorothy L. Sayers, Agatha Christie, and Josephine Tey—than into the underworlds of Sam Spade or Spenser. But those who do remain with "murder in the vicarage," to use W. H. Auden's phrase, trade in nostalgia, and these "cozies" do not grapple with the problems and conditions of our own time. W. H. Auden argues in his essay by the same name that they cannot so engage, for the more complete the initial state of innocence, ("the vicarage"), the greater the outrage of murder, and consequently, the greater the reader's gratification when evil is finally expunged from the community.

This is undoubtedly true; but what is aesthetically satisfying can be morally blunting. The closed society, the innocent world to which Auden refers is rigid and homogeneous. By adhering to the status quo, fiction derived from the Golden Age novel of manners reproduces sexism, racism, and class hierarchy. Conservatism of this stripe permeates the novels of Charlotte MacLeod, which are set in enclaves of privilege. Max, the husband of a MacLeod detecting husband and wife team, though Jewish and an outsider to the closed WASP society to which his wife still belongs, interestingly enough is not used by the author as a social critic despite his outsider position. Rather, the establishment as she depicts it is full of lovable eccentrics, similar to their English forebears. MacLeod does not tax or even address their assumptions of class and religious superiority. By contrast, a much more originally conceived crime novel, *Return To Sender* by Dick Lochte, shows this same society to be rife with anti-Semitism and snobbery.

Although Carolyn Heilbrun asserts that she doesn't read science fiction because it is "dreamy" and takes place in "la-la land," her own Amanda Cross novels, unmistakably descended from the English tradition, transpire in a life so idealized as to be as false to women's experience as are the heroines of the "new" romance. Consider the perfection of the heroine's life: Kate Fansler, Amanda Cross's detective, is married to a good-looking, articulate, professionally dedicated man who treats her as an equal and with whom she holds witty, civilized conversations. The relation between them is affectionate but restrained. Furthermore, they have no children, thus enabling Kate to control a schedule to which her husband happily accommodates. She has a tenured job at a distinguished university, no financial worries, no responsibility for aging parents, no health problems of her own. She is fortunate both in her interesting colleagues, and in a warm and understanding relationship with a niece and nephew (showing her to be feminine enough for all practical purposes). She is also WASP, slim, and attractive.

Of course detective stories, even the "hard-boiled" type, are all wish-fulfilling to some degree, and we, the readers, rely on the identification and/or capture of the criminal at the end. This is its primary escape: it provides the mystery buff with the gratification produced by poetic, rather than civil, justice. In P. D. James' *Devices and Desires*, the local detective-fiction-reading rector, weary of an employee's spiritual crisis, longs to return to his book: "He wanted to get back to Inspector Ghote, Keating's gentle Indian detective, who, despite his uncertainties, would get there in the end, because this was fiction: problems could be solved, evil overcome, justice vindicated and death itself only a mystery which would be solved in the final chapter."[9]

The Amanda Cross novels offer the reader the escape provided by the reliable administration of poetic justice and also by the fantasy of the perfected life enjoyed by its detective, Kate Fansler. Despite this, reality intrudes into Cross' mysteries in her unmasking of academic sexism, racism, and ageism.

What happens if we look at some women who are not part of the genteel amateur tradition, but are professional private eyes, conventionally more "realistic"? Can we make generalizations about them? Certainly we meet examples of female sleuths possessing "street smarts," and involved in social problems—for example, V. I. Warshawski, the detective protagonist created by Sara Paretsky, and Jenny Cain, the series detective of Nancy Pickard. V. I. (as Warshawski is known) comes from a working class family, and knows the outsiderness that immigrant status confers. In the novels of Marissa Piesman, the heroine is a social worker, immersed daily in the struggles of the disadvantaged. Furthermore, she is not set apart from the ordinary; she has her own worries. She is single, chubby, financially insecure, with an elderly widowed mother. She is not privileged by birth, ethnicity (she's Jewish), or the insulation of money. Sue Grafton's sleuth Kinsey Milhone also comes from a working class family; moreover, because she was orphaned young she had to become independent and savvy at an early age. These women detectives, and others like them, operate successfully in a world of violence (Kinsey Milhone mentions "injuries sustained on the last case I was working on"), corruption, racism, and corporate greed, which they deplore. And, like Sam Spade and Philip Marlowe, they succeed in creating a personal code of integrity and trust within the evil world they prowl.

For these "tough gal" detectives, however, being a private eye raises complex new questions their male models did not have to face. First, these heroines must confront the thorny problem of their relation to violence. Investigator Eliza Pirex reflects, "The day I applied for a permit to carry a concealed weapon, I felt sick. Today, I pat the gun like an old friend." [10] Both Carlotta Carlyle and Kinsey Milhone have killed while engaged in investigations; Milhone, in *I Is for Innocent*, takes part in a shoot-out she compares to the O.K. Corral. V. I. Warshawski is less persuaded; she owns a gun, but often, tellingly, forgets to carry it. At a time when issues of women's roles in the military and the extent to which they may enter combat are being debated, this extension of traditional female roles meets a mixed reception from both men and women.

Second, now that we have women detectives who carry and use guns, are women's sexual roles in these crime novels also going to conform to the profoundly macho conventions of the genre? Can we imagine Philip Marlowe with a wife at home keeping the stew hot? With a steady girlfriend? Can we imagine Sherlock Holmes consulting his wife's dinner arrangements rather than Bradshaw's, the English railway timetable necessary to pursuit? The male detective, by being a loner, incidentally confers a sexual tension upon the novel in which he operates, augmenting its drama.

What is appropriate for the new women private eyes, or is the question of their sexual behavior now inappropriate? Contemporary women sleuths fill in the years left blank between the young Nancy Drew and the elderly Miss Marple, the first too young, and the second too old to lend romance to their plots (though Nancy Drew does have "crushes"). Grafton's Kinsey Milhone, Paretsky's V. I., Linda Barnes' Carlotta Carlyle, and Joan Smith's Loretta Lawson follow their instincts with equanimity and without much afterthought. Does this reflect changing sexual mores in the society at large, or will readers resist this liberalization though the detective's amorous activities have been a mainstay of male detective fiction? [11]

Detective Eliza Pirex reminds us of the independence conferred on protagonists in the genre: "Women tend to be more monogamous than men. . . . I don't know why I stray against the odds every once in a while. Probably because I'm a detective and we detectives have a yen for romance and adventure *as the literature bears witness*" (emphasis added). [12]

Though now women do not find sleuthing and desire mutually exclusive, these detectives find no precedent or pattern for their female sexuality. As we have seen in preceding chapters, the expression of women's sexual desire is problematic enough in the mainstream male literary canon; predictably, this is particularly so in a genre as macho as the crime novel—hence, elderly Miss Marple and adolescent Nancy Drew. Masculinist crime fiction narrowed the field to two unacceptable types of woman: the dumb blonde, a sex object, Marilyn Monroe; and the scheming brunette, Barbara Stanwyck. Although women sleuths are no longer killed off as punishment for sexual freedom (as women were in the Travis McGee mysteries), they operate in societies in which women are betrayed, raped, made into the objects of pornography, their own desire silenced.[13] It comes as a candid novelty, therefore, to find the amateur sleuth Calista Jacobs acknowledging in Kathryn Lasky Knight's *Trace Elements* the sexual frustration she experiences as a widow.

The inner conflicts women experience are finding voice now that women are writing crime fiction involving life-like contemporary women protagonists. This entails expanding the crime novel's formulaic plot to consider seriously problems of interest to women but peripheral to the crime. We are told, for instance, that V. I. Warshawski worked in an abortion counseling clinic while in college, before we meet her as a "private eye." In P. M. Carlson's *Murder Unrenovated*, two of the female characters are pregnant: For the unmarried one, Nancy, the decision about whether to have an abortion is painful. "It's a decision that's going to hurt someone, no matter what she decides. There's no painless choice," Nancy's lover is told.[14] The other pregnant character, Maggie, *is* married but harbors the superwoman fear: Can she do everything? Can she do everything well? "I want to be the best mother. The best wife. The best statistician. The best business partner for Dan. It seems such a big job."[15]

The sequel to *Murder Unrenovated*, *Rehearsal for Murder*, takes place after the baby has arrived. Maggie and her husband Nick share parental chores, both, for example, carrying Sarah around in a Snugli, even, occasionally, while sleuthing. We may endorse the blending of private and professional lives, but the level of risk for the infant carried along on the chase compromises the plausibility of this *modus vivendi*. What *is* highly convincing to the general reader is not the logistical solution but the picture of the frustration of both husband and wife, working professional adults, in their necessity to accommodate to their infant's demands. At one stage this even endangers the relationship between them. Although there are murders and mysteries in the novel, it is, at the same time, significantly the story of the detectives Maggie and Nick, and how a baby upsets the equilibrium they had achieved as equal adults.

Notably, for many of the men in these recent novels the issues are the same as for the women; in a choice between love and duty, the choice which sundered Dido and Aeneas, men do not pledge themselves to duty as reflexively as did the Trojan hero. Nick, investigating a murder, ruefully muses, "Who was the Don Juan of diaper changes, the Thoreau with drool on his shoulders? The Lone Ranger who walked the baby instead of sleeping with his wife? Where were the heroes he needed now?" [16]

His ruefulness is transitory: The anti-heroic bent of this novel remains in place. Additionally, Nick's anti-heroic stance puts in perspective the destructiveness of what Maggie identifies as "silly teen-male fantasy." [17] Playing out this fantasy of adventure and escape from commitment, the villain of the piece, Steve, dreams of escape from domestic and financial entanglements, and kidnaps his own daughter for the ransom money his father-in-law will stake.

Rehearsal for Murder concludes with a subversion, undertaken complicity by Maggie and Nick, of official justice. True, many older crime novels ducked the actual dispensation of justice or gave the villain the option of "honorable" suicide. What is worth remarking in its newness is the rationale of the subversion in *Rehearsal for Murder*. "If he got what the law prescribes, he'd be ruined," Nick points out to Maggie. And she answers, "More to the point, the family would suffer." [18] The family has become the preemptive consideration.

Two corollaries ensue from the infiltration of domesticity into the crime novel. First, children become a standard part of the cast of characters. For instance, series detectives Sarah Kelling and her husband Max have a child, Davy, but continue, with interruptions, as a detective team. They don't just have him; they are shown, especially the father, to be constantly checking on the child's welfare. Dorothy Cannell's *Mum's the Word* allows Ellie, nine months pregnant, to go detecting with husband Ben. The two children in *All the Muscle You Need*, by Diana MacRae, occupy the emotional center of the two lesbian heroines' lives. Occasionally, they even accompany the heroine who detects on her investigative forays. The children have credible personalities and dialogue, and precisely because the author does not consign them to some convenient background place, they are real and not stage props for the reader, either. Children, then, are recognized as a part of life in this previously macho genre, which, if it rendered women as victims and villains, omitted children altogether. In Sara Paretsky's *Indemnity Only*, on the other hand, V. I., the tough gal sleuth, divorced, childless, feels wistful watching another woman's daughter asleep on her couch. Her maternal feelings toward this young girl, whose father's murder she is investigating, have led her to remove the child from an uncaring, neglectful family, and bring her temporarily to her own apartment. Further, even when funds run out, she continues the investigation into the father's murder because of her protectiveness toward the girl. Again in this same book, V. I. describes herself as having "small stirrings of envy"[19] when she glimpses a woman picnicking with her children in the park.

The second corollary in the crime novel's new domestic arrangements reflects our rapidly changing ideas about what constitutes a family and a family life; the absent perspective of the woman is now present. Many of the women sleuths are married but do not sacrifice equality or independence. Just so, Kate Fansler's husband, Reed Amhearst, is conveniently dispatched from home whenever the need arises for Kate to be off detecting on her own; sometimes, upon her own initiative, she puzzles out the case with him, benefiting from his trained legal judgment. Sarah Kelling's husband, Max, and Maggie Ryan's husband, Nick, work cooperatively with their wives as professional as well as personal partners. Gay couples, both male and female, are part of the novels' households, and lesbian investigators like Eliza Pirex are no longer exceptional. Widows far outnumber widowers in our society, and their emotional and financial insecurities are expressed by characters like Calista in the novel *Trace Elements*, previously mentioned, and Julia in *Murder Unrenovated*.

In a development of equal importance, many of these fictions provide their heroines with deep emotional attachments which nevertheless are not romantic, a particularly striking innovation in the case of female detectives who operate "independently." V. I. Warshawski is close to an older Austrian woman doctor, a mentor, to whom she repairs for comfort and advice in book after book in the series. Beginning with the first novel of the series, *Indemnity Only*, this relation is made clear. Lotty, the doctor, says to V. I., "You have no mother, but you are a daughter of my spirit."[20] In *Blood Shot*, V. I. herself becomes honorary sister to a younger woman, Caroline, promising her, "Till death do us part, kid."[21] The first part of the sentence is from the marriage ceremony, though the final word reverts to the Humphrey Bogart diction of tough guy movies. Linda Barnes' sleuth, Carlotta Carlyle, also adopts a little sister. Sue Grafton's Kinsey Milhone has strong ties with her elderly landlord, Henry, and with a neighborhood restaurateur, Rosie, recurrent figures in the Milhone series. Intense female friendship is a major theme in Amanda Cross's *No Word from Winifred*.

Moreover, the novels form emotional alliances with new configurations that work to unfold the plots. In *Trace Elements*, a widow and her son, bonding closely after the death of the husband/father, sleuth together to find the killer of the man they both loved. The teenager Serendipity Renn

Dahlquist and private eye Leo J. Bloodworth form an unlikely detecting team and an unlikelier friendship in Dick Lochte's *Sleeping Dog*. Significantly, in the latter book, not only is the function of detective split between the two protagonists, but the narrator's function as well. As a consequence of this new emphasis on relation, the single voice of authority that characterized the crime novel gives way to chapters narrated, in this case, first by one protagonist, then the other.

Relations with others, then, both male and female, help to sustain these women protagonists pitted against corrupt institutions, and in turn, these women, even when operating alone professionally, alter conventional conceptions of the detective as necessarily an emotional loner. For example, some of these young women sleuths are orphans but acquire surrogate "parents" in order to buttress their emotional health. The quality of healing these women find in personal relations is different and apart from the general restoration of a *past* order which the traditional crime novel accomplishes. Personal relations are part of the composition of the *present*.[22]

One of the most significant changes in crime fiction written by women and featuring women investigators is this emphasis on the importance of relations between people. In the same survey of feminist crime novelists cited earlier, Mary Bowen Hall found that the authors who answered perceived no conflict for their sleuths between being independent and maintaining close ties with others. As crime writer P. M. Carlson testifies: "The new wave of female protagonists first showed that women could do the jobs and have the adventures that had previously been a male preserve. Today we're taking a second step—a reaffirmation of the value of connections—family, friends."[23] That is, the values women espouse in their own lives are reflected by those of the new women detectives.

Maureen Reddy, who has examined the relation between feminism and the crime novel, finds women "borrowing familiar features of detective fiction in order to turn them upside down and inside out, exposing the genre's fundamental conservatism and challenging the reader to rethink his/her assumptions."[24] What the feminist crime novel, despite its substantial innovations, does not do is to offer broad, alternative visions for society. However, I'd like to discuss briefly four novels that do push the limits of the crime novel outwards in the way Reddy suggests.

Of these four, the first two centralize the deeply rooted social issues of sexism and racism: Valerie Miner's *Murder in the English Department* and Barbara Neely's *Blanche on the Lam*. Miner's professorial sleuth, Nan Weaver, confronts the failure of liberal education in the very institution of learning to which she is attached. Though the novel would seem, by virtue of its setting and the occupation of its heroine, to belong to the novel of manners which conserves the status quo, it confounds expectations. Sexism here does not take the form of such inequities as a struggle for tenure or promotion or admission to the faculty club; rape is the crime of this novel. A female student, attempting to ward off rape by a male professor, accidentally kills him in self-defense. Though the murdered man was disliked by his colleagues, academic ranks close in self-protection. The department does not want the murder fully investigated, because they don't want the circumstances surrounding the crime to be uncovered. The reader's sympathies are skillfully enlisted by the description of the power relations between professor and student in the scene leading up to the event.

After committing the crime, the student becomes stonily silent, even though her account would change her plea to one of self-defense. She is frightened, but also humiliated, despite the fact that the death was accidental, but the attempted rape was not. This is the rape victim's usual reaction. Sleuth Nan Weaver must patiently, over time, extract the girl's story in the face of the hypocrisy and false witness of her colleagues, their efforts to intimidate her and the student. We encounter an institutionalized moral corruption which leaves the student *and* Weaver outsiders.

Barbara Neely's *Blanche on the Lam*, the first crime novel by an African-American woman about an African-American woman, tackles the issue of racism. Within the framework of a chase and suspense, of clues and a mystery, issues of class and race retain the spotlight. In this work, the abuse of power is *inescapable*; it is shown in all its daily insults, its divided world of blacks and whites. Consequently, the escapism characteristic of the genre is rendered impossible. Blanche, whose only ally in the white world is the retarded son of the family employing her as a servant, escapes with her life at the end. But her future is problematic; innocence is nowhere restored. She never lived in an innocent world that bears restoration; her very name is ironic. And though as an "invisible" servant she hears and sees evidence about the identity of the killer, she has no influence. All she can do is flee and hope.

One of the most innovative contemporary renderings of the crime novel, pushing its conventions to the extreme, is *Glory Days* by Rosie Scott. The protagonist, Glory Day, a professional painter and nightclub singer, erupts with energy and anger against female stereotypes. She is fat, yet she has an active erotic life. She lives in domestic chaos, untidy and warm, with her daughter; she is not a solitary hero/ine, even though she hunts down a murderer with intrepidity and purposefulness. The novel is not about an anti-hero/ine either. Almost as much a documentary in its replication of place and event as it is a police procedural novel, it reports the hostility between white and aborigines and the connection between the drug world and the criminal underworld of New Zealand. What is most curious about *Glory Days* is that this novel ultimately transcends its own gritty social realism. This book is not about "glory" in the heroic sense (though survival is always at risk), but about compassion, a new "glory" defined by its eponymous heroine.

Glory Day carries back to her own home from the nightclub where she sings a comatose young woman who has overdosed on drugs. She cares for her, drawn increasingly into the stranger's frightening story. The novel acquires a second level of meaning through the use of archetypal female figures, such as the witch. Glory's lover tells her daughter: "She's [Glory] a good witch, Rina. There are good witches and bad witches. In fact, very few witches are bad. They're usually just women who want to live on their own" (i.e., without a man).[25]

In the character of Glory Day the novel presents a Demeter figure of redemption—maternal, loving, restorative, united with Kore (Rina). Compassion, rather than the promise of money or a passion for puzzle-solving, draws the protagonist into the plot. Glory Day brings a new motivation and breadth to the genre.

The last example of these boundary-breakers is Joan Smith's second mystery *Why Aren't They Screaming?*, featuring Loretta Lawson. To an extraordinary degree, this crime novel flies in the face of major conventions of the genre. Like Milhone and Paretsky, Lawson does battle with a corrupt world, and again like her counterparts, she tries to redeem as much of it as possible. But this amateur sleuth panics, runs from the scene of the crime, unthinkingly disturbs evidence—in short, she allows the normal human emotions of fear and confusion to color her responses to crime. She often berates herself for wrong steps or oversights. She is not omniscient, she is fallible. She is not extraordinarily brave. More significant even than Lawson's departure from the conventional picture of the detective is Smith's profound departure from the expected poetic justice of the end. We are given an ending but no resolution, not even one that transpires offstage.

In *Why Aren't They Screaming?*, women peace workers encamped to protest a nuclear building site at Greenham Common, England, arouse hostility among the village property owners. As a direct outcome of their dissent, their tents are burned in a gesture of intimidation. The author points her finger not at a criminal or gang of criminals responsible for this arson, but at the very organizations that supposedly uphold order—the police, various government bureaus, local politicians. Evil no longer has the ambient air of an underworld; to the contrary, it is the miasma of the overworld.

In this novel, we move from the criminal invasion of the social order by an anomalous or abnormal situation or person such as Auden described, to a condition in which violence and corruption are the norm. This is the prevailing condition of modern times that Hannah Arendt characterized as "the banality of evil," so pervasive as to be reabsorbed into the fabric of society.

"Clara and Peggy are dead and the whole thing's sorted out without the police having to ask awkward questions. What sort of world are we *living* in?" demands Loretta Lawson of no one in particular.[26] Clara's murder results from her allowing the peace women to camp on her property despite the outcry of her neighbors; Peggy, one of the campers, is killed because she possesses proof of the guilt of Clara's murderer. The officially *uninvestigated* deaths of Clara and Peggy make them casualties in the war between powerful and powerless, disproving the assumption upon which the crime novel is based—that evil will be pursued even if not apprehended.

There isn't even a pretense of justice at the conclusion of *Why Aren't They Screaming?* Piling one successful crime upon another, the key criminal, a Conservative Member of Parliament, clears the way to be named a Cabinet member by arranging the murder of a political competitor. Evil triumphs; the new Minister appears smiling on television. Loretta Lawson, knowing his guilt and seeing the announcement of his appointment on the screen, is left hugging her cat for comfort, protesting, "No! They can't! They just can't!" but she does so "quietly and without conviction."[27] "They" can. Lawson, the detective, knows the truth, and now the reader does. But nothing changes. No one is screaming because there is no one to hear; cover-up is one of the rules of the game, the charges cannot be made to stick.

In sum, as all these new developments and departures illustrate, the genre is slowly yielding up its formulaic and masculinist disposition. The subordination of character to plot is no longer standard; in the P. D. James "mystery novels," "novel" is as descriptive as "mystery." A more leisurely pace, permitting a rich background for the sleuth/protagonist, characterizes Linda Barnes' *Steel Guitar*. Independent female sleuths are successful "private eyes." Maternity and detection are not seen as mutually exclusive. Holmes and Watson are not the paradigmatic pair. Women's sexuality finds expression. Relations between people are seen as a necessary and wise antidote to the brutality of the world. The voice of authority is no longer always singular. Feminist values, sometimes propounded by men as in Dick Cluster's anti-heroic *Return to Sender*, are entering the crime novel. All of these shifts move in the direction of a more comprehensive, humanistic view; importantly, they reflect new gender relations.

My contention is that these novels are, nevertheless, hampered by the genre itself, with its conservative bias and central event of violence, which operates from the conviction that we are stuck with evil, that it is institutionalized. What these feminist novels undertake to do, and do well, is to expose this evil and the powerful institutions of patriarchy which uphold its justice and its order. Next I will look at feminist science fiction, the third and last sub-genre, which has been the vehicle for presenting a more sweeping vision of change.

7

Gender and Genre:
Science Fiction and the Feminist Utopia

What would it mean to live
in a city whose people
were changing despair into hope?—
you yourself must change it.—
What would it feel like to know
your country was changing?—
you yourself must change it.—
Though your life felt arduous
new and unmapped
what would it mean to stand on the first
page of the end of despair?
  —"Dreams Before Waking," Adrienne Rich

Of the three sub-genres—the "new" romance, crime fiction, and science fiction—it is the last, as an arm of fantasy, which affords the broadest opportunity to upset gender stereotypes and, beyond that, present visions of societies different from the one we inhabit. The author of science fiction, unlike the social realist, can do more than record or even criticize social problems such as environmental pollution, violence towards women, and the impulse toward militarism. By implicitly or explicitly comparing a utopian and a dystopian society, she can enable us to envisage alternate possibilities, can show us how societies could be reorganized to eliminate such disorders. Science fiction shows the *what, how, why, where,* if not the *when* of change. As Paul Ricoeur asserts, utopianism is necessary for ethical thinking, the literal succumbing to the imaginative "what if " before designing a new reality.[1] The utopias we will discuss in this chapter are not nostalgic glances backward at some prelapsarian, pre-patriarchal past, but proposals for a better world, imagination's world to come.

Although since the 1970s we have seen women writers fashioning female tycoons and sleuths, it was left to science fiction to become the vehicle *par excellence* for the expression of feminist values, attracting to what had been only recently a male purview, a slew of women writers: Suzy McKee Charnas, Dorothy Bryant, C. J. Cherryh, Mary Staton, Jane Yolen, Doris Lessing, Ursula Le Guin, Marge Piercy, and Octavia Butler, among others. Their advent, the changes they've wrought, make one ask what the word "science" is doing there at all, what validation it confers upon their novels. Certainly these women do not equate science and technology with a myth of progress. Feminist science fiction is both futuristic and utopian, fulfilling the French feminist description of what women's writing should be. In fact, I suggest that the most telling note of feminist science fiction is its utopian character. Whereas a myth of progress implies that betterment will come about regardless, these works postulate that radical change is required. And while they discard a myth of inevitable betterment their fictions remain optimistic, confronting issues and making concrete proposals.

The futures they imagine are facilitated by the fact that fantasy as a genre not only can project a future we might not extrapolate from the present, but it can also eradicate a past. Joanna Russ's *The Female Man,* for example, erases the event of the great Depression of the 1930s. Such license is liberating; future change is easier to conceptualize if we free ourselves of contrary historical precedent and prejudice. For example, science fiction may enable us to imagine societies in which the Oedipal myth has *not* been the governing myth of development for both sexes in the twentieth century. Despite post-Freudian objections to the Oedipus complex as the central explanation of human development, it continues to be common cultural coinage. In fact, in her essay "Paradigm," Monique Wittig found it necessary to coin the term "Anti-Oedipus" to articulate her different interpretation of human sexuality and development.

So imaginative creation becomes the new reality and not what our limited experience in "real" life leads us to call facts. What we believe, what we can credit as possible, changes. We can reject the present for the future, can hover between "reality" (fact), and "fiction."

The salient question is obviously which, or rather whose, future? Different authors purvey different values: in C. S. Lewis's Narnia fantasies, Christianity is the prevailing belief-system; in Sir Francis Bacon's *New Atlantis*, scientism. What they share is the faith of each that his system will produce a better world. They are, then, political in their advocacy. This chapter will focus upon the system of values these feminist metafictions embed. I would emphasize that these values embrace the whole society, but that in order to envisage enormous social change, two profound shifts in gender relations must have already occurred: first, women must have control over their bodies, including reproductive rights; second, women must participate equally in leadership and governance, which posits that child-rearing is shared between women and men. The new societies described in feminist science fictions either assume that such changes have already been instated, or propose schemes for bringing them about.

Certain fictional modalities seem particularly hospitable to a vision of change. The editors of *Bitter Healing: German Women Writers from 1700 to 1830* suggest that women are drawn to genres like the fairy tale that allow them to criticize "things as they are" and to present a vision of "things as they might be." A contemporary writer in this line is Ursula Le Guin. Her science fiction can be seen as a modern modification of fairy tale.

Paradoxically, then, fantasy offers women the opportunity to realize most fully the reality of themselves. Since women are accustomed to think of themselves as "the other," Simone de Beauvoir's "second sex," it is but a short step to the world of sci-fi "aliens," and even to inter-galactic mates who are free from ideas of gender hierarchy. Some women science fiction writers explore "otherness" in lands in which no men have dwelt for generations, a device employed in Charlotte Perkins Gilman's *Herland* (1915), not the first but probably the most influential prototype for feminist science fiction. Joanna Russ's land of Whileaway in *The Female Man* is another such single-sex country, a benevolent female realm set among three other warring, patriarchal worlds. Still other feminist authors create utopian societies in which the sexes cohabit but without gender strife, lands such as Lessing's Zone Three in her *The Marriages Between Zones Three, Four, and Five*, or the world of Luciente in Marge Piercy's *Woman on the Edge of Time*. In sum, contemporary feminist fantasies centralize the question of the status of women in society as an essential prerequisite for further, wider, change.

The change in women's status in these novels occurs as a result of their repudiation of old assumptions about women's "nature." For example, mother/child relations are re-examined as part of this project, and alternative systems of mothering, such as collective mothering and professional mothering, are proposed. In Piercy's *Woman on the Edge of Time*, women and men are both engaged in child-rearing. Or, following the precedent set in Charlotte Perkins Gilman's *Herland*, Marge Piercy's *Woman on the Edge of Time* and Suzy McKee Charnas' *Motherlines* challenge the assumption that "maternal feeling" resides "naturally" in all women, i.e., that all women desire children.[2] (We know that Gilman felt that her own experience proved this a false article of faith.) These novels may also question the widely held belief that women's "natural" sexuality is always heterosexual. But whatever the various plot permutations, what these and other sci-fi novels by women share is the creation of autonomous heroines—in itself empowering for women readers. In Octavia Butler's *Dawn* women mate with "aliens" or clone in a version of the Virgin Birth. In both cases, conception and birth occur without the aid of men, women are self-sufficient, and the "norm" of the nuclear family is abolished. Extravagant out-of-the-body creation of children also removes women from the "messy" world of women's biology, used so often to signify inferiority.

Predictably, science fiction by men does not reconsider questions of sex and gender, but rather retains, despite other fantastical departures, old assumptions about women's sexual and gender identity.[3] In the current acrimonious struggle over women's reproductive rights (abortion, birth control, the use of reproductive technology), feminist science fictions present a world in which that battle has been won, in which women have the absolute authority over their bodies that they don't have in the "real world" of patriarchy (insofar as it is given to *any* human being to have such control). Just as we earlier asked about the organizing bias of any utopia, "Whose future?" so we must now ask, "From what real world does the writer take off?—that of the male or the female? Or both?" Moreover, depicting the redistribution of household and child-rearing tasks is rightfully seen by feminist sci-fi writers as the way to an *un*fantastic, realistic accommodation between the sexes, necessary to gender equality. Thus Gilman's fantasy *Herland* is foreshadowed by her earlier book on domestic economy, *The House: Its Work and Influence* (1903), which argued for the centralization of domestic work, including child care.

Let us return to the question of whether women need to construct a fantasy to imagine such changes. The fantasy of science fiction clearly is not the only modality for presenting feminist values. Poetry, drama, sociology, psychology, biography, autobiography, mainstream fiction, film—all have presented characters impelled by feminist values or understood in the light of them. But science fiction, precisely because as fantasy it initiates an encompassing, inclusive, different, futuristic vision, is an excellent modality for presenting an entire *society* sustained by feminist values. We have never been protagonists in the places these novels represent, which are "elsewhere," correcting current inequities of power between the sexes. Moreover, the authors of these novels insist the goal of gender equality must include not only the private, but also the public sphere. As Drucilla Cornell aptly remarks, "Our political obligations cannot be separated from our dreams and fantasies."[4] And so, as we have noted, these utopian visions show women (certainly affected to the same degree as men by what the public world decides) participating fully in public policy-making, as they do not in present society.

Thus the second enabling feature for women in these feminist science fictions is that they present women who are leaders: rational, intelligent beings who debate (Gilman), use persuasive rhetoric (Lessing), and govern wisely (Le Guin). Of necessity, therefore, these protagonists are speakers, as the passive, silent heroines of yesteryear typically were not. These hypothetical societies constitute one response to the running question of this book, "What can women *do*?" They can visualize substantial change, developing models of female leaders and models of cooperative governance. Such pictorialization is important insofar as it helps to counteract age-old traditions which deny women leadership and leave them uncomfortable with it. Women must assume leadership if, as ordinary heroines, they are to be agents for change.

Science fiction produced by men is closer in general to the realistic novel than that produced by women. First, because, though initially fantastical, masculinist prediction of machines capable of conferring superhuman power upon people accords with our knowledge that technology *is* ever-expanding. We now take for granted the space ships, the submarines, the rockets that were predicted before they existed. They are easily assimilated through the popular media of film and video games, extrapolating into an indefinite future our familiar world-with-machines—e.g., the computer, the fax—until tomorrow becomes today on the screen.[5]

Despite retaining some of the more typical devices of science fiction (movement backward and forward in time, travel through outer space, machinery that can perform unheard-of deeds) feminist sci-fi departs not only from social realism, but also from male predecessors in the genre, who often proceed from the idea of the world as a giant Meccano set or, worse, a stage-set for the apocalypse.[6]

Margaret Atwood pushes science fiction, traditionally clinical, impersonal, and potentially dangerous, to the extreme in her dystopian novel, *The*

Handmaid's Tale.[7] Familiar from prior dystopias such as George Orwell's *1984*, Aldous Huxley's *Brave New World*, and Anthony Burgess's *A Clockwork Orange*, these traditional qualities of sci-fi serve Atwood's scarifying account of the absolute repression of women and of male control of reproduction in a military dictatorship. Although Atwood does not resort here to technology as the mechanism of control, an invisible and therefore even more menacing control nonetheless pervades the fiction. There is a strange suggestion of a technology of thought and mind control whose workings we the readers understand only partially. Control is reflected in the strict dress code, the complex hierarchy within the rulers' organization, the fearful concern with visibility and invisibility; "eyes" are everywhere and nowhere, watching. Women are forbidden to read. Big Brother has become an agent of gender subjugation. We dare not leave this world alone to right itself, and in the imagined worlds of Le Guin and Lessing we find necessary correctives.

Because of their more sweeping recommendations for social change, these feminist science fictions are harder than traditional ones to accept; unfortunately, their goals and their process are further from the observation and experience of most people. In other words, we're familiar with technology, but have no experience of a better world to guide us. Thus when people dismiss science fiction as depicting a "la-la land" they are expressing their conviction that a better world *cannot* be brought about, that our best strategy is defense. Dystopias are lent credibility by life; utopias are not. We read these feminist science fictions not for the pleasure of recognition, but as we do all utopian fiction, to find answers or, at least, resolutions. How can life on earth be arranged better? How can societies be governed equitably? How can peaceful negotiation become the means of settling dispute? How do we learn respect for difference? These are the large moral questions beyond gender relations, though significantly rooted in them, which these novels confront. If we re-examine straightforward male utopian fantasies, such as Edward Bellamy's *Looking Backward*, Thomas More's *Utopia*, or Sylvester Judd's *Margaret*, we find that despite all the meliorist schemes offered, not one changes either the status of women or their relation to men. None of them even raises these issues. As practiced by writers such as Lessing, Le Guin, and Russ, science fiction poses better worlds for men as well as for women, for the individual and for the community. In the hands of these writers, fantasy becomes the serious vessel for a counter-reality which in no way resembles the sheer escapism and heightened individualism of books such as James Hilton's *Lost Horizon* —fantasies which pander to our dream of personal immortality but care nothing for ideals.

In contrast to such entertainments, both Joanna Russ's *The Female Man* and Doris Lessing's *The Marriages Between Zones Three, Four, and Five* evince a strong communitarian impulse. Their ethos compels women to attempt the reformation of crueler societies which lie far from idyllic utopias they call home, from their "Whileaways," as Russ's community is named. Their female protagonists are not lotus eaters, but responsible leaders whose communal impulses shine through. Leaders among the women in *A Door Into Ocean* by Joan Slonczewski are, tellingly, called Sharers; in Octavia Butler's *Dawn*, it is the women leaders' function "to teach, to give comfort, to feed and clothe, to guide"[8] newcomers to their land. This is a marked change from the alienation and dis-ease characteristic of much male-authored science fiction: The new feminist novels stress the hopeful possibility of cohesive, workable social structures. Even when direct engagement does not take place, the enactment of feminist values converts the male observer, as it does, for instance, the three stray male travellers in *Herland*, or in "Houston Houston Do You Read?" by James Tiptree Jr. (Alice B. Sheldon). In these fictions, male characters are initially discomfited by, but come to accept, almost without exception, the paradigm of cooperation and its corollary, a diminished emphasis upon individualism in the society into which they have been introjected.

Before we proceed to a discussion of what constitutes the embracing social vision of these sci-fi novels, we must consider the charge of anti-individualism, levied by male protagonists in the novels, as well as by some critical readers of both sexes. The charge is deserved, but not unanticipated by these writers of feminist science fiction. It may even be that they provoke it, and that it is proleptic. Precisely because these books are concerned with innovations in gender relations, they focus more on the development of a new psychology of *women* than on that development of a particular female character's psychology necessary in order to write a female *Bildungsroman*. Now sci-fi in general is a genre in which character is usually sacrificed to plot—even subordinated to the invention of exotic scenery. But in developing a new psychology, the lack of characterization aids the writers' new purposes. For example, the emphasis upon gender identity rather than personal identity may surface in, simply, the use of matronymic rather than patronymic surnames, as is the case with one of Joanna Russ's heroines in *The Female Man*, whose surname is Evason, or Eva's/son, Eve's son. This device resonates with our keen interest in the past lineage of her/story.[9]

More important, concentrating on changing accepted gender roles rather than on developing individual characters has meant the disappearance of the stock female characters and traits still tolerated in the novel of realism (which, after all, still does reflect current cultural values) and masculinist science fiction. As we have already remarked, it comes as a welcome relief to the intelligent woman reader, long accustomed to the slur on women's rationality, that the mothers of *Herland* by Charlotte Perkins Gilman or the governing council of women in Zone Three in Lessing's *The Marriages Between Zones Three, Four, and Five* are sweetly reasonable, open to inquiry, level-headed, even-handed. The female protagonist of Joanna Russ's *The Female Man* is a whiz with machines, a technical expert; in *Herland* women are foresters, engineers.

Like today's female sleuths and tycoons, then, these heroines of science fiction can do whatever a *human being* can do, because in the worlds in which they function there is no mind/body problem for women, no cultural directive about the marriage plot and gender roles. In fact, the questions "what is masculine?" and "what is feminine?"—perhaps most pointed in the work of Joanna Russ—are the sub-text of the majority of these feminist science fiction novels. To put it differently, how, they ask, do we develop? These feminist stories teach, as do many fairy tales and folk tales. We escape, but—as Carl Gustav Jung and Bruno Bettelheim explain—we learn. This gives feminist science fiction an importance most critics overlook; though fantasizing, these authors are thinking deeply about how children should be educated. They are thinking about the wisdom of androgynous roles, about the relation of biology to destiny.

Once the feminist sci-fi writers discussed here have pictured a future society in which gender relations are no longer the crucial, the primary issue, *even for women*, writer and reader are free to reflect on the larger moral designs which inform their novels.

What to call these novels? So far, I have allowed myself to blur the distinction between the terms "feminist science fiction," the more generic "fantasy," and "feminist utopia," because no one of them is completely descriptive of the writing we're considering, yet each is partially so. The works we are discussing require a *new* name.

Marleen Barr has created the term "feminist fabulations" to describe this development of the genre, an improvement on two counts: First, it eliminates the label "science fiction" which carries inaccurate connotations of progress based on technology and scientism. Equally, labelling Le Guin's and Lessing's books "space operas" (a common tag for sci-fi) suggests erroneously that their promise of peace for all and equality for women lies in dominance over nature, conquest of "space." And as for "opera"—that art form has proven lethal for most of its heroines! Second, I endorse this new descriptive phrase because "fabulations" places feminist science fiction within the fabulist tradition, that is, one tradition of stories with a moral lesson. Finally, the word "fabulations" implies a fictive or imagined reality apart from social realism.

What does Barr's adjective "feminist" denote before "fabulations"? I would answer first that, far from being launched into the ether of space, the novels by Lessing and Le Guin which belong to this category, and at which we'll be looking shortly, are grounded in human relations. Kristeva feels the need to invent a new name for the radical counter-societies proposed by women, places outside the law which go beyond realism and even beyond male utopias, and she comes up with "a-topia." A new vision cannot be contained in a compromised word laden with previous connotations.

Feminist fabulations necessarily vary in literary merit, style, and the importance placed on character and plot. Some, like Le Guin's, are rich in poetic language and the interweaving of literary, visual, and even musical effects. Others are best-sellers—breathlessly paced, threatening the female realm, and retaining strong plot lines. Still others may include the appeal of travel literature or description of bucolic pleasures. Some, like many of Joanna Russ's, are humorous. The enjoyment we derive from them has a variety of sources, as does our enjoyment of novels in general. We don't read Hemingway and Virginia Woolf for the same delights. We don't turn the pages of *To the Lighthouse* to find out whether the Ramseys' party ever gets to that titular destination.

Presumably, we enjoy these feminist sci-fi fictions partly because we find our own values dramatized, and our own sex empowered in a way that they are not in the realistic novel. The realist novel does not present us with many heroines who "show us what it is like to live as a free and fully human female being in a patriarchal society."[10] Its very realism precludes such a portrait because women as a sex are *not* fully empowered. They are still subjects in the making. Thus, while literary critics may urge that some of the women of Chekhov, Lawrence, James, Forster, are the most *human* characters within their novels, meaning that the moral intelligence rests, finally, with them; what these women can *do* with it (to revert to our original question) is another matter. In fact, enacting the moral view was frequently a burden, given the limited scope of the average female protagonist. These putative "heroines" gain in awareness, but do not acquire commensurate powers of resistance. In feminist fabulations, however, the individual woman is not charged with unique moral responsibility. Thus these fictions stand as a corrective to the mainstream realist novel which, Myra Jehlen argues, is socially irresponsible for posing as individual problems that are really social. Moreover, because the works we are looking at do not picture separatist worlds peopled only by heroines, we read these books with a broader interest as well. Feminist values have never been put into practice on a broad scale, as, say, Communist values have; we read these books in part to see how these visions, now living on the margins, look when centralized.

Taken together, what is this new vision, what commonality emerges from these feminist fabulations? The values they promulgate can be summarized as: the indictment of war, weapons, destruction, and violence; the rejection of a heroic persona; the assumption of intimate bonds between different creatures and even with natural forces; extended kinship; the replacement of hierarchy by partnership in the private world and responsive short-term leadership in the public realm.

Taking Ursula Le Guin's *Always Coming Home* and Doris Lessing's *The Marriages Between Zones Three, Four, and Five* as my points of departure, but drawing illustrations from other feminist sci-fi novels as well, I now want to place in context these social and spiritual values, and show how the brave new worlds in which they flourish operate, what heroinism means in "literary feminism."

The fact that the worlds of both Lessing's Zone Three and Le Guin's Valley of the Kesh are matrilinear is not surprising—what is so, is that both writers develop from this shared initial condition whole societies substantively similar. The inference is that the kind of society they picture is a natural outgrowth of matriarchy. On the other hand, neither novel creates worlds separated by gender, a crucial reason for my choice of these particular two works for extended examination. In many other feminist sci-fi novels we find a powerful bond with nature, communion among species, pacific organization. But in many this is restricted to a female world since, the argument runs, such feeling originates there. But if we are to see the feminist science fiction novel as prescriptive, it must be adaptable for both sexes. For this reason, both Le Guin's and Lessing's fantasies are concerned with the individual's relation to the community and her *or* his responsibility for the spiritual well-being of that community.

Moreover, both of these books face the problem of human violence; unlike the crime novel, however, both reject the idea that it is ineradicable. Importantly, because they confront the issue and yet refuse to blame "human nature" and thereby shrug it off, both trace sources of violence unexplored in previous examples of the genre. Thus traditional science fiction such as Edward Bellamy's *Looking Backward* may establish a relation between property and violence, yet stop short of probing a further relation: *women's relation to property and therefore to violence.* Women, counted as part of material wealth, are traditionally possessions and not possessors in patriarchy. As such, they remain vulnerable properties in utopias which are male-authored.[11]

Furthermore, since these feminist fictions posit equality between the sexes and are at the same time pacifist, a new question arises. Are we correct in inferring a causal relation? In other words, are Le Guin, Lessing and other feminist sci-fi writers implying that violence in the society in general proceeds from a cultural acceptance of violence toward women? A cultural pathology? They may be, though which specific violence is the Prime Mover in a world dedicated to violence is open to debate.

What can be maintained with certainty is that since gender definitions have never been revised we cannot tell, except speculatively, how a gender-free society would behave. Violence, whether towards women, children, the earth, other nations or races, does stem from the same pathology, one which builds on a primary relation of powerful/powerless. We have seen Marxian blueprints for economic change, Kantian blueprints for political change, which ignored to their detriment multifarious manifestations of the incipiently violent relation of power/powerlessness. For example, Francine du Plessix Gray reports in *Soviet Women: Walking the Tightrope* that, despite the sweeping economic changes in the Soviet Union at the time of her visit in 1991, the lot of women living there today remains deplorable. In the then U.S.S.R, women did not control their own reproductive functions (as they still do not in that region); and the damage she witnessed, both physical and psychological, is incalculable.

In our own society violence toward women is escalating. Film critic Jay Carr notes a growing trend toward "woman bashing" in Hollywood, citing as evidence the films *Blue Steel*, *Revenge*, and *Pretty Woman*, all released in the same week.[12] Actress Meryl Streep deplored the cinematic mistreatment of women in a speech to the Screen Actor's Guild in August 1990. The actual battering of women as well as widespread representation of that violence is symptomatic of a disseminated not a localized disease.

In the important sense that the imagined world of Lessing's Zone Three or Le Guin's Valley of the Kesh improve upon the real, the most significantly utopian feature of both is that their people live in peace, a prevalent theme in feminist science fiction, e.g., James Tiptree Jr.'s (Alice B. Sheldon) "Houston, Houston, Do You Read," Joanna Russ's *The Female Man*, and Joan Slonczewski's *A Door Into Ocean*, among many others. This alone would be an important reason for taking cultural relativism seriously, even in a so-called "entertainment."

A warless world, like a gender-free world, may be a fiction and not a fact, but to consider either war or sexism "the real" is to suggest their permanence, even their naturalness, their propriety. It is also to obscure the profound connection between the two. To depict the overthrow of war and of gender strife, to visualize and describe societies which have eliminated material power as well as private and national imperialism, is an imaginative leap. The risk of that leap provides much of the tension of these utopias. That is, we as readers know these are imagined worlds, we are constantly aware they may never be actualized, even though visualized. We project onto them the conflict between our experience and our yearning toward the good, informed by our conviction that we must imagine something before we can move toward it.

These imaginings also, importantly, develop rituals we lack for preserving a spiritual dimension in our lives. From the Nuremberg rallies to American football games, rituals sacralize social practices and unify people. But where are the rituals that mark individual rites of passage, a life and its sanctity? Where are the rituals extending beyond those surrounding entertainment and war that would bind us to a community? As the hold of mainstream religion has weakened on the twentieth century mind and spirit, almost all rituals have become secular and trivial. Thus, Ray Raphael claims that American men invent rituals to simulate a rite of passage no longer culturally observed: "join the army, compete in sports, get a job, graduate from college, climb mountains, pledge fraternities, screw girls, get drunk with the guys." [13] That is, even coming-of-age rites once central to the initiate's integration into the larger adult community have lost all but the most superficial social character for most participants, who do not, in truth, feel themselves transformed. [14]

As for women, Naomi Wolf's analysis of the devastating effects of the beauty myth upon women concludes that the myth exists to a spiritual vacuum: "The beauty cult attests to a spiritual hunger for female ritual and rites of passage. . . . Can we evolve more widely among friends, among networks of friends, fruitful new rites and celebrations for the female life cycle?" [15] Though the rituals Wolf would like to see created would celebrate female experience, our culture *as a whole* lacks, and would benefit from, a richer ritualistic expression of emotional life.

The books of Starhawk, Carol Christ, D. Budapest and many other women writers who belong to special present-day groups organized around feminist values attempt just that. They describe new rituals, new occasions selected as worthy of notice. Their governance delineates very carefully the proper dress, food, drink, and setting for the enactment, respectively, of rituals recognizing loss, arrival of puberty, joining the community, rituals to celebrate the natural world and our common human vital connection to it, rituals of cleansing and purification, and many more. In the specificity of their practices, they dispel the charge of "dreaminess." They are the day-to-day, trial-and-error experiment of living the visions of *Always Coming Home* and *The Marriages Between Zones Three, Four, and Five*; or, to put it conversely, the novels are blueprints of the feminist principles these communities practice.

It could be argued that such rituals, lacking the resonance of historical practice, can't be grafted successfully onto our contemporary world, would lack conviction and authenticity. But some present-day societies in fact do, even self-consciously, reach back through history for context and precedent. They reach back just because contemporary lives pay so little attention to meaning that we must seek it out. Even more than in fictive creation, it takes courage, optimism, and imagination to organize functioning groups in which feminist values prevail and new rituals can develop. Such rituals stand in contradistinction to Pindar's dictum that "success is the first of prizes. To be well spoken of [fame] is second," [16] or to rituals of glory still drama-tized on football field and battlefield. A sense of social responsibility in-clines these novels to qualify the terms of conflict. For instance, the novel *A Door Into Ocean*, nominally science fiction, remakes traditional classifica-tions; it depicts a new epic struggle, one between pacifists and "forcers" or aggressors, not between two opposing forces.

Also, conflict redeems the characters from the flatness of idealization—they experience struggle, loss, pain, grief and even defeat. When, for in-stance, Al-Ith, leader of Zone Three in Doris Lessing's *The Marriages* re-turns to her land after enforced residence in Zone Four, she finds her sister ensconced in her place as ruler. There are hard lessons to be learned; if lead-ership is responsive, no one is indispensable. Love can be unrequited, friends desert, death come. The people of these novels do not exist merely to enjoy a perfected world. In fact, we are left with the basic problem of imperfect human nature that prompted eighteenth century Enlightenment thinkers to try and formulate governing principles that would successfully channel anti-social, or self-interested, impulses. But the failure of the Enlighten-ment can be at least partially ascribed to its reification of reason and mo-dernity, and its consequent detachment from both the natural world and the world of feelings. But neither then nor now does one need to posit the perfectability of humankind, only its educability. This is why the question "How can we develop?" is centralized. Feminist values, as we have summa-rized them earlier in the chapter, propose different relations to nature and to one another.

For both Le Guin and Lessing, attempting to implement feminist values uncovers a basic and profoundly important confusion in our culture between fact and fiction, or, in the sense that we have been using fiction, fact and fantasy, and the value and uses of each. Though both authors attack this imprecision in terms of a debate over narrative mode (we have already mentioned the limitations of the realistic novel), it is much more than that. It is a debate about how and where to locate truth; the relation of narrative to truth; and the question of whether truth is gendered. Hélène Cixous's words are particularly apt: "I am that which I speak." One question which has preoccupied feminist scholars is the gendering of discourse: Whose version of truth does the "reality" of speech convey? Julia Kristeva invents the neologism the "True-Real" to acknowledge that both words were necessary because they are not perfectly coincident in meaning. Both Le Guin and Lessing, using feminist fabulation, tackle the problem of gendered truth and its relation to realism.

Le Guin focuses the question of gendered truth in *Always Coming Home* by contrasting our own culture with the imaginary Kesh culture where feminist values do prevail.

> If fact and fiction are not clearly separated in Kesh literature, truth and falsehood, however, are. A deliberate lie (slander, boast, tall tale) is identified as such and is not considered in the light of literature at all. In this case I find our categories perhaps less clear than theirs. The distinction is one of intent, and we often do not make it at all, since we allow propaganda to be qualified both as journalism and as fiction; while the Kesh dismiss it as a lie.[17]

Thus Le Guin exposes the hypocrisy of our society which labels what it finds in non-fiction as "real" and what it finds in fiction as "false." This system of labelling enables "real" and "false" (made up) to become, by extension, as Le Guin notes, identified respectively with the ethical terms "truth" and "lie." That is, the labels "non-fiction" and "fiction" have become evaluative not merely descriptive terms; they refer not to genre but to worth. Because our own time is surpassingly the age of docudrama, as practiced by writers like Norman Mailer and Truman Capote, this observation has particular implications for us. We infer that journalism and television are our carriers of information/fact/truth, delivered as "the real," though (in truth) the version we see is always selective, edited, even censored. Fantasy may hold up for inspection moral truths which resist, or even find no place in, seemingly factual account.

Always Coming Home reconsiders with even more particularity than the paragraph quoted above this unresolved question of the relation of truth to narrative:

Narrative [in our culture] is either factual (nonfiction) or nonfactual (fiction). The distinction is clear, and the feeble forms such as "novel-ized biography" or "the non-fiction novel" that attempt to ignore it only demonstrate its firmness. In the Valley the distinction is gradual and messy. The kind of narrative that tells "what happened" is never clearly defined by genre, style of valuation from the kind that tells a story "like what happened." [18]

The information that in the Valley of the Kesh "the kind of narrative" was "never clearly defined by . . . valuation" tells us that fiction and fantasy were not, there, *sui generis*, discredited, at the bottom of the hierarchy of genres hallowed by the male canon which esteems epic far above lyric.

Now this perception of narrative that Le Guin introduces through her imaginary Kesh society is not just temporally progressive or developmental, i.e., proceeding from a flawed present into a future utopia, but a gendered perception. The distinction between fact and fiction that exists in the Kesh society, which is the feminist culture of the book, is "gradual and messy," recalling our earliest chapters which consider woman as process, as flux. Narrative flexibility, then, can be seen to parallel female development as it is viewed by commentators like Nancy Chodorow and Miriam Greenspan—more fluid, less boundaried, than male. Carrying this further, Jacques Derrida speculates in *Spurs* that woman's nature lies in the undecidable, suspending the tension between truth and falsehood, perhaps building on Freud's characterization of women as *unheimlich*. There seems to be widespread acceptance of the notion that gender and genre intersect significantly, and that one place we observe this is in the entrance to the unconscious, whose images flood those fantasies.

We can postulate that female development, *and* the plot which reflects it, is nonlinear, repudiating that march of events which ideally expresses heroic action. [19] We can identify the lyrical organization, the narrative mode Le Guin adopts, (or Monique Wittig in *Les Guérillères* also) as most expressive of female development. Broadly, both *Always Coming Home* and *The Marriages* are organized lyrically, which is to say in a nonlinear mode, but both are nevertheless dynamic, bearing titles which imply movement. [20]

As we have seen, a new vision often gives birth to a new form, gender helps determine genre. Returning to the genre of science fiction and the feminist fabulations within it, there is no question but that the innovation of *Always Coming Home*, for example, lies as much in its lyrical form as in its content, the former complementing and substantiating the latter. Le Guin's novel transgresses genre boundaries by including drawings, visual symbols, poems, stories, descriptions of dances, songs; she and the composer Todd Barton have even produced a tape of music to accompany the book. The circular symbol which repeats at intervals through the book as well as at the conclusion of each chapter, is another example of this principle of structural inclusiveness. By closing her chapters with a circle and not a final period, Le Guin problematizes the very notion of closure.[21] Geographical as well as narrative space is circular; the Valley of the Kesh, located somewhere in the Pacific Northwest is described thus: "The lands go on and on to the sea again, you know . . . and so on round till you come back to the Valley."[22]

Of course, many stylistic characteristics of this work parallel those of postmodernism: Multivocality, pastiche, fragmentation, inclusiveness. This is no coincidence. The style which is called postmodern testifies to a radical change in contemporary sensibility; the silence in Samuel Beckett's work extends almost to muteness, silence becomes a static and monumental force, subverting dialogue. Similarly, these a-topias subvert the silence which in the past swallowed the expression of female desire. In these fantasies speech swells to a choric voice, with many different narrators. For example, in *Les Guérillères*, both the single voice of authority and the direct line of narrative are subverted. Both postmodernism and feminist literary expression cultivate the introduction of what is stylistically new and different. Specifically, the works we're looking at share with postmodernist writing innovations in narrative authority, as well as linguistic and temporal departures.

Le Guin's and Lessing's novels are closer to the time we experience in myth, with its cyclical connections to birth, death and renewal (nature) than to epic or tragedy and the deeds of the hero.

The time of *Always Coming Home* is as non-specific as its locale, weaving constantly among past, present, and future so as to suggest timelessness and indivisible connections. The Kesh people live with a past which is always present, reflected in a poem within the book entitled "From the People of the Houses of Earth in the Valley to the Other People Who Were on Earth Before Them." And the very title *Always Coming Home* extends a continuing present into the future, resembling in this way the title of Audre Lorde's poem, "Now That I Am Forever with Child." Both refer to a present which transcends individual life. Time, in this interpretation, is seen as flux, as a feminine principle, as it is also in Paula Gunn Allen's *The Sacred Hoop: Recovering the Feminine in American Indian Tradition*. Gunn Allen suggests: "There is some sort of connection between colonization and chronological time."[23] "Indian time" to the contrary, "rests on the perception of individuals as part of an entire gestalt . . . the revolving of the seasons, the land, and the mythic reality that shapes all life into significance."[24]

In sum the senses of time and space, influencing genre in literature, impinge also upon language. Feminist writing in general has, in the effort of "making it new," exhibited extraordinary attention to playfulness of language, punning, neologisms which refresh and entertain the reader. As in the poetry of John Ashbery, a consummate player with words, we learn to expect the unexpected. For feminists, what such linguistic departure or rupture from accustomed usage concerning gender boundaries, syntax, and grammar, accomplishes is to open discourse to new ideas, new ways of seeing. Feminism and postmodernism agree that the difference between truth and falsity, fiction and non-fiction, is illusory, or at best, elusive; to paraphrase Magritte, the text is not a text. One consequence for both is that sexual differentiation is blurred—viz., the frequent appearance of the androgyne character in feminist fabulations, that of the transvestite in the postmodern novel.[25]

Doris Lessing's moral fable *The Marriages Between Zones Three, Four, and Five* shares a striking number of features with Le Guin's *Always Coming Home*. First, Lessing's metafiction or neo-realistic fiction, like Le Guin's, shows the relation of genre to gender by breaking with conventional narrative as it breaks with conventional patriarchal values. It, too, interpolates songs and poems into the multiple narratives that comprise the book. Second, in *Marriages*, as in *Always Coming Home*, the disruption of narrative into many voices leads to distrust of the rigid boundaries between "fact" and "fiction." The following passages from *Marriages* illustrates this:

> When storytellers say: And then there appeared a dwarf with a hump or an exquisite girl made of the wind—well, their audience always thinks that this is a manner-of-speaking but perhaps after all these storytellers, or their ancestors, *did* see little gnarled strong men and women who live deep in mountains, or a race of people so rare and fine they could pass through walls and who were at home in flames or in the wind . . . or at least such beings were part of the consciousness of the lower Zones, to an extent that the thoughts of these minds, or the words of the storytellers, could bring them to life—there they were now, vivid, alive, moving in Al-Ith's mind's eye, perfect and created, yet so far away, yet she could see them, and yet she might not touch them. And there were the strange beasts of the realm of the storytellers, and the familiar beasts, too.[26]

This *maybe*, this *once upon a time*, recasts history as imagination, not fact; it is a story, a version recounted by women and not a record. That is, at the point where gender and genre intersect great importance is attached to storytelling, referring to a language of poetry, of metaphor, of magic, of myth. Storytelling is itself one of society's rituals, a safe-keeping of beliefs. Its power is not the prevailing power of the father tongue which organizes our institutions and professions, and which is, in any case, a written tongue. Writing as law, history, theology, political manifesto, the record of property, has long been a tool of male domination, omitting women's experience and excluding women contributors.

Contrariwise, Lessing's sense of the past in this book is imparted and strengthened through storytelling, which in its conflation of past, present, and future, enables her to assert the connectedness of all things over time. "We are the visible and evident aspects of a whole we all share, that we all go to form." [27] There is, in the longer passage quoted above, reference to all kinds of metamorphoses. If history is not a museum of dead lessons but an inextricable part of ourselves, no one is excluded. This conclusion of Lessing is one for which Le Guin's visual symbol of inclusiveness and organic growth, already mentioned, is a correlative. [28]

Lessing's story is told by female narrators, the "Chroniclers" of Zone Three, just as Le Guin's novel is told by the woman, Stone Telling, and as female narrators are likewise the fable-tellers of Monique Wittig's *Les Guérillères.* Similarly, Joanna Russ's *The Female Man* contains women narrators who tell sacred stories in special sacred places. As Sarah Lefanu's study informs us, *The Book of Mrs. Noah*, by Michèle Roberts, nominally science fiction, is in essence about the telling of stories. Because Le Guin and Lessing insist upon the living continuity of history, (embedded for instance in Lessing's subtitle, *Canopus in Argos: Archives*), it is especially true that women, as chroniclers, as narrators, hold a central place in the society. This is an important role for women to reclaim, but also one vital to the imaginative life of the entire community. By contrast, in our culture "storytellers" are now an entertainment act, sustaining but feebly the illusion of shared community.

In Grace Paley's story "Zagrowski Tells," he *tells* because "to breathe, you got to tell." [29] Telling is healing, an act of wholeness. His story, any story told aloud, presumes an audience in a community. The palpable lack we feel of community and of a shared oral history is the basis for the enthusiasm which greeted Garrison Keillor's simulacrum, Lake Woebegon.

In neither Le Guin's nor Lessing's novel has the written word replaced oral communication. Lessing's society of Zone Three, like Le Guin's Valley of the Kesh, derives its authentication from oral tradition; Memory, as a crucial function, is capitalized throughout the book. Now Memory, or Mnemosyne as she is called, is a female goddess, and mother of the muses. Thus with the female narrators of Zone Three we return to a different language, "the mother tongue," derived from the language of conversation, of the colloquial, of gossip, of the quotidian, and also the language, if not the discourse, which includes the material female body. [30] Women's writing is opening up present-day patriarchal discourse to the inclusion of women's experience as well as to substantial stylistic innovation.

Let us look now in closer detail at the feminist values, summarized earlier, which infuse both Lessing's and Le Guin's novels under consideration here, remembering too that these values obtain widely in other feminist fabulations.

The Indictment of Hunting, Weapons, and Destruction: A Hatred of War and Its Derivative Games and Rites

Hunting, which after war is the quintessential male initiation rite, is scorned, whereas constructing personal relations *is* seen as an appropriate undertaking for an adult male in the Kesh society. Le Guin reappraises male and female values here, and judges male "virtues" to be destructive to a humanistic society: "Hunting for food and skins was primarily an occupation for children. . . . A man who spent much time hunting after he had outgrown the Bay Laurel Lodge and was of marrying age was looked upon as either childish or shiftless. Hunting, in general, was not seen as appropriate behavior for an adult."[31]

By contrast with the Kesh people, their neighbors, a people symbolically named Condor (a bird belonging to the vulture family), pursue a policy of military aggrandizement, but do not prosper: "Do not fight with these sick people, cure them with human behavior," and "very sick people tend to die of their own diseases," or "destruction destroys itself," are typical Kesh responses to the Condor.[32] As the author points out, this Kesh attitude is a reversal of the current values of our own society. (Any resemblance between the Condor world and ours is purely intentional.) "What we call strength, it calls sickness; what we call success, it calls death."[33]

Lessing similarly turns male virtues upside down:

> Three comes before Four.
> Our ways are peace and plenty.
> Their ways—war![34]

The three lines above are chanted by women of Zone Three at the beginning of *The Marriages Between Zones Three, Four, and Five.*[35] Zone Three is a peaceful kingdom ruled by women whose leader is Al-Ith, whereas Zone Four, the neighboring country, a dystopia, led by the tyrant Ben-Ata, supports a military system and force. The contrast between them serves the evaluative purpose of the novel.

The Marriages is the story of the forced marriage between the two leaders of Zones Three and Four and Al-Ith's subsequent removal to her husband's land, undertaken to afford the bride an opportunity to educate her husband beyond the militarism and brutishness to which he's been socialized since childhood. Her husband's Zone Four even boasts Children's Regiments, a creation which has historical precedent. Since we as readers watch the obstacles Al-Ith must overcome, her final exodus in heartbreak, and her ultimate replacement by a wife from Zone Five, the novel is far from static. Overall, its drama derives from her experience, teaching her (and us) that education beyond aggression is neither easy nor quick. For example, the reader shares Al-Ith's dismay when she is escorted to inspect the military machine of Zone Four:

> Walking again in the mists and splashings of the gardens, with the drum everywhere, in their blood, and in their minds, she called his attention to the files of soldiers down below, deploying among the wet hazes of the meadows . . . and she knew he was marshalling praise and criticism and orders, for the perfection of that work of his, the army.

> "And who," she asked, in a way that would make him know she was in earnest, "are your enemies? . . . Who do you fight?" . . . She knew he was remembering the pillage and the rapine of innumerable campaigns, and thinking if these had in fact been for some ghost of a mistaken idea then . . . "We are not your enemies—it is not even possible for one of us to cross the border without bad effects—yet you have forts all along our frontier from one end to the other, just as close as you can get to it."[36]

The inevitable accompaniments of a martial mentality are rank, hierarchy, show, intimidation, and civilian poverty. Al-Ith rebukes her husband, "Why do you have to have ranks, and a hierarchy? Is it because you are so poor?"[37] Ben-Ata's land is variously described as arid, farmed out, or swampy; its homes, tools, fences, animals, as ruinously neglected. Thus, Al-Ith, though speaking from the perspective of a fantasized world speaks the unmistakable truth of the real world: Foreign entanglements are a political strategy to distract the citizenry from domestic problems.

The common misery that accompanies military power in Ben Ata's Zone Four likewise is attacked in Le Guin's *Always Coming Home*: "To construct a tank or a bomber was so difficult and so unnecessary that it really cannot be spoken of in terms of the Valley economy. After all, the cost of making, maintaining, fueling, and operating such machines at the very height of the Industrial Age was incalculable, impoverishing the planet's substance forever and requiring the great majority of humankind to live in servitude and poverty."[38]

As *three* comes before *four* in arithmetic, so *A* comes before *B* in the alphabet; thus the ruler of Zone *Three*, the feminine principle is named *Al-*

Ith, the masculine principle of Zone *Four*, *B*en-Ata. By this device, Lessing presents the reader with two clues, numerical and alphabetical, about their respective status in her eyes. More tellingly, since the plot turns on the premise that through *marriage* between the leaders of Zones Three and Four a more civilized, humane view of the world will filter down from Three to Four, and eventually to Zone Five, the most primitive of the Zones, we as readers know we are to understand that it is through the heart, the bonds of affection, friendship, and sexual love, that transformation will be effected.

The Assumption of an Intimate Bond Among Different Creatures, and Even Natural Forces

In *Always Coming Home* the reader encounters ant dances, bee dances, puma dances, dances of wind, clouds, and rain. The Kesh people consider themselves related to both creatures and forces, all the dwellers in one's House: "To call an olive tree grandmother or a sheep sister, to address a half-acre field of dirt plowed for corn as 'my brother,' is behavior easily dismissed as *primitive* or as *symbolic*. To the Kesh it was the person who could not understand or admit such relationship whose intelligence was in a primitive condition and whose thinking was unrealistic."[39]

In *Marriages* the leader of Zone Three, Al-Ith, is able to ride the fiercest horse without benefit of saddle or bridle; she is able, as are her subjects, to understand and talk to animals. One of her countrywomen, recalling a scene with their leader imaged at the center, might be describing an oleograph of St. Francis: "All kinds of little animals have crept into this picture. Birds hover around her head. A small deer, a great favorite with our children, has stepped on to the dust of the road, and is holding up its nose to the drooping nose of Al-Ith's horse, to comfort it, or to give it messages from other animals. Often these pictures are titled 'Al-Ith's Animals.' Some tales tell how the soldiers try to catch the birds and the deer, and are rebuked by Al-Ith."[40]

In Zone Three nature is animistic, creatures are interdependent. When Al-Ith is unhappy, the fauna and flora of her kingdom sicken. This same note is struck in Whileaway, the feminist utopia of Russ's sci-fi novel *The Female Man* where, we are told, Whileawayans "provide human companionship to Whileawayan cows, who pine and die unless spoken to affectionately."[41]

Extended Kinship

The congeries of relationship in *Always Coming Home*—this society, matrilinear and matrilocal, practices a system of extended kinship—demonstrate the same belief in wholeness and inclusion as do both the narrative structure and the interpretations of time and space. The wide-flung net of kinship includes "four kinds of relatives:"

> People who lived in one's House: one of the five great divisions of the human and other beings of the Valley, the Obsidian, Blue Clay, Serpentine, Red and Yellow Adobes. The relationship was called maan.
>
> People who were related by blood (consanguines)—chan.
>
> People who were related by marriage (affines)—giyamoudan.
>
> People who were related by choice—goestun.[42]

Both Le Guin's novel and Lessing's *The Marriages Between Zones Three, Four, and Five* introduce the same notion, alien to us, of "kinship by choice."

Thus the individual is related to all around him or her—animals, birds, friends, blood relations, clan members—and this vast network of connection, maintained by those who are official chroniclers, is a foundation for peaceful co-existence, among people and between species.

Moreover, the mothers in Lessing's Zone Three, believing that much is to be learned from many, and that wisdom is not singular, select father figures whose nurture will supplement that of the biological father of their children. Women adopt "brothers"; relations between the sexes are not necessarily sexual and not, in any case, possessive. The lack of possessiveness also shapes child-rearing practices; many surrogate mothers help the biological mother raise and tend the children. Al-Ith, after the birth of her child by Ben-Ata, whose kingdom, unlike her own, follows conventional parenting, reflects: "This *mine, mine, mine* about a child paid every kind of reverence to the flesh, but where was the acknowledgment of the high and fine influences that fed every child—each child, that is, who *was* supplied and fed with them? . . . one might not, most definitely *could* not, say of a child, 'mine, mine' or 'ours, ours'—meaning, only parenthood."[43]

In *The Marriages* this interrelatedness brings peace among people, the common weal being, in actuality, more common. So the women of Zone Three declare: "When those women [from Zone Four] strove and struggled to lift their poor heads up so they could see our mountains towering over them it was as if they were secretly pouring energy and effort into springs that fed us all."[44]

Similarly, Russ's *The Female Man* refers to a "kinship-web," and the novel's Whileaway children have more than one mother. Marge Piercy's *Woman on the Edge of Time* becomes a member of a "tribal family." In Gilman's *Herland* child-rearing is entrusted only to professionals, thereby raising its status as an occupation in the community and simultaneously freeing those mothers who are not maternal. Women, because ongoing definitions of nature and nurture have landed them in subordinate roles, have more of a stake than men in re-examining the roots of these issues in the legal and economic protection of paternity. This is no less true today than in Gilman's time.

The notion of extended kinship deepens and broadens the sense of community in both *Always Coming Home* and *The Marriages*. It stands in opposition to the pessimistic, even apocalyptic note typical of the sci-fi which is more sci- than fi-, a tone struck, for example, by H. G. Wells. The name of the female narrator of *Always Coming Home*, Stone Telling, seems oxymoronic to us but in the land of the Kesh, animistic belief, pre-dating science, prevails. This belief, except in the religion of indigenous peoples, has long been put by as "naive." Many feminist books revive this idea in an effort to reconnect us with the natural world. For example, the spirituality leader Starhawk writes: "Community includes not just the human but the interdependent plant, animal, and elemental communities of the natural world." [45] These quests—redeeming women, redeeming the earth—conflate in the movement called Ecofeminism, reflected in Mary Daly's book titles, *Gyn/Ecology* and *Outercourse*.

Rejection of the Heroic Persona

The tenets of feminist belief we have cited thus far—the indictment of hunting, weapons and destruction, and the assumption of extended kinship—are consistent with the novels' dismissal of heroic gestures, and indeed both Lessing and Le Guin question the need for heroes at all. [46] Le Guin writes:

> There was a story told about a group of Finders exploring down the Outer Coast, who got into a chemically poisoned area; four of the group died. The four survivors mummified their companions' bodies, with the aid of the bone-dry desert climate of the South Coast, and so were able to carry them home for burial—four alive carrying four dead for a month's journey. The feat was spoken of with sympathy, but not with admiration; it was a bit excessive, a bit too heroic, for Valley approbation. [47]

In *The Marriages*, Ben-Ata, the prototype of the military hero, is the focus for Lessing's rejection of that persona. As the absolute ruler of Zone Four, the ruler with complete "power-over," he rules a kingdom in which women are particularly oppressed. That is part of the economic and social contract of his territory; his female subjects are "resigned," "accepting." It comes as no surprise that, disparaging women, he selects the word "monster" to describe them, the word we have already encountered as a synonym for witch. "It seemed to him that half his realm, the female half, was a dark dangerous marsh, from which monsters might suddenly appear." [48] But in

Zone Three, the women's kingdom, where peace, prosperity, and community prevail, the vocabulary expresses transcendence and celebration: Instead of "dark," "dangerous," and "monstrous," we find the women described as "light," "delicate," and "funny;" "laughing," "amusing," possessing "lightness, gaiety, wit, fire." Indeed, a shared characteristic of *Herland*, *The Marriages Between Zones Three, Four, and Five*, *Always Coming Home* and *The Female Man* is the positive value accorded playfulness and humor.[49]

When travellers from the martially organized Zone Four come to the more humane Zone Three, the prospect that unfolds before their eyes is not heroic contest, but a sacral domesticity reminiscent of the humility of the flight into Egypt, and transcendent in its light.

> Taken detail by detail there was nothing in it so remarkable: a man telling a small child how to sit well at the table, a woman smiling at a man— her husband? If a husband, certainly not like one from Zone Four!— but looked at as a whole, it all seemed suffused with a clear fine pale light that spoke to them of the longing that is the inner substance of certain dreams: it was the knowledge of bitter exile.[50]

This luminosity the women from Zone Four perceive as ideal, a glimpse of a paradise from which they have been expelled in some pre-history, shares nothing with the armored brilliance of their zone. Rather, this tableau clarifies for them (literally in its quality of light as well as metaphorically) the poignant contrast mentioned earlier between our experience and our yearning for the good.

In sum, the visions of Le Guin's *Always Coming Home* and Lessing's *The Marriages Between Zones Three, Four, and Five* envisage radical change. Things-as-they-*should*-come-to-pass are for both writers closely linked to their own feminist values and the long history of women's involvement with the quality of human life. As long ago as 1845, for example, before the vindication of the rights of women, before medicine advocated a meat-free diet, Margaret Fuller and many other feminists condemned meat-eating as barbarous practice.[51] Fuller believed that the integration of women into public life would lead to a culture of "plant-like gentleness." Feminists like Elizabeth Cady Stanton and those in the Women's Loyal League were abolitionists before their own cause had triumphed; they campaigned to end slavery far in advance of a women's suffrage bill. They looked forward to a humane society, not only to equal rights for women.

To achieve humane societies Le Guin and Lessing offer the reader not just idle, idiosyncratic, or arbitrary confabulations and speculations, but prescriptions rooted in feminist history. Technology may play a part in such fictions, but their shared major concern is with people, not with machinery, alien creatures, sheer novelty. Though they may be set in a future or erase a past, these novels are alive with propositions for a here and now that can carry us into the future. The final adventure they celebrate is not a heroic exploit, some rescue by a superwoman, but better relations among peoples and between the sexes, nothing more nor less than a mature society which would eschew the reductionism of failure/success for a recognition of the profound cultural complexities of right and wrong.

Fantasy, that is, may effect what reason cannot. It is a startling realization that we have never, through the study of past causes, averted an impending war. We may be unequal to the task of keeping the peace and preserving the universe if we expect reason alone to be our guide. The Enlightenment was not a deterrent to colonialism or religious intolerance. A feeling of compassion for others makes relations of peace and mutual respect the goal of each life. With ethnic wars blazing in all corners of the earth, and the necessity to find some global harmony pressing, we need paradigms for peace.

Jeanette Winterson's uncategorizable fantasy, *Sexing the Cherry*—historical, fantastical, satirical, scatalogical—is unlike fantasies by Calvino, Nabokov, or Borges because its pervasive inventiveness as well as originality of structure, admirable in themselves, are put to the service of a larger moral purpose. They signal the novel's message: guard the environment; be skeptical about heroism and rhetoric; believe in the transformative power of love; understand that control, personal or political, is destructive.

Similarly, the novels of Lessing and Le Guin we have been examining offer specific recommendations for the evolution of humane societies: First, *community* must be strengthened, not individuality.[52] Though we pay lip service to the ideas of social connection and harmony, they actually run counter to some of our most strongly held Western twentieth-century assumptions. Our culture's goal is personal "self-fulfillment," and the language we perceive as the key to this goal, namely, the therapeutic language, is aimed at procuring *personal*, not social happiness. Moreover, personal happiness, defined in contemporary America as instant gratification and informed by a strong sense of entitlement, justifies a power relation of power-over, based most often on the accident of wealth or class. Conversely, there is little language for *communitas*. Individual acts of benevolence are insufficient. Modern Western literature itself centralizes the singular consciousness, not the one-in-all. We have few shared rituals that retain any spiritual dimension, that are not tarnished by commercialism, and still fewer channels for the encouragement of spiritual growth. Recognizing this, both Le Guin's and Lessing's novels celebrate ritual and ritualize celebration. Ritual both marks and effects transformation. Who, by contrast, commemorates our rituals? Who are our storytellers? The CNN or MTV anchorpeople? The National Public Radio commentators who do first person "stories?"

Le Guin and Lessing reject conventional notions of heroism and the heroic as by definition conservative, dominating, and unresponsive; they offer instead a much more flexible model of leadership which does not include power over or provide a system of self-perpetuation codified by law. Rather, the privileged relation between two individuals is a partnership; that among many individuals, a leadership which is organized flexibly and co-operatively. Importantly, they do not repudiate the notion of leadership itself.[53] Were these changes implemented the violence that results from autocratic rule, from the doctrine of universalism and its suppression of demands that arise from difference, could be averted.

Third, both authors honor love, sexual and platonic, and view it as a potential agent for change that includes equality between the sexes. Equality for women as it is presented here includes economic, political and reproductive rights. Until such equality between the sexes is achieved, domestic violence, which accounts for a high percentage of violent crimes against women, will not be eliminated. Violence against women is growing exponentially. A 1990 government-funded study estimated that 12.1 million American women have been raped at least once,[54] and in 1992 Surgeon General Antonia Novello reported that violence is the leading cause of injury to women aged 15-44.[55]

Finally, both fictions are deeply anti-bourgeois, partly out of recognition that the domestic sphere has not been the haven for women it is commonly supposed, but, to the contrary, frequently a locus of abuse and silencing. More largely, anti-bourgeois sentiment informing these works apprehends the firm connection between bourgeois values and violence. What notion of community can there be in a society living with burglar alarms, guns and watchdogs, closed-circuit television? We multiply the safeguards, but leave the major source of violence, the economic power/powerlessness polarization of our country, unchecked.

Rightly, both Le Guin and Lessing regard the attachment to property and to material goods as coeval with the domination of nature, and as conducing, ultimately, in their possessiveness and acquisitiveness, to war. Gender exploitation, class exploitation, race exploitation, spring from a common impulse of greed and the desire for power, the initial struggle to get it, the ongoing struggle to retain it. The connection between our wanton consumption of resources and goods, the death of nature, and war as the consumer of us, the death of us, is incisively drawn for us by these novels.[56]

Now these appear to be wonderfully grandiloquent aims. And, in fact, they return us to the charge that science fiction, as a genre, is wide-eyed. This accusation is, I think, partly attributable to a naive or optimistic outlook which feminist fabulation shares with utopian literature in general. But, as Irving Howe, one of the foremost political savants of our age argues, though "utopian" is a term of dismissal in much intellectual discussion, today "utopianism is a necessity of the moral imagination."[57] Maybe to achieve even limited change, to avoid paralysis, optimism is necessary. The crime novel's operative principle is the constancy of evil, and it is ultimately a conservative genre. Science fiction rejects both the Christian and Freudian belief in sin as an unswerving impulse of human nature, but the consequence, as I've attempted to show, is not that conflict is excluded. Rather, writers like Russ, Le Guin, and Lessing show conflicting interests within their invented society to be already subdued to a general good, shifting the burden of struggle to the education of the unconverted, locating it in a nation or community threatening but not contiguous to their a-topias. Tension still exists in that struggle of unknown outcome, the struggle to educate illustrated in the clash between female and male worlds in *The Female Man*, *A Door Into Ocean*, or *The Marriages*. Moreover, the omission of that special conflict we have come to expect in the traditional novel between the highly individuated protagonist and the society, may bar these science fictions from aesthetic excellence as we presently define it but leave space for broader issues to be developed. In any event, their premise is that prizing individuality we nevertheless suffer from anonymity.

Whatever one's stand on this point, on other grounds these imagined worlds can not be disbarred from serious consideration. The specificity of their social, political and economic arrangements; their introduction into the genre of the issue of sexual domination; their contribution to the ongoing dialogue of contemporary thought about what is masculine and what is feminine, as reflected in gender development; the particularity of their suggestions for new rituals and spiritual emphases; their insistence on the value of community, redeem them from any charge of irrelevance or frivolity.

So although feminist fabulation may be faulted for not presenting political process, for not providing a fool-proof plan to transform a militaristic nation into a pacific one, it is "dreamy" only if one accepts that nothing can be changed, that human nature dooms history to repetition, that human nature is irreducibly ineducable. Were this to be the case, fantasy could never educate toward change, and in that way, presage reality. If these novels could not be read as blueprints for a future, at best they would be diverting. But as Irving Howe affirms: "They are efforts to indicate possibilities of renewal. They provide materials for developments some of us will never live to see."[58]

As it is, they seem to me less fantastic than many a "realistic" crime novel, in which the inevitable identification of the criminal implies a just as inevitable restoration of innocence to the society at large. That *dénouement* acts as a pacifier for the reader, who need not then contemplate profound alterations in our society, however pernicious some of its institutions. Even those crime novels which introduce female detectives, and more rarely, even those such as we have singled out which end with neither poetic nor civil justice served, do not shake off the burden of the status quo. Science fiction, on the other hand, gives us something to strive toward: whatever is educative, is futuristic. For heroines in the making, what could be more fitting than an ethical world in the making?

Ironically, it is the *fantasy* of science fiction which poses the question: of what does our *real* estate consist? and then paints a brave new world, peace-filled and gender-free, and as yet, an a-topia.

Epilogue:
The New Heroine

In Sally Potter's feminist film *Thriller* (1979), a cinematic version of the opera *La Bohème* (1896), the contemporary protagonist Mimi announces that she is looking for a theory for her life, something that will enable her to understand herself. While the character whose namesake she is, Mimi the operatic seamstress, dies of tuberculosis and for love in the best unreflective operatic tradition, this contemporary Mimi scrutinizes literature and people in an effort to discover a revelatory or interpretive theory for herself.[1] In so doing, she deconstructs the romantic heroine/victim, a central operatic tradition, and takes responsibility for self-knowledge and direction. Intelligence becomes an agent of destiny; the melodrama of pathos in *La Bohème* is transformed into a "thriller" of detection and connection.

In this book I have searched for a new theory of women that will help us to understand our lives, as women and as readers, and to draw some conclusions about where we stand now, what we can do, and whether that doing requires a heroine. She is, and we are, subjects in the making.

In *Thriller*, a long beginning sequence depicts Mimi at the mirror, the narcissistic, initial stage of her search for self-understanding. She peers at her image, twisting and turning her neck so that her angle of vision as well as the viewer's is distorted, fragmented, even grotesque; this view of the self derives from narcissism. By the end of the film, which closes with a shot of Mimi embracing another woman, with no mirror in sight, she knows this. Although in this instance I interpret the embrace as lesbian, the implications of the film and the gesture extend beyond sexuality and sexual preference. Exploring what differences really exist between herself (the good suffering girl) and Musetta (the naughty girl, the vamp), modern Mimi challenges the good girl/bad girl polarization which opera, like so many representations of women, takes for granted. In *Thriller* these operatic feminine principles are united, casting retrospective doubt upon myriad other pairings of this sort, such as de Sade's Juliette and Justine. Acknowledging "the other," the cinematic Mimi finds an integrated self.[2] As women, we authenticate each other in our bodies, our experience, our language, just as men bestow manhood upon other men. The recovery which ultimately connects us to the larger community succeeds this recovery of the self and the "other."

To initiate and implement this recovery, as well as to counter false theories about women that maintain gender inequality, feminism undertakes ongoing explorations of women's sexual, political, religious, and social issues. In fact, the lack of such a strong theoretical base may well have weakened the women's movement in the early 1970s. In Chapter 5, we have seen feminist creation of emancipatory strategies that contribute to a new psychology of women. In another sphere, women's letters, journals, diaries, cookery books, and housekeeping accounts, the records that in fact constitute their own social history are being unearthed and published, a development which has begun only in the last twenty years. Additionally, the positive influence of women's biographies and autobiographies cannot even be reckoned yet; these lives between book covers function as surrogate mentors in the imagination, empowering generations after them.

Paralleling and enriching these developments, contemporary poetry and fiction by women provide numerous examples of a shift toward matriarchy: E.D. Broner's *A Weave of Women*, Jill McCorkle's *Tending to Virginia*, Janet Kaufman's *Places in the World a Woman Could Walk* as well as her *Obscene Gestures for Women*, Mermer Blakeslee's *Same Blood* are only a few examples. The enormous popular success of books such as Marion Zimmer Bradley's *The Mists of Avalon*, which retells Arthurian legend from a woman's point of view, shows how women are seizing upon sources of authentication.

For all these reasons, and despite the backlash about which Susan Faludi justifiably cautions us, we are now achieving the selfhood women have lacked heretofore and which is an absolute prerequisite for equality. Recovery through equality was the initial goal of the women's movement both in its nineteenth century incarnation and in its revival in the 1970s. Suffrage, property rights, divorce laws were at issue then; equality of status, pay, health care, professional opportunity are now. But over the last decades of women's liberation, as we have gained some measure of economic and social equality, we have realized that equality by itself, though crucial, is insufficient because it will not automatically correct other social malpractices.

This is where the fortunate women whose lives have improved the most—educated, middle-class, white Western women—are now, in the

1990s. Though there have been in the past individual women with broad
social concerns, as well as a history of cultural feminism which supports
those concerns, for the first time women are beginning on a large scale to
imagine a condition beyond equality, to visualize the immense changes required of any society which seeks to foster feminist values. Feminists stand
behind many causes such as human rights and the anti-nuclear movement
because they interpret these causes, in their engagement with the quality of
life, as feminist in the broadest sense. What difference will this shift in
emphasis from gender equality to a wider social vision make for the heroine in the story? For the individual woman outside the text?

In fact, the two questions are not truly separable. What women propose is the acknowledgment of another's separate, distinct, and participatory presence. Whereas the hero ignores this, the heroine realizes that consent to "otherness" is the essence of both dialogue and relation. (Interestingly, an anti-hero such as Willy Loman in *Death of a Salesman* cannot maintain dialogue. The play is as much about this inability as about anything else.)

Now the implications of opening discourse to dialogic relations go,
for the individual, far beyond the text of the individual life to principles of
governance and moral judgment. Once "truth" and "reality" are not the
pronouncements of a single authoritative voice, the way clears to new formulations of the desirable relation of the self to society, as this book has
attempted to show. Justice, truth, reality, authority, are opened to disruptive debate. When "otherness" has an active voice in the debate, hierarchies
based on race and class as well as on gender can be destabilized.

In both text and life counter-views introduce the theme of "disorder:"
first, in the narrative itself, the *disorder* of the text ruptures patriarchal discourse, making room for new voices; next, the *disordering* of traditional views
of women's "nature" challenges the assumption that "otherness" is inferior
or anomalous; finally, *disorder* strives to replace hierarchical modes in personal and public relations. We need therefore, to reorient ourselves with
regard to terminology generally (as we had to with regard to the terminology of heroism and the terminology of genre) and to regard *disorder* not as
a threat but as a promise, a means of inducing openness and change. This is
why I interpret Jane Flax's title for the final chapter of her book *Thinking
Fragments*, "No Conclusions," as a positive statement.[3]

Thriller, for example, opens and concludes with Mimi sitting alone in
a bare room laughing and laughing. Laughter, one of a cluster of symptoms
of the emotional disorder of hysteria, breaks open the discourse of the film,
enabling change. Even more broadly, comedy, as social critique, proceeds
by disruption. Laughter subverts the binary opposition of self and other.

Mimi's laughter at the film's opening is self-directed mockery. At its close, following the embrace of the two women, the laughter is triumphant.[4] In short, "disorder" can accomplish something.

In order for Mimi to find her voice, a new and contemporary voice, the original nineteenth-century Puccini score of *La Bohème*, upon which *Thriller* is based, is melded with the sound track of Alfred Hitchcock's horror film *Psycho*. But *Thriller* does not segué tidily from one to the other, because as long as the original operatic music is played, Mimi's role is prescribed: she must die for love. To settle the score, the score must be interrupted. We are watching process. Discordant music functions here in the same way as laughter.

If we consider what new interpretations can come to light when disorder questions order, we recall Carol Gilligan's landmark study *In a Different Voice*, which reported that women's interpretation of justice, tempered by skepticism about an abstract, rigid, and uncontextualized justice, differs from men's. Or another example: Making *dialogic* relations a principle is first to make relations a principle: when women enter the lists of crime fiction and science fiction, genres previously dominated by men, they bring an emphasis on relation that found no place when "loners" were the heroes of these fictions.

Disorder as subversion of the status quo lies behind the new-found energy women bring to satirical writing, another conventionally masculinist genre. Insofar as satirical purpose is a judgment upon the public realm, authors such as Fay Weldon, Margaret Atwood, Djuna Barnes, Jeanette Winterson, and Angela Carter offer broad contemporary critiques of society, their satires often expressed in fantasies. Their works are undergirded by feminist values. There is, as Susan Rubin Suleiman phrases it, "subversive intent."[5] If women are "getting back to the meeting," in Carolyn Kizer's phrase, once there they are questioning parliamentary procedure. This is why the comic mode, which requires both intelligence and an outsider's perspective, is a persuasive one for the new heroine. It is especially appealing to women writers and readers who do not wish to be circumscribed by "relational" feminism.

What women can do as individuals in their own stories likewise has shifted its focus from personal development and representation to the goal of dislodging the present powerful/powerless organization of society. As Carolyn Merchant has warned us, the ideology of dualism is based on conquest. And Jean Baker Miller in *Toward a New Psychology of Women*, Starhawk in *Truth or Dare*, Carol Gilligan in *In a Different Voice*, and Ursula Le Guin in *Dancing at the Edge of the World* all separately distinguish "personal power," i.e., power from within, inner strength that comes through a process of trans-formation, from "power-over." This is an important way to think about the disposition of power, and in the implementation of this very project of dis-mantling "power-over," the heroine takes shape. Whereas the epic hero advances with increasing power, and the tragic hero loses his power in a fall (and that's the tragedy), the contemporary heroine resists power-over.

To women, who have excellent cause to distrust it, power seems safer when it is distributed among many agents. The merits of this idea have long been urged. The idea of the decentralization of power has roots going back to Aristotle and has continued since the seventeenth century through the political tradition of liberalism. Thomas Jefferson and James Madison both advocated it, and to this pluralistic tradition, feminism gives a strong as-sent. This means from the outset that the solution to destructive social pa-thologies inflicted on women cannot be a shift from patriarchy to matriar-chy, which would simply constitute a different skewing of power, again com-promising principles of diversity and equality. Oppressive power, power-over, is at the heart of the pathologies we are trying to extirpate from the society at large. Consequently, the functions of a heroine, including a voice of authority, are distributed among many competing protagonists in the text (as we saw in our discussion of feminist crime novels and science fictions). In different terms, the multivocality we are implementing in literature can be extended into political principle.

It is my belief that today's heroine need not be an extraordinary per-son, endowed with extraordinary powers and set apart from her fellows in the manner of the hero. If in the past the heroine was difficult to identify because she was overshadowed by the construct of the hero, she has emerged from the nexus of ordinary women into a position of leadership—but with a modest silhouette, a small *h*. The heroine is ordinary, in the positive and specific sense that she remains concerned with ordinary life; Paula Gunn Allen informs us that even warrior-heroines in Native American fiction do not partake of the customary detachment of soldiers. Rather, they retain an "attachment to self, to relatives, to earth and sky."[6] They neither become nor worship abstraction. Not concerned, for instance, primarily with her own immortality and the honor she must win to ensure it, the heroine need not court death as does the hero. Instead, freed from the hero's obsession with his own mortality and desire to transcend it, she can view the future not as end, but as beginning. She is attached to life.[7]

Breaking down barriers which limit women's contribution to society will enrich the culture by adding complexity through difference, but what's at stake here is larger than female self-expression, obsessed though our society is with self-expression. The heroine reaches beyond the satisfaction of a self as materially based, a core of desire; rather, the first thing individual women can do, in contrast to the many earlier fictional heroines who had moral conviction but no public voice, is to bear witness *aloud*, inside and outside the text. These raised voices have been one of the most encouraging results of the women's movement.

Walter Benjamin regards the loss of community and the basis for shared experience as a lamentable characteristic of modern times. Individual women insist that it is vital for *all* to recognize that child care, abortion, welfare, education, are not "women's issues" any more than AIDS is, or the environment is, or peace is. These problems are, as ordinary heroines, heroines with a small *h* like Helen Caldicott or Rachel Carson argue, human issues urgently requiring the efforts of the whole society. They are, in fact, problems of such global scope as to be almost overwhelming; ultimately, the most important function of the resurgence of feminist utopian fiction may be to help us regain a sense of possibility.

The ordinary heroine, then, is a moral voice and presence; her moral bravery is her criterion of maturity. Furthermore, unlike the hero, whose extraordinary deed occupies a moment in time, her witness continues. And, as literate, educated women increase in numbers, we may perhaps for the first time be of sufficient number for our presence to make a practical difference.

Finally, when women challenge the will to control them, the personal struggle between the sexes for gender equality leads to the broadest social considerations. This is because public issues—the domination of other peoples and nations, the conquest of space and of nature—are, like personal ones, issues of power relations, operating in a manner destructive to the entire society. Suzy McKee Charnas' dystopia *Walk to the Edge of the World* paints the destruction of the world as the result not only of a nuclear explosion but also of the exhaustion of the earth itself, a planet known as "Wasting." Even the reification of youth in our culture, damaging to both men and women, is rooted in this same presumption of control, in this case control over time. Hubristic arrogance permeates modern Western thinking. If everything is manipulable, then everything is an object, and the manipulator is honored only by his ability to subdue, an attitude that may be traced in some measure to the privileged position accorded scientific epistemology. The Faustian myth appears a truer key to understanding our central cultural pathology than does the Oedipal one.

But the pervasive will to conquest, whether Oedipal or Faustian, will not be contested as long as our primary interpretation of the universe is mechanistic rather than organic. The incessant clamor of violence in all corners of the world testifies to the fact that, far from returning to a view of the world as organic, humankind has lost a sense even of *itself* as organic. Order rests upon control, and control in turn relies upon violence. A fascinating sidelight on this shift from organic to mechanistic imaging is the practice at nuclear power plants of bestowing women's names upon the bombs, patting them, addressing them as "baby," to sexualize and thereby animate but also control them in a parody of domestication. Reporting about her experience as an observer of scientists at a nuclear station, Carol Cohn reports that they "gave birth to male progeny with the ultimate power of violent domination over female Nature."[8] That is, the female role, with its imagery of birth and creation, is paradoxically appropriated by nuclear scientists who are at the same time inventing instruments of unthinkable violence toward the archetypal Mother, "Mother Earth."

The new heroinic paradigm, opposing power/over as the *modus operandi* of choice, is as much a responsibility of accountable, flexible leadership in the public domain as it is a partnership in the private one.[9] Pluralism is the logical political extension of the feminist insight into connection and equality. Social hierarchy generally proceeds from economic advantage and protectionism but is supported also by the rationalizations of prejudice. But just as women subvert literary structures, they may deconstruct hierarchical social categories which uphold inequity. They can substitute important ideas of community and difference as indispensable to social equity.

Perhaps any heroine we could define *exactly* would be static, conservative, and inflexible, as heroes are. Women's "disorderliness" may be instrumental in creating a breach through which the whole society may advance—away from patterns of binary opposition, violence, materialism, intolerance, and the no longer unimaginable destruction of nature and humankind.

Endnotes

Prologue

[1] In Yaeger, *Honey-Mad Women*, 126.

[2] Wolf, *Cassandra*, 260.

[3] Revisionist versions of the western hero appear in movies such as *Dances With Wolves*, *The Unforgiven*, and *Posse*; the comic book character Superman is officially defunct. Surely these are significant indicators of new post-heroic directions in our thinking.

[4] *Shakespeare's Sisters* is the title of a collection of essays on women poets, edited by Sandra Gilbert and Susan Gubar.

[5] The contemporary writer Gloria Hull reminds us that though Shakespeare's sisters may be brought to light, they do not speak for black women writers (Gilbert and Gubar, *Shakespeare's Sisters*, 68). In direct contrast to the hero, the heroine for today creates herself in a cultural climate in which multiculturalism has received public recognition, for example, in President Clinton's inaugural address, January 1993.

[6] Marcus, "Laughing at Leviticus," 225.

Chapter 1

[1] "Despite the many taboos surrounding a career on the stage, it was through this profession that women first achieved an individual identity and public recognition." Pauline Schmitt Pantel, ed., and Arthur Goldhammer, trans., *A History of Women in the West*, Vol. 1 (Cambridge: Belknap, 1992), xiii.

[2] In Showalter, *Female Malady*, 230.

[3] Erica Jong's heroine Fanny is much more autonomous, almost a Psyche figure, rescuing her child despite her spineless husband. Adrienne Rich offers a substitute rescuer figure in the person of another woman, a heroine, rather than a hero.

[4] Edmund Spenser, *The Faerie Queene* (Boston: Houghton Mifflin, 1908), Book 1, Canto 1, 1.

[5] See Brownstein, *Becoming a Heroine*.

[6] Gillian Clarke, "Letter From A Far Country," *Selected Poems* (Manchester: Carcanet, 1985), 55.

[7] "Marriage is to girls what war is to boys." *Annales*, E.S.C. 6 (1959-1973). Pantel, *A History of Women in the West*, 525, fn 25.

[8] In these matches of equality, the hero, having abjured 'manliness,' suffers the romantic fate, i.e. dying for love. He voluntarily pursues the Love Plot instead of the Quest.

[9] In order to become part of the male world, Russian science fiction writer Katerina Clark suggests, "the youth is taken away from the mother or female dominated world in which he has lived until then." Green, "Asteroid," 131.

[10] Greenspan, *New Approach*, 212-13.

[11] Marianne Hirsch identifies what she describes as a separate female novel of growth, "Spiritual Bildung: The Beautiful Soul as Paradigm," in Elizabeth Abel, Marianne Hirsch, Elizabeth Langland, eds., *The Voyage In: Fictions of Female Development* (Hanover N.H.: University Press of New England, 1983). The problem is that such a view facilitates an unfortunate separation, explored in a subsequent chapter, between spiritual and physical powers. Nevertheless, *The Voyage In* remains a seminal work about the relation between female *Bildungsroman* and genre itself.

[12] Lessing, *Diaries of Jane Somers*, 196.

[13] Work is organized largely along gender lines. That is, at issue here is not only equal pay for equal labor, but the rules of labor assignment. Those occupations with a preponderance of women workers are those, like nursing, which have been seen as appropriate to women's 'natural' proclivities. What women do is changing now, in part as a result of challenging these 'natural' boundaries. One example is that of women athletes, who are revising previous estimates of the limits of women's bodies in competitive athletics. Another aspect of 'women's work' is the enormous back-up and service work that women supply in times of military engagement. See Cynthia Enloe, *Does Khaki Become You?: The Militarization of Women's Lives* (Boston: South End Press, 1983).

[14] J. D. Broverman, D. M. Broverman, F. E. Clarkson, P. S. Rosencrantz, and S. R. Vogel, "Sex-role stereotypes and clinical judgements of mental health," *Journal of Consulting and Clinical Psychology* 34 (1970), 1-7.

[15] Interestingly, during the Gulf War, the *Boston Globe*, (January 20, 1992), 33, reported that Saddam Hussein was "holed up with . . . a cache of 16mm prints of movies by his favorite actor, John Wayne."

[16] Ernst Junger, cited in the *Times Literary Supplement*, August 10-16, 1990, 842.

[17] See Hartsock, "Masculinity, Heroism," 139.

[18] Rigoberta Menchú's self-portrait, *I, Rigoberta Menchú: An Indian Woman in Guatemala*, shows her as a "spirit-warrior," one concerned with humanity at large, whose task is, importantly, to educate: "Women have had a great history. They've all experienced terrible things, whether they be working-class women, peasant women, or teachers. . . . We don't . . . want power, but . . . something [to] be left for human beings. And this gives us the courage to be steadfast in the struggle, in spite of the danger." Trans. Ann Wright (New York: Verso, 1983), 233. Menchú's work, as Barbara E.Gottlieb points out, "unites indigenous and European-descended Guatemalans in the struggle for human rights, demilitarization, and decent treatment for agricultural workers." *CovertAction* (Spring 1992), 37. I am grateful to Judith Nies for drawing Roberta Blackgoat, to my attention.

[19] Carter, *Passion*, 53.

[20] The Hero and his derivatives are firmly attached to conservative values. His conception of honor, of chivalry, are fixed by that society whose best exemplar he is. He has to be, as it were, preconceived, since his function is to restore and

redeem his society to its prior state from whatever blight temporarily overwhelms it. He is conservative because he is literally a conservator of the status quo.

[21]By definition, masquerade, circus, carnival are inclusive, (circus even literally taking place in a circle) and therefore have a correspondence to the definition of Woman/Space discussed here and developed in Chapter 2. These sub-genres of comedy are about variety, multivocality (think of the exuberance of having three rings!), not about singularity of narrator or narrative. They deliberately confound reality and fantasy. Their strong element of fantasy enables us to ask "What if . . ?" even more than we do in most other fictional proposals, and this is a vital question for women who are trying to image different worlds for their changed roles. That is, these modes of comedy are asking the same questions raised at the intersection of genre and gender and discussed in this chapter: "What is the relation of truth to fiction?" and "How is that truth gendered?"

Moreover for women, whose designation as "other" incurs for them the continual risk of being Freud's *unheimlich* or uncanny, being "grotesques," what comedies such as Angela Carter's *Nights at the Circus* and Djuna Barnes' *Nightwood* present in their language is a diction for "otherness," a hybrid discourse of high style juxtaposed to obscenity and slang. These novels exercise inventiveness outside a familiar *weltanschauung*, presenting instead a *subfusc* world peopled by dwarfs, creatures half animal-half human, a nighttime world brought up to daylight for scrutiny. In their marginalized characters and concern for the oppressed they speak to the reality of women's experience. The openness and accommodation of their language allows women to occupy their stage. Certainly postmodernism shares the innovative layering of diction, but hybridization serves a different function in Barnes' and Carter's comedies; in them, the marginalized body becomes the normative body. The carnivalesque body, like the hysteric body, speaks the unspeakable, dramatizes the grotesque and hybrid. Women comprise one sector of this reality.

This deliberate comic strategy, centralizing what is marginal, employing marginalization to fix attention on the grotesque, is necessary because our western Judeo-Christian culture offers strong resistance to any idea of hybridization. We are fearful of losing our homogeneity. According to Paula Gunn Allen, spiritual traditions which lie outside the mainstream, such as those of Native Americans, are perceived as "other" and therefore as contaminants. The co-existence of differing spiritual beliefs has historically been difficult to attain; the validation that the traditions of many indigenous peoples accord hybridization makes them even more suspect to mainstream culture. Whereas stories of transmogrification (flora, fauna, animal, human changing into and out of each other) were once accepted as tokens of our commonality and continuity with all natural life, a way of understanding the universe as in the *Gilgamesh* epic or Ovid's *Metamorphoses*, in our culture at this time transmogrification survives only in occasional revels such as Mardi Gras, where celebrants don animal skins and furs, bird feathers, masks of other creature/kinds, flouting, *with permission*, for a discrete period, the injunctions against hybridization. To the contrary, acceptance of transmogrification is still integral to Inuits, Africans, Native Americans, and many other cultures.

Costume affects and announces change of identity, and that is why it can be threatening. Foucault maintains that *masquerade* is about the change of sexual identity; this is preeminently clear in the adoption of drag. Drag targets the boundaries between bodies, between sexes, and incorporates grotesquerie to turn definitions of identity inside out. Some of this unruliness or disorder operates within the framework of established institutions, as Mardi Gras before Lent, for example, is tolerated within the Catholic Church. But this containment of the King of Misrule should not blind us to the fact that there are profound implications to cross-dressing, as Marjorie Garber's recent book *Vested Interests: Cross-Dressing and Cultural Anxiety* informs us. We must recognize that such outbreaks of disorderly conduct defy not only Christian but intellectual faith, the Enlightenment legacy which joins Christian faith in privileging mind over body. More immediately, for women drag actualizes the separation of sex and gender, demonstrating that the two are not identical, that gender is a social construct. Moreover, the shifting definitions of gender and sex are blended. For the heroine, who must emerge from the construction of a gender role which deprives her of leadership, public acknowledgement of the separation of sex and gender is crucial. Circus, masquerade, carnival are licensed precisely in this separation.

[22] *Radcliffe News* (Winter 1991), 5.

[23] Bei Dao, "Comet," in *The August Sleepwalker*, trans. Bonnie S. McDougall (New York: New Directions, 1988), 69.

[24] Jane Flax's theoretical interpretation of our cultural experience as *Thinking Fragments*, finds its literary parallel in the 'fantastic realism' of Sylvia Townsend Warner's *Lolly Willowes, or The Loving Huntsman* (New York: Viking: 1926); Joanna Russ's *The Female Man*; and Angela Carter's *Nights at the Circus*.

[25] Wolf, *Cassandra*, 262.

[26] Joanna Russ, "What Can a Heroine Do? Or Why Women Can't Write," Cornillon, ed., *Images of Women*, 12.

[27] See Hite, *Other Side of the Story*.

[28] Russo, "Female Grotesques," 219.

[29] Walter Pater quoted in Fraya Katz-Stoker, "Feminism vs. Formalism," in Cornillon, ed., *Images of Women*, 323. Here we may note that Robert Lowell criticized Anne Sexton's later poetry for its lack of adherence to formal structure, whereas she felt she was forging an instrument which would convey the experience of madness. Middlebrook, *Anne Sexton*, 181.

[30] Showalter, *Female Malady*, 219. Also for a fictional treatment of male hysteria induced by war, see Pat Barker's recent novel, *Regeneration*, which focuses on the breakdown and subsequent treatment of World War I infantryman and poet, Siegfried Sassoon.

[31] See Poovey, "Scenes of an Indelicate Character," and Kaledin, "Dr. Manners."

[32] Some feminist psychologists point out that women are socialized to be attuned to flux. Because of their key role in child development, the argument runs, they are closer to the actual dynamics of change within the social unit. See Sara Ruddick, *Maternal Thinking*.

Chapter 2

[1] Bartky, *Femininity*, 68.

[2] De Lauretis, "Desire in Narrative," in *Alice Doesn't*, 143.

[3] Lesser, *Life Below the Ground*, 128.

[4] Mary Daly, *Gyn/Ecology: The Metaethics of Radical Feminism* (Boston: Bea-

con, 1978), 2. Perhaps more than any other single fiction, Angela Carter's novel of an apocalyptic world after a war of the sexes, *The Passion of New Eve* delineates the frightening proportions of this fear.

[5] Showalter, *Female Malady*. Statistics from the National Association of Anorexia Nervosa and Associated Disorders show that seven million American women suffer from anorexia and bulimia. *Boston Globe*, April 29, 1992: 47.

[6] There are innumerable contemporary literary examples of the connection between hunger for food and erotic hunger, and the relation of both of these to power; for an extended fictive treatment see Margaret Atwood's novel, *The Edible Woman*. See also "The Cardinal's Third Tale," in *Last Tales* by Isak Dinesen (herself possibly an anorectic); Lucille Clifton's poem, "to thelma who worried because I couldn't cook," in *Good Woman: Poems and a Memoir*; Anne Sexton's *The Awful Rowing Toward God*, in which she incorporates the metaphor of the communion service, "Here, take my body and eat."

The most explicit reference to the intimate connection between erotic hunger and the hunger for food which I have come across occurs in the Japanese film, *Tampopo*, in which the two lovers, in preliminary love play, pass an egg back and forth between their mouths. For a theoretical discussion of the relation of food to eroticism, see Michie, *Flesh Made Word*; Gilbert and Gubar, *Madwoman in the Attic*; Yaeger, *Honey-Mad Women*; and Suleiman, ed., *The Female Body in Western Culture*.

[7] For a full-length discussion of the relation of women to the rise of the novel see Brownstein, *Becoming a Heroine*.

[8] In his recent book *The Good Enough Mother*, Bruno Bettelheim tries to lighten the almost inevitable maternal guilt our society induces by making 'good' a signification of degree, rather than kind. For a further exploration of this point see Susan Rubin Suleiman's "On Maternal Splitting: Apropos of Mary Gordon's *Men and Angels*," and Chodorow and Contratto's "Fantasy of the Perfect Mother."

[9] Benjamin, "Desire of One's Own," 84.

[10] Miller, *Good Mother*, 23.

[11] Kennedy, *Ironweed*, 52-53.

[12] See also Hilde Bruch's study of anorexia entitled *The Gilded Cage: The Enigma of Anorexia Nervosa*.

[13] Alicia Borinsky, "Jean Rhys: Poses of a Woman," in Suleiman, *The Female Body*, 299.

[14] Such reversal is conspicuously operative in Degas' painting "The Interior," and many of the Balthus portraits of young girls.

[15] For a discussion of genteel employments such as embroidery which enabled women to "kill time," see Michie, *Flesh Made Word*.

[16] These values are upheld and promulgated in the cinema: from *Mildred Pierce* to *Working Girl*, ambition is presented as the nether pole to femininity. Even talent does not justify ambition. For example, in the film *Autumn Sonata*, the mother's pianistic career is shown to have been achieved by her sacrifice of the daughter, and at the ultimate price of her own unhappiness.

[17] Doane, *Desire to Desire*, 179.

[18] Not surprisingly, the motif of arson is not uncommon as a female response to "the cage." Dido is the example *par excellence*, first burning with desire, then consumed on a pyre. I am indebted to Jane Marcus for the example of Marguerite

Yourcenar's heroine in *Fires* (New York: Farrar, Straus, Giroux, 1981).

[19] Two other examples: Mary Oliver's poem, "Sleeping in the Forest" from her collection *Twelve Moons*: "I thought the earth / remembered me, she / took me back so tenderly" (Boston: Little, Brown: 1979), 3; and Isak Dinesen's heroine in "The Caryatids: An Unfinished Gothic Tale," whose heroine plaintively inquires "Might we not . . . want to . . . sleep in the woods at night?" in *Last Tales* (New York: Random House: 1957), 132.

[20] The motif of flying is another response to "the cage," and figures prominently in women's fantasies. In Isak Dinesen's story, "The Supper at Elsinore," the dinner table discussion includes a hypothetical argument about whether the heroine Fanny should accept a pair of wings if she were offered them. She declares that she would, and is reproved by the gentlemen present, including the Bishop, who states that women should not fly. Though the gentlemen wish for an "angel in the house," they foreground the house and repress the wings; they demand she be that oxymoron, an earth-bound angel. See also Erica Jong's *Fear of Flying*. Flying, for both sexes, is also a metaphor for creating, as in "a flight of the imagination." Poet Nikki Giovanni, seizing a grand role of autonomy and freedom, declares in "Ego Tripping":

> I am so perfect so divine so ethereal so surreal
> I cannot be comprehended
> except by my permission
> I mean . . . I . . . can fly
> like a bird in the sky . . .

Like Fevvers, the heroine of Marguerite Yourcenar's novel *Fires* is an aerialiste, a symbolic profession for a heroine.

[21] This raises a debatable point for feminists: is the woman character empowered, made a heroine, through an identification with Nature, or does Nature's own vulnerability to man-made force inevitably render this empowerment problematic?

[22] For a full discussion of this, see Frank Kermode, *The Sense of an Ending: Studies in the Theory of Fiction* (New York: Oxford University Press, 1967), and Roland Barthes, *The Pleasure of the Text* (New York: Hill and Wang, 1975).

Chapter 3

[1] Fetishism depends upon the acceptance of essentialism. Since it is far more common among men than among women, one may speculate that it is easier for men to credit the existence of "an essence of womanhood" than vice versa. For discussion of this point, see chapter 9, "The Disembodied Body of Marilyn Monroe," in Wendy Lesser, *His Other Half: Men Looking at Women Through Art*.

[2] Bottigheimer, *Bad Girls*, 87.

[3] Carter also produced an anthology, *The Old Wives' Fairy Tale Book* (New York: Pantheon, 1990), in which she questions "good girls and where it gets them." This same viewpoint informs Jill McCorkle's short story, "Sleeping Beauty, Revised," in *Crash Diet: Stories*.

[4] Kenneth Clark, *The Nude* (London: John Murray, 1956).

[5] Miles, *Carnal Knowing*, 142.

[6] Rubin, "Traffic in Women."

[7] Gubar, "Blank Page," 303.

[8] Sexton, "Self in 1958," in *Live or Die* (Boston: Houghton Mifflin, 1966), 73; Fenton, "Masks," in Howe and Bass, eds., *No More Masks*, 298.

[9] Michie, *Flesh Made Word*, 87.

[10] Gubar, "Blank Page," 293.

[11] Ibid., 298.

[12] See Linda Ray Pratt, "The Abuse of Eve by the New World Adam," in Cornillon, *Images of Women*, 162.

[13] Lillian Robinson and Lise Vogel,"Modernism and History," in Lillian Robinson, *Sex, Class, and Culture* (Bloomington: Indiana University Press, 1978), 41.

[14] Wolf, *Cassandra*, 227.

[15] In Robinson and Vogel, "Modernism and History," 42.

[16] In Lesser, *His Other Half*, 78.

[17] Robinson and Vogel, "Modernism and History," 42.

[18] Cornillon "The Fiction of Fiction" in Cornillon, *Images of Women*, 126.

[19] Benjamin, "Desire of One's Own," in de Lauretis, *Feminist Studies*, 92, 98.

[20] Acceptance of the lack of signification leads Lacan to join Freud in postulating that women are castrated, and therefore unable to be satisfied.

[21] "And O that awful deepdown torrent O and the sea the sea crimson sometimes like fire and the glorious sunsets," James Joyce, *Ulysses* (New York: Modern Library, 1961), 783.

[22] Carol M. Armstrong, "Edgar Degas and the Representation of the Female Body," in Suleiman, *Female Body*, 228.

[23] Kristeva, *Powers of Horror*, 163.

[24] In the *New Yorker*, Ingrid Sischy looks at the work of the Edwardian Clementina Lady Hawarden and the contemporary photographer Cindy Sherman: "Together, they suggest how dressing up could be used as a thread to weave in and out of the history of photography in order to help find what has been missing: the presence of women" (May 6, 1991), 96. The point is that between these two women photographers, a period of almost a century, the same absence prevails.

[25] Both the aestheticization of Foucault and that of the representations in painting which we've been discussing also leave out the important idea of the self-in-relation, to use Jean Baker Miller's term.

[26] Kristeva, *Powers of Horror*, 163.

[27] Reporting on fashions for the coming season, Holly Brubach in the *New Yorker* notes the male fantasies expressed in the world of fashion design for women, and queries: "Where, I wonder, are women's fantasies?" (July 6, 1992), 66.

[28] Bartky, "Foucault, Femininity and the Modernization of Patriachal Power," in *Femininity and Domination*, 78. As an extension of Bartky's point about the yet-to-be-imagined, it will be interesting to watch whether women's fantasies produce pornography about male bodies. Currently, pornography is assumed to be visual violence against women, and feminist critics like Catharine MacKinnon link pornography to actual violence against women. But we have yet to see whether the absence of pornography created by women is a consequence of the broader missing expression of female desire.

[29] The new look at women on the part of women film directors created new representations of women and a focus on their concerns. At the Telluride Film

Festival in 1991 directors Martha Coolidge (*Ramblin' Rose*), Jody Foster (*Little Man Tate*), and Nancy Savoca (*Dogfight*) brought women's issues to the screen for the first time in the Festival's 18 years of existence.

[30] An interesting sidelight on the "femininity" of the heroine are the larger-than-life female figures painted by the seventeeth century artist, Artemisia Gentilleschi, herself a rape victim. Women like Judith, Gael, Salome, are created as heroinic. Though they are active, assertive, passionate, as large as classical Heroes, they are not evil. I am grateful to Professor Nancy Scott of Brandeis University for calling my attention to these unusual representations.

[31] Jong, *Fear of Flying*, 9, 10-11, 96-97.

[32] Alther, *Kinflicks*, 350.

[33] Though Diane Wood Middlebrook's biography of Anne Sexton makes Sexton's relation to her daughter's body literal not metaphoric, the poem expresses a relation frequently found in other women's writing. For a discussion of the erotic strand in the mother/daughter relationship, see Alicia Ostriker's *Stealing the Language*.

[34] Jong, *Fear of Flying*, 11.

[35] See Butler, *Gender Trouble*, 121.

[36] See also Marianne Hirsch, *The Mother/Daughter Plot*. Hirsch argues on the opposing side of this point. Uncovering a submerged mother/daughter plot in *La Princesse de Clèves*, Hirsch sees that close relation as creating expectations of affiliation that are misleading and doom the Princess to disillusioning repetitions.

[37] Butler, *Gender Trouble*.

[38] Carter, *Passion of New Eve*, 7.

[39] Weldon, *Life and Loves*, 5.

[40] This issue is developed by Nancy K. Miller in *Subject to Change: Reading Feminist Writing*.

[41] Wendy Lesser corroborates this interpretation. In her discussion of Cecil Beaton's obsession with the vanity and narcissism of the feminine, and his consequent use of mirrors and other reflecting surfaces in his portrayal of them, Lesser concludes that Beaton depicts women actually looking at something other than themselves. See *His Other Half: Men Looking at Women Through Art*. For a book-length discussion of the mirror and its role in the identity of women, see *Herself Beheld: The Literature of the Looking Glass* by Jennijoy La Belle.

[42] Linda Tschirhart Sanford, *Women and Self-Esteem: Understanding and Improving the Way We Think and Feel About Ourselves* (Garden City: Anchor, 1984), 229.

[43] Elizabeth Fenton, "Masks," in Howe and Bass, eds., *No More Masks*, 298.

[44] If, as D.W. Winnicott maintains, the mother is the only mirror of the infant, her own underdeveloped or postponed self-regard may be a positive function of her self-in-relation.

[45] Ostriker, *Stealing the Language*, 187.

[46] Virginia Woolf, *A Room of One's Own* (Harmondworth, Middlesex:Penguin, 1965), 37.

[47] Miles, *Carnal Knowing*, 125-139.

[48] Fraser, "Poem in Which My Legs Are Accepted," in Howe and Bass, eds., *No More Masks*, 253.

[49] Barba, "A Cycle of Women," in *Rising Tides: Twentieth Century American Women Poets*, Laura Chester and Sharon Barba, eds. (New York: Washington Square, 1973), 356.

⁵⁰ Clifton, "What the Mirror Said," in *Good Woman*, 169.

⁵¹ Weldon, *Life and Loves*, 5.

⁵² Fainlight, "It Must," in Couzyn, ed., *The Bloodaxe Book*, 139. If the older woman is commonly presented as unworthy and therefore invisible to the mirror, the younger woman, if she displays an excess of unbridled emotion—the violation of feminine decorum—is also grotesque. See Mary Russo, "Female Grotesques."

⁵³ Cooper, "The Knowledge That Comes Through Experience," in Howe and Bass, eds., *No More Masks*, 161.

⁵⁴ Jong, *Fear of Flying*, 311.

⁵⁵ Dinesen, "The Supper at Elsinore," in *Seven Gothic Tales*, 220.

⁵⁶ Macdonald, "The Stained Glass Woman," in *Transplants* (New York: George Braziller, 1976), 3.

⁵⁷ Michie, *Flesh Made Word*, 125.

⁵⁸ Levertov, "Abel's Bride," in Gilbert and Gubar, eds., *Norton Anthology* (New York: W.W. Norton, 1985), 1949.

⁵⁹ Gilbert and Gubar, "The Mirror and the Vamp."

⁶⁰ Sexton, "Double Image," in *To Bedlam and Part Way Back* (Boston: Houghton Mifflin, 1960), 60.

⁶¹ Kizer, "Pro Femina," in Howe and Bass, eds., *No More Masks*, 174.

⁶² Sexton "Snow White and the Seven Dwarfs," in *Transformations* (Boston: Houghton Mifflin, 1971), 3.

⁶³ In Lacanian terms, *jouissance* exists outside the male symbolic order, anyway. Lynda Hart's *Making a Spectacle: Feminist Essays on Contemporary Women's Theatre* (Ann Arbor: University of Michigan, 1989) is a book-length elaboration of the application of this idea to theater.

⁶⁴ Bulfinch, *Mythology: The Age of Fable, The Age of Chivalry, Legends of Charlemagne* (New York: Crowell, 1970), 116.

⁶⁵ Another example of the power held to reside in the hair is, of course, the famous one of Samson and Delilah. Shearing his locks is a symbolic castration by which she renders him powerless.

⁶⁶ Neumann, *The Great Mother: An Analysis of the Archetype*, trans. Ralph Manheim (New York: Pantheon, 1955), 38.

⁶⁷ Napier, "Greek Art." The castration myth as a variant of death is not only associated with a "monster" like Medusa, but because of her double-valenced power, with Aphrodite, Goddess of Love. Legend has it that she shaped herself out of the "immortal flesh" of the sexual organs of the oldest god, Uranus, who was castrated by his son Kronos at the behest of his raped mother, Gaea (earth). Interestingly, we meet castration myths in matriarchal as well as patriarchal mythologies, where the function of the hero (the obverse of the young maidens sent to Minos once a year for sacrifice to the Minotour) was to unite with the tribal mother annually in a "sacred marriage," and then to be sacrificed (castrated?) in a solemn ceremonial. The male fear of castration may well have origins in historical events.

⁶⁸ Cf. the following invocation in which we discover that in-dwelling of opposites, generative/dissociative, for which women prize the goddess:

in one hand she holds the sun
and the moon in the other. . . .

The moon the virgin
mother
patroness of harlots. . . .

She dangles the dark key of the infernal regions
between her imperious fingers
Queen of the Underworld Empress of Demons.

Maze-queen corn-queen barley-queen
fructifier quickener pestilence-bringer
queen of the crucible. . . .

Kali Maria Aphrodite
Jocasta
Jocasta. Jocasta. Jocasta.

Carter, *The Passion of New Eve*, 61-62.

[69] Charles Blinderman takes note in his essay, "The Servility of Dependence: The Dark Lady in Trollope," of Trollope's assumption that the female gaze is emasculating. He cites Trollope's novel *The Bertrams*, in which Lotta Schmidt "stares back when stared at," and is described by Trollope as possessing "'no feminine softness,' no 'young shame.'" Since she is a Jewess, this impropriety is attributed to her Oriental exoticism, but nonetheless, the author characterizes her as "the breath of destruction." In Cornillon, *Images of Women in Fiction*, 63.

[70] Freud, "Medusa's Head," in *Freud on Women: A Reader*, ed. Elisabeth Young-Bruehl (New York: Norton, 1990), 272.

[71] Kristeva, *Powers of Horror*, 155.

[72] Adcock, "Kilpeck," in Couzyn, ed., *The Bloodaxe Book*, 203.

[73] Sarah Lefanu, in her study of feminism and science fiction, points to a feminist revision of the vampire. She writes, "The image of the vampire represents transgression, the breaking of social codes, a denial of death. It is interesting to note that so many women writers are attracted by this image for the vampire is traditionally a male figure, active over his female victims' passivity. . . . It is perhaps that identification with the vampire figure allows a claim to be made for a libertarian sexuality for women, a transgression . . . from the constraints of social order." *Feminism and Science Fiction*, 83.

[74] Elias-Button, "The Muse as Medusa," 202. Jefferson Humphries speculates that "the male poet listens to the muse and brings a report; the female poet turns into muse or siren and sings a music which she will not translate into theory." "Muse Figures: Notes on Gender Difference in Poetry." *The Michigan Quarterly Review* (Winter 1991): 106.

[75] Wittig, *Les Guérillères*, 52.

[76] Sarton, "The Muse as Medusa," in Gilbert and Gubar, eds., 1777.

[77] Lindsey, "Medusa," in *Falling off the Roof* (Cambridge: Alice James, 1975), 22.

[78] Noteworthy for its relevance to this topic is E. Ann Kaplan's *Motherhood and Representation: The Mother in Popular Culture and Melodrama* (New York: Routledge, 1992).

Chapter 4

[1] Pratt, *Archetypal Patterns*, 174.

[2] Weldon, *Life and Loves*, 277.

[3] Since many women psychologists such as Miriam Greenspan and Jean Baker Miller draw a sharp line between "personal power" and "power over others," I have used the words autonomy or subjectivity to keep this distinction clear.

[4] Agosin, "Fairy Tales and Something More," in *Witches*, 17.

[5] Sexton, "Snow White," in *Transformations*, 6.

[6] Agosin, "Fairy Tales and Something More," in *Witches*, 17.

[7] Jean Baker Miller reports, to the contrary, in *Toward a New Psychology of Women*, that the language of women even in the description of the sexual act, centers on the idea of the gift.

[8] We should note in passing the many charming books for children starring beneficent witches, e.g., *Lolly Willowes* by Sylvia Townsend Warner, *The Wizard of Oz* by Frank Baum, and *The Golden Key* by George MacDonald.

[9] I am grateful to Miriam Goodman for pointing out to me that the "ordinary eighties witch" may be a woman cast out by her husband, impoverished by divorce, who takes on a witch's identity: outrageous in her appearance, outspoken in her language, a dangerous model for young girls, and an object of fear on the part of society.

[10] See Miles, *Carnal Knowing*.

[11] Aeschylus, *The Oresteia*, in Wolf, *Cassandra*, 222.

[12] Shakespeare, *King Lear*, act 4, scene 6, line 20.

[13] Klee, in Djikstra, *Idols of Perversity*, 282.

[14] But these paintings and writings also contain a more covert message. By moralizing about the undesirability of animals, and at the same time juxtaposing them to the figures of desirable women, we are made to feel, beyond the sexual sphere, a profound threat of hybridization, the elision of boundaries, of the loss of racial homogeneity and ethnic purity. See chapter 1, endnote 21.

[15] Djikstra, *Idols of Perversity*, 325.

[16] Carter, *Passion*, 87.

[17] Jarrell, "In Nature There Is Neither Right Nor Left Nor Wrong," in *The Complete Poems* (New York: Farrar, Straus & Giroux, 1972), 331.

[18] Carter, *Passion*, 59.

[19] W. B. Yeats, "Sailing to Byzantium," *The Collected Poems* (New York: Macmillan, 1956), 191.

[20] Bogan, "The Crows," in Howe and Bass, eds., *No More Masks*, 70.

[21] I am grateful to Mary Russo's work on the female grotesque for bringing to my attention these figures.

[22] Sexton, "The Gold Key," in *Transformations*, 1.

[23] Pratt, *Archetypal Patterns*, 176.

[24] These terms, black and white, standing respectively for evil and good, are descended from the original German and the tales of witches in the Black Forest. Though this color distinction strikes us today as objectionably racist, it obtains in any situation in which the outsider (bad) is contrasted with the representative of the dominant group (good). In literature, for example, we encounter the fair heroine of the Victorian novel juxtaposed to the dark-haired Jewess; or the innocent white-clad

hero, Billy Budd, confronting a Captain, his tormentor, garbed in black. Though our awakened consciousness may deplore it, color is widely used as a moral index.

[25] Wittig, *Les Guérillères*, 89-90.

[26] Sonya Rudikoff, "How They Thought About Sexuality in Late Antiquity," *Hudson Review* (Summer 1989), 312.

[27] Characteristically, as Jean Baker Miller informs us, any dominant group retains for itself the power to impose its own stories and repress alternative stories. Yet our definition of history itself is finally changing from one which chronicles power to a more inclusive social history along the lines Walter Benjamin proposed.

[28] Scarf, *Unfinished Business*, 388.

[29] Ibid., 389.

[30] Showalter, *Female Malady*, 154.

[31] Scarf, *Unfinished Business*, 400-401.

[32] Rich, "Snapshots of a Daughter-in-Law," in Howe and Bass, eds., *No More Masks*, 195.

[33] In Chapter 7 we will see how the lyric organization of language is able to retain some of the compositional structure of the garden and the quilt.

[34] Stimpson, "Adrienne Rich and Lesbian/Feminist Poetry," in *Parnassus: Poetry in Review* (1985), 263.

[35] Randall, "To William Wordsworth From Virginia," in Howe and Bass, eds., *No More Masks*, 159.

[36] Weldon, *Life and Loves*, 11.

[37] Shakespeare, *The Tempest*, act 1, scene 2, 364-365.

[38] Agosin, "Witch They Call Me," in *Witches and Other Things*, 15.

[39] Elizabeth Bishop, "Invitation to Miss Marianne Moore," in *The Complete Poems* (New York: Farrar, Straus and Giroux, 1969), 94.

[40] Wolf, *Cassandra*, 161.

[41] Leo Steinberg, unpublished Leventritt Lecture, Harvard University, 1986.

[42] Stephen Dobyns "Katia Reading," *The Balthus Poems* (New York: Atheneum, 1982), 36.

[43] Jane Gallop, "Annie Leclerc Writing a Letter, with Vermeer," in Nancy K. Miller, ed., *The Poetics of Gender* (New York: Columbia, 1986), 139.

[44] Zbigniew Herbert, "The Discreet Charm of the Bourgeoisie," in *Still Life With A Bridle: Essays and Apocrypha*, trans. John and Bogdana Carpenter (New York: Ecco, 1991), 71.

[45] Sexton, "The Gold Key," *Transformations*, 1.

[46] Lauter, *Women as Mythmakers*, 65 ,69, 76.

[47] W. B. Yeats, *The Collected Poems* (New York: Macmillan, 1956), 252.

[48] Goethe, *Faust*, in Wolf, *Cassandra*, 280.

[49] We should note here that the pre-verbal or pre-oedipal stage as it is also termed, has been defined by Nancy Chodorow as the maternal stage of influence for both sexes.

[50] Rosemary Dinnage, "White Magic: Persuasions of the Witch's Craft: Ritual Magic in Contemporary England," *New York Review of Books* (October 12, 1989), 6.

[51] Gwendolyn Brooks, "The Crazy Woman," in *Blacks* (Chicago: Third World Press, 1987), 360.

[52] Margaret Walker, "Molly Means," in *This Is My Century: New and Collected Poems* (Athens: University of Georgia Press, 1989), 26.

⁵³ D.H. Lawrence in Wolf, *Cassandra*, 245.
⁵⁴ Lucille Clifton, "the coming of Kali," in *Good Woman*, 135.
⁵⁵ Lessing, *Diaries of Jane Somers*, 12.
⁵⁶ Le Guin, *Dancing*, 5.
⁵⁷ Ibid., 4.
⁵⁸ For a full treatment of this topic see Carolyn Heilbrun, *Writing a Woman's Life*, and Margaret Morganroth Gullette, *Safe At Last in the Middle Years: The Invention of the Midlife Progress Novel: Saul Bellow, Margaret Drabble, Anne Tyler, and John Updike* (Berkeley: University of California Press, 1988).

Chapter 5

¹ As Nancy Willard has pointed out, a priestess, according to Webster's dictionary, is defined as "a girl or woman who officiates in sacred rites, especially of a pagan religion." Significantly, however, Webster's does not mention the word "pagan" in its definition of a priest.
² Curiously, Freud termed Christianity "regressive" because he felt the position it accorded the Virgin was a step toward the reinstatement of the Mother Goddess.
³ Ann McCoy, *Arts Magazine* (February 1989), 69.
⁴ Tennyson, "Guinevere," *Poems of Tennyson* (London: Oxford University Press, 1926), 597.
⁵ Gillian Clarke, "Letter from a Far Country," in *Selected Poems* (Manchester: Carcanet, 1985), 64.
⁶ See Gimbutas, *The Civilization of the Goddess: The World of Old Europe* and endnote 59, below.
⁷ The title of one of Nancy Spero's paintings, *Active Histories*, as well as the inter-positioning of ancient and contemporary figures, lends additional support to the notion of past "mothers" informing and enabling present "daughters." *Nancy Spero: Works Since 1950* (Syracuse: Everson Museum of Art, 1987).
⁸ Wolf, *Cassandra*, 195.
⁹ Naomi Scheman, "Missing Mothers, Desiring Daughters." 85, n. 45. In this light, it is interesting to read Toni Morrison's *Beloved* as a retelling of the Medea story, with the revenge contextualized so that the heroine's desperation, resulting in infanticide, transforms the motive of revenge into what is, by her lights, deliverance from slavery.
¹⁰ For additional discussion of this point, see Cynthia Navaretta, ed., *Voices of Women: Three Critics on Three Poets on Three Heroines* (New York: Midmarch Associates, 1980).
¹¹ Gilbert and Gubar, "The Mirror and the Vamp."
¹² Women's values seek new structures for expression. Women's values must also discover a concrete, accepted, and consensual vocabulary. As psychiatrist Jean Baker Miller informs us, there is, for example, no psychiatric vocabulary yet to express women's values, though there is a vast psychiatric discourse. In fact, fascinating questions arise in the consideration of women's discourse, a discourse capable of conveying both immanent and transcendent experience. For instance, will there be a "feminine sublime," Patricia Yeager wonders, that will enable women "to seize the grand roles formerly allotted to men?" Yet one that will not be hierarchical, male, and martial, as she perceives the style characterized as "the sublime"

now to be? Will such language blend with the feisty, personal, colloquial style which is emerging in much of femininst creative writing? French femininst scholarship, particularly the work of Julia Kristeva and Luce Irigaray, explores a feminine specificity in language, the notion that difference is signified in speech.

[13] Relational feminism, as commentators make clear, argues in favor of de-emphasizing the cult of the individual.

[14] Jong, *Fear of Flying*, 100.

[15] Adrienne Rich, "Natural Resources," *The Dream of A Common Language: Poems 1974-1977* (New York: Norton, 1978), 67.

[16] May Sarton, "My Sisters, O My Sisters," in Gilbert and Gubar, eds., *Norton Anthology*, 1773.

[17] Wittig, *Les Guérillères*, 58. This novel presents problems for many readers, aside from the issue of commonality vs. individuality. The woman warrior is not constrained by the law of the Father; she indulges her own sexual desires; she is a combatant on the field of war. That is, the book proceeds by role reversal and so differs from a configuration of the ideal society in feminist utopias. Indisputably, the violence in this work, implicit in its Amazonian origins, makes these women resemble male warrior-heroes. Therefore, though they destabilize gender identity, thereby changing the distribution of power, their sovereignty veers toward revenge. About violence, Wittig herself has written that a work of literature may be a tool of war between women and oppressors.

[18] Sexton, "In Celebration of My Uterus," in Gilbert and Gubar, eds., *Norton Anthology*, 1999.

[19] Lessing, *Diaries of Jane Somers*, 199-200.

[20] Adrienne Rich, "North American Time" in Catharine Stimpson, "Adrienne Rich and Lesbian/Feminist Poetry," in *Parnassus: Poetry in Review* (1985), 263.

[21] Ibid., 261.5

[22] Mamonova, *Russian Women's Studies*, 172.

[23] Both Joyce Carol Oates' *Invisible Woman: New and Selected Poems 1970-1982* and Robin Morgan's poem "The Invisible Woman" echo the much earlier *The Invisible Man* by Ralph Ellison, a classic portrayal of black invisibility.

[24] Audre Lorde, "From the House of Yemanja," in Gilbert and Gubar, eds., *Norton Anthology*, 2252.

[25] Stephen Dobyns, "Patience," *Balthus Poems*, 15.

[26] May Sarton, " My Sisters, O My Sisters," in Gilbert and Gubar, eds., *Norton Anthology*, 1775.

[27] Scheman, "Missing Mothers, Desiring Daughters," 75.

[28] *Jouissance* has notably been taken to refer to bodily experience. Julia Kristeva, for example, says *jouissance* refers to the undifferentiated infantile reaction to the mother, while Hélène Cixous states that *jouissance* is what has been repressed (by women) and must be expressed.

[29] Vance, *Pleasure and Danger*, 24.

[30] Olga Broumas, "Days of Argument and Blossom," in *Parnassus*, 24.

[31] Wittig, *Les Guérillères*, 104.

[32] Sappho "To Anaktoria," trans. Willis Barnstone (Garden City, N.Y.: Anchor, 1965), 7.

[33] See Gillian Clarke's poem "Sheila Na Gig at Kilpeck," in *Selected Poems*, 76.

[34] Harold Bloom, *Ruin the Sacred Truths*, 35-36.

[35] Lesser, *The Life Below*, 114.

[36] Gilbert and Gubar, "The Mirror and the Vamp."

[37] Goethe, *Faust* in Wolf *Cassandra*, 285.

[38] Lesser, *The Life Below*, 114.

[39] Sexton, "Housewife," in Howe and Bass, eds., *No More Masks*, 188.

[40] For a further discussion of the significance of the cave as a metaphor for woman/space, see Sandra Gilbert and Susan Gubar's *The Madwoman in the Attic*.

[41] See Elaine Showalter, *Sexual Anarchy*, 150-156.

[42] Greenspan, *A New Approach*, 165.

[43] Carter, *Passion of New Eve*, 11.

[44] Cynthia Macdonald, "Objets d'Art," in Howe and Bass, eds., *No More Masks*, 209.

[45] Diane Ackerman, "A Fine, A Private Place," in *Jaguar of Sweet Laughter: New and Selected Poems* (New York: Random House, 1991), 196.

[46] Ostriker, *Stealing the Language*, 197.

[47] Heilbrun, *Writing a Woman's Life*, 64.

[48] Diane Wakoski, "Belly Dancer," in *Emerald Ice: Selected Poems 1962-1987* (Santa Rosa: Black Sparrow, 1988), 20.

[49] Kathleen Fraser, "Talking to Myself Talking to You," in Ostriker *Stealing the Language*, 204.

[50] Wittig, *Les Guérillères*, 66.

[51] Ibid., 72.

[52] Adrienne Rich, "Images for Godard," *The Will to Change*: *Poems 1968-1970* (New York: Norton, 1971), 47.

[53] Adrienne Rich, "I Am in Danger—Sir—," in Gilbert and Gubar, eds., *Norton Anthology*, 2030.

[54] Sexton, "Little Girl, My String Bean, My Lovely Woman," in *Live or Die* (Boston: Houghton Mifflin, 1966), 64.

[55] Denise Levertov, "The Goddess," in Gilbert and Gubar, eds., *Norton Anthology*, 1943.

[56] Denise Levertov, "Song for Ishtar," ibid.

[57] See E. Ann Kaplan, *Motherhood and Representation: The Mother In Popular Culture and Melodrama* (New York: Routledge, 1992).

[58] See Lois W. Banner, *In Full Flower: Aging, Women, Power and Sexuality* (New York: Knopf, 1992).

[59] See Esther Harding Davis, *Women's Mysteries, Ancient and Modern*; Carol Christ, *The Laughter of Aphrodite*; Buffie Johnson, *Lady of the Beasts: Ancient Images of the Goddess and Her Sacred Animals*; and Carol Christ, *Journey to the Goddess*. Cf. endnote 6, above.

[60] Lucille Clifton, "she is dreaming," in *Good Woman*, 138.

[61] Angela Carter, *The Sadeian Woman* (New York: Pantheon, 1978), 5.

[62] Kaja Silverman, "*Histoire d'O*," in Vance, *Pleasure and Danger*, 346.

[63] Wittig, *Les Guérillères*, 110-111.

[64] Julia Budenz, "Exiles," *Crazyhorse* 45 (Winter 1993).

Chapter 6

[1] Clément, *Opera, or The Undoing of Women*.
[2] *New York Times* Book Review, August 26, 1990, 4.
[3] Krantz, *I'll Take Manhattan*, 311.
[4] Ibid., 197-198.
[5] Dennis Porter, *The Pursuit of Crime in Art and Ideology in Detective Fiction* (New Haven: Yale, 1981).
[6] In a review of Amanda Cross' *Death in a Tenured Position* reviewer Mary Cantwell speculates that so many women find mystery writing congenial precisely because it *is* 'safe' as far as the demands of the genre itself. That is, it has modest ambitions, "narrowness of vision or shallowness of perception . . . [would not] truly flaw a mystery novel," *New York Times* Book Review, March 22, 1981, 3.
[7] Nancy Pickard, *Sisters in Crime/National Project Survey Newsletter*, 1990.
[8] Mary Bowen Hall, ed., ibid.
[9] P. D. James, *Devices and Desires* (New York: Warner, 1990), 402.
[10] McRae, *All the Muscle You Need*, 245.
[11] For a corresponding point about women and sexual realism in the visual arts, see Linda Nochlin, *Women, Art, and Power, and Other Essays*.
[12] McRae, *All the Muscle You Need*, 82.
[13] Although in the PBS series *Prime Suspect*, based on the novel by Lynda La Plante, starring Detective Chief Inspector Jane Tennison, commitment to her career costs her her lover.
[14] Carlson, *Murder Unrenovated*, 85.
[15] Ibid., 142.
[16] Carlson, *Rehearsal for Murder*, 118.
[17] Ibid., 207.
[18] Ibid.
[19] Paretsky, *Indemnity Only*, 211-212.
[20] Ibid., 221. Interestingly, V. I. and Lotty quarrel in Paretsky's latest novel, thus imparting new tension.
[21] Paretsky, *Blood Shot*, 376.
[22] In fact, they presage the concept of "extended kinship" we'll examine shortly in our discussion of science fiction.
[23] P. M. Carlson in *Sisters in Crime/National Project Survey*, 1990.
[24] Reddy, *Sisters in Crime*, 2.
[25] Scott, *Glory Days*, 158.
[26] Smith, *Why Aren't They Screaming?*, 213.
[27] Ibid., 214.

Chapter 7

[1] See Cornell, *Beyond Accommodation*, 169-171.
[2] Cf. Erica Jong's assertion in *Fear of Flying* that non-reproductive sexuality is "selfish" in Chapter 3.
[3] For a full discussion of such questions, see Sarah Lefanu's *Feminism and Science Fiction*.
[4] Drucilla Cornell, "What Takes Place in the Dark," *Differences: a Journal of Feminist Cultural Studies*, 4:2 (1992), 69.

⁵ An early feminist satire, *The Republic of the Future* by Anna Bowman Dodd, does indeed use the imagined technology of the future to promote women as the dominant sex by the device of having machines free them from housework. How optimistic this seems!

⁶ As with all generalizations, there are exceptions. For instance, Josef Nesvadba's story "Captain Nemo's Last Adventure" plumps for poetry and music and an end to technical progress; Samuel R. Delaney's fiction engages feminist concerns; Octavia E. Butler's *Dawn*, to the contrary, presents a post-nuclear apocalyptic world. Moreover, such works lack the strong utopian bias that characterizes feminist fantasies which, in the main, carry strong social and spiritual messages.

⁷ I see parallels between Atwood's *The Handmaid's Tale* and Mary Shelley's *Frankenstein*, insofar as they are both female visions of the male as dark and ready to implode.

⁸ Butler, *Dawn*, 116.

⁹ Le Guin's *Always Coming Home* echoes the title of Carol Pearson's study "Coming Home: Four Feminist Utopias and Patriarchal Experience," in Barr, ed., *Future Females*. In this context, coming home signifies a return to the mother and to the self, putting the fragmented self which existed in patriarchy together into wholeness. See also Joanna Russ's "Recent Feminist Utopias" in the same collection.

¹⁰ Ellen Morgan, "Humanbecoming: Form and Focus in the Neo-Feminist Novel," in Cornillon, ed., *Images of Women*, 204.

¹¹ The feminization of poverty today relies on this traditional equation of women and property, which in turn makes a statement about the respective value of male and female in society. See Ruth Sidel's sociological study *Women and Children Last: The Plight of Poor Women in Affluent America* (New York: Viking, 1986).

¹² Jay Carr, *Boston Globe*, March 25, 1990, B30.

¹³ Ray Raphael, *The Men From the Boys: Rites of Passage in Male America* (Lincoln, Neb.: University of Nebraska, 1988), 23.

¹⁴ For the intriguing theory that the mushrooming of self-help groups in America provide a secularized form of religion, see *Boston Sunday Globe*, April 29, 1990, 1. The communes of the sixties, with their "flower power," their systems of shared work, their slogan "make love, not war," their emphasis on storytelling, their repudiation of private property, were another testing ground for pieces of this vision. Though the sixties communes were not feminist-inspired, the formation of "alternative" schools, magazines, newsletters, all that came to be known as "the counter-culture," sprang from many of the same values. Conversely, Rosemary Radford Ruether speculates in *Sexism and God-Talk: Toward a Feminist Theology* (Boston: Beacon, 1978) that the continuous attempt of our masculinist society to separate itself from the feminine is responsible for some of the sociological and moral crises we now face.

¹⁵ Wolf, *The Beauty Myth*, 279. Wolf continues: "We have baby showers and bridal showers, but what about purification, confirmation, healing, and renewal ceremonies for childbirth, first menstruation, loss of virginity, graduation, first job, marriage, recovery from heartbreak or divorce, the earning of a degree, menopause?"

¹⁶ Pindar, "Phythian Ode 1," in *Victory Odes*, trans. Frank J Nisetich (Baltimore: Johns Hopkins, 1980), 5, 77-78.

[17] Le Guin, *Always Coming Home*, 536.

[18] Ibid.

[19] One might go so far as to reflect whether that linear march of events is not a death-march, since there are no points along the line at which the line is broken, escaped from, and at which the idea of rebirth, as in natural cycles, intercedes.

[20] Perhaps at this point of connection with Native American literature, we can take the opportunity to summarize briefly *many* similarities between feminist values and Native American traditions. Some noteworthy examples are: kinship rules based on an elaborate system of rights; respect for human beings extended to other living creatures; the circular perception of time, e.g., Misha Gallagher's story entitled "Stories Don't Have Endings" in Allen, ed., *Spider Woman's Granddaughters*; the belief that storytelling is a practice of community; the looseness of genre definition, and the belief in multivocality in fiction; the belief in history as a living force without which the present loses meaning; separation as a loss (rather than maturation or liberation).

[21] See Appendix 1. Counterparts of this are Monique Wittig's circular symbol in *Les Guérillères*, Starhawk's circular symbol in *Truth or Dare*, and the Wiccan circle comprising all directions and elements. (Wicca was the old form of the word witch.)

[22] Le Guin, *Always Coming Home*, 483.

[23] Gunn Allen, *The Sacred Hoop: Recovering the Feminine in American Indian Traditions* (Boston: Beacon, 1986), 151.

[24] Ibid., 154.

[25] In fact, Le Guin's *Left Hand of Darkness* goes even further and, by imagining a country of human hermaphrodites, questions how sexual identity acquires meaning.

[26] Lessing, *Marriages*, 196-197.

[27] Ibid., 197.

[28] See Appendix 1.

[29] Grace Paley, "Zagrowski Tells," *Later the Same Day*, 161. For an interesting exploration of the role of storytelling in community, see Patricia Meyer Spacks, *Gossip* (New York: Knopf, 1985).

[30] It is this language that Monique Wittig terms *"l'écriture feminine"* in her essay "One Is Not Born a Woman," though she rejects it as "essentialist" for her own writing.

[31] Le Guin, *Always Coming Home*, 448.

[32] Ibid., 403, 405.

[33] Ibid., 405.

[34] Lessing, *Marriages*, 3.

[35] Zone Five, whose female leader Vashti, is anarchic, plays a less significant part in the structure or conception of the novel.

[36] Lessing, *Marriages*, 71-72.

[37] Ibid., 75.

[38] Le Guin, *Always Coming Home*, 405. For an extended treatment of this point, see Carolyn Merchant, *The Death of Nature: Women, Ecology and the Scientific Revolution* (San Francisco: Harper and Row, 1983).

[39] Le Guin, *Always Coming Home*, 451.

[40] Lessing, *Marriages*, 10.

[41] Russ, *Female Man*, 51.

[42] Le Guin, *Always Coming Home*, 451.

[43] Lessing, *Marriages*, 156.

[44] Ibid., 142.

[45] Starhawk, *Truth or Dare*, 23.

[46] I share with the reader Le Guin's reminder that Virginia Woolf in her "Glossary" to *Three Guineas*, defines heroism as botulism, and hero as bottle. In other words, the hero's story is poisonous!

[47] Le Guin, *Always Coming Home*, 94.

[48] Lessing, *Marriages*, 179.

[49] Full-bodied and direct humor, rather than gallows humor, marks the emergence of the heroine in all genres. One example is the following section of Marge Piercy's poem "The Woman in the," in Howe and Bass, eds., *No More Masks*, 247.

[50] Lessing, *Marriages*, 222.

[51] For a full discussion and bibliography on this subject, see Donovan, "Feminism and Animal Rights."

[52] Nancy Berry pinpoints this difficultly. "The American tendency to see leadership as the remarkable individual we call leaders creates a profound barrier inhibiting social progress. Because Americans see leadership as an expression of individuality, we fail to perceive leadership as an expression of community." *Utne Reader*, (May–June 1993), 93. In fact Berry suggests that we are slowly moving away from our old notions of what hero/leaders must be, and are accepting more flawed individuals, mortal and with their own inconsistencies and vulnerabilities. Most interesting is her speculation that as a consequence of both postmodernism and pluralism, we may be unable to agree on a national hero, to achieve consensus.

[53] As Julia Kristeva comments in "Women's Time": "The difficulty . . . is how to avoid the centralization of power, how to detach women from it and how then to proceed, through their critical, differential and autonomous interventions, to render decision-making institutions more flexible," 202.

[54] *Boston Globe*, April 24, 1992, 1.

[55] *Boston Globe*, October 3, 1992, 3.

[56] For a recent non-fiction exploration of this theme, see Susan Griffin's *A Chorus of Stones: The Private Life of War* (New York: Doubleday, 1992).

[57] Irving Howe, "The Spirit of the Times," *Dissent* (Spring, 1993), 133.

[58] Ibid., 132.

Epilogue

[1] Clément, *Opera, or The Undoing of Women*.

[2] One of the repeated lessons of this book is the danger inherent in the system of binary classification. Whether Nature/Culture, Black/White, Virgin/Whore, Good Mother/Terrible Mother, such classification leads to stereotyping, exclusion, and hierarchy, sometimes in the guise of complementarity.

[3] See Prologue, Chapter 1, Chapter 7 for discussion of genre.

[4] Jacques Derrida in *Glas* asserts that laughter, coming from the unconscious, questions and ridicules the essence, the "truth" of man—and presumably, that of

women. Hélène Cixous' essay "The Laugh of the Medusa" is more specific, maintaining that laughter shatters the opposition between self and other.

[5] Suleiman, *Subversive Intent.*

[6] Gunn Allen, *Spider Woman's Granddaughters*, 30. I am grateful to Judith Nies for calling my attention to this book.

[7] It is rather a tired speculation that the desire to overcome mortality may, for women, be satisfied by childbearing rather than fame.

[8] Cohn, "Sex and Death," 701.

[9] Along the same lines, Rosemary Radford Ruether urges "we have the responsibility and necessity to convert our intelligence to the earth. We need to learn how to use intelligence to mend the distortions we have created." *Sexism and God Talk*: *Toward a Feminist Theology* (Boston: Beacon, 1983), 89.

Appendix 1

NARRATIVE MODES IN WESTERN CIVILISATION

FACT: NONFICTION   NONFACT: FICTION

Journalism   Biography   Annals   History   Myth   Legend   Folktale   Parable   Tale   Story   Novel   Propaganda
Description
Report   LIES,
                                                               JOKES

WHAT HAPPENED   LIKE WHAT HAPPENED

NARRATIVE MODES IN THE VALLEY

Ursula Le Guin, *Always Coming Home*

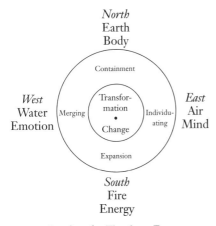

North
Earth
Body

Containment

West   Merging   Transfor-mation • Change   Individu-ating   *East*
Water   Air
Emotion   Mind

Expansion

South
Fire
Energy

Starhawk, *Truth or Dare*

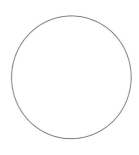

Monique Wittig, *Les Guérillerès*

Ursula Le Guin, *Always Coming Home*

Starhawk, *Truth or Dare*

Appendix 2

Le Guin summarizes the distinction between the current (masculine) structure of society and her projected (feminine) society by selecting widely varying metaphors and working out their ramifications for the society through a series of *relations*. These clusters she terms "generative metaphors," itself a feminine metaphor of giving birth or creating. Since Le Guin's terminology represents with justice both her own and Lessing's visions, recalling many of the themes we have just explored, culminating in the terms of Change, which are feminist goals, I quote them below.

The Metaphor: THE WAR.
What it generates: STRUGGLE.
Universe as war: The triumph of being over nothingness. The battlefield.
Society as war: The subjection of weak to strong.
Person as warrior: Courage; the hero.
    Medicine as victory over death.
Mind as warrior: Conquistador.
    Language as control.
The relationship of human with other beings in war: Enmity.
Images of the War: Victory, defeat, loot, ruin, the army.

The Metaphor: THE LORD.
What it generates: POWER.
Universe as kingdom: Hierarchy from one god down. Order from chaos.
Society as kingdom: Hierarchy from one king down. Order from chaos.
Person as lord/subject: Class, caste, place, responsibility.
    Medicine as power.
Mind as lord/subject: Law. Judgement.
    Language as power.

The relationship of human with other beings in the kingdom: Superiority.
Images of the Kingdom: The pyramid, the city, the sun.

The Metaphor: THE ANIMAL.
What it generates: LIFE.
Universe as animal: Organic, indivisible wholeness.
Society as animal: Tribe, clan, family.
Person as animal: Kinship.
  Medicine as rest.
Mind as animal: Discovery.
  Language as relationship.
The relationship of human with other beings as animals: Eating. Interdependence.
Images of the Animal: Birth, mating, dying, the seasons, the tree, the diverse beasts and plants.

The Metaphor: THE MACHINE.
What it generates: WORK.
Universe as machine: Clock and clockmaker. Running and running down.
Society as machine: Parts, functions, cogs; interrelations; production.
Person as machine: Use. Function.
  Medicine as repair.
Mind as machine: Information.
  Language as communication.
The relationship of human with other beings as machines: Exploitation.
Images of the Machine: Progress, ineluctability, breakdown, the wheel.

The Metaphor: THE DANCE.
What it generates: MUSIC.
Universe as dance: Harmony. Creation/destruction.
Society as dance: Participation.
Person as dancer: Cooperation.
  Medicine as art.
Mind as dancing: Rhythm, measure.
  Language as connection.
The relationship of human with other beings as dance: Horizontal linkings.
Images of the Dance: Steps, gestures, continuity, harmony, the spiral.

The Metaphor: THE HOUSE.
What it generates: STABILITY.
Universe as household: Division within unity; inclusion/exclusion.
Person as householder: Selfhood.
    Medicine as protection.
Mind as householder: Belonging.
    Language as self-domestication.
The relationship of human with other beings in the house: Inside/Outside.
Images of the House: Doors, windows, hearth, home, the town.

The Metaphor: THE WAY.
What it generates: CHANGE.
Universe as the way: Mystery; balance in movement.
Society as the way: Imitation of the nonhuman; inaction.
Person as wayfarer: Caution.
    Medicine as keeping in balance.
Mind as wayfarer: Spontaneity. Sureness.
    Language as inadequate.
The relationship of human with other beings on the way: Unity.
Images of the Way: Balance, reversal, journey, return.

It is most interesting to note in connection with Le Guin's metaphors above that Starhawk's *Truth or Dare* employs similar metaphoric projections: LORD is Master of Servants, Censor, King, Defender, Avenger, Orderer, Controller, Comptroller. Atwood's *The Handmaid's Tale* presents the Republic of Gilead as a military dictatorship whose ruler is Commander. Gilman's heroine Ellador *[Herland]* reflects about authoritarianism, "God says so — the King or the Captain says so — the Book says so — and back of it all, the Family, the Father-Boss." Starhawk's LORD, Le Guin's LORD, and Gilman's LORD extrude word-clusters of patriarchy.

Select Bibliography

Abel, Elizabeth, ed. *Writing and Sexual Difference*. Chicago: University of Chicago Press, 1982.

Agosin, Marjorie. *Witches and Other Things*. Translated by Cola Franzen. Pittsburgh: Latin American Literary Review Press, 1984.

Allen, Paula Gunn, ed. *Spider Woman's Granddaughters: Traditional Tales and Contemporary Writing by Native American Women*. New York: Ballantine, 1990.

Alther, Lisa. *Kinflicks*. New York: Knopf, 1975.

Atwood, Margaret. *The Edible Woman*. Boston: Little Brown, 1969.

————. *Surfacing*. New York: Simon and Schuster, 1972.

————. *Selected Poems*. New York: Simon and Schuster, 1976.

————. *The Handmaid's Tale*. Boston: Houghton Mifflin, 1986.

Auerbach, Nina. *Communities of Women: An Idea in Fiction*. Cambridge: Harvard University Press, 1978.

Bakhtin, Mikhail. *Rabelais and His World*. Translated by Helene Iswolsky. Cambridge, Mass.: MIT Press, 1968.

Barnes, Linda. *Steel Guitar*. New York: Delacorte, 1991.

Barr, Marleen. *Future Females: A Critical Anthology*. Bowling Green, Ohio: Bowling Green State University Popular Press, 1981.

Bartkowski, Frances. *Feminist Utopias*. Lincoln: University of Nebraska Press, 1989.

Bartky, Sandra Lee. *Femininity and Domination: Studies in the Phenomenology of Oppression*. New York: Routledge, 1990.

Bateson, Mary Catherine. *Composing a Life*. New York: Atlantic Monthly, 1989.

Beauvoir, Simone de. *The Second Sex*. Translated by H. M. Parshley. New York: Vintage, 1974.

Belenky, Mary Field, Blythe McVicker Clinchy, Nancy Rule Goldberger, and Jill Mattuck Tarule. *Women's Ways of Knowing: The Development of Self, Voice, and Mind.* New York: Basic, 1986.

Benjamin, Jessica. *The Bonds of Love: Psychoanalysis, Feminism, and the Problem of Domination.* New York: Pantheon, 1988.

————. "The Bonds of Love: Rational Violence and Erotic Domination." In *The Future of Difference*, edited by Hester Eisenstein and Alice Jardine. New Brunswick, N.J.: Rutgers University Press, 1980.

————. "A Desire of One's Own: Psychoanalytic Feminism and Intersubjective Space." In *Feminist Studies/Critical Studies*, edited by Teresa De Lauretis. Bloomington: Indiana University Press, 1986.

Benjamin, Walter. *Reflections: Essays, Aphorisms, Autobiographical Writing.* Edited by Peter Demetz. Translated by Edmund Jephcott. New York: Harcourt Brace Jovanovich, 1978.

Berger, John. *Ways of Seeing* New York: Penguin, 1972.

Bernheimer, Charles and Claire Kahane, eds. *In Dora's Case: Freud, Hysteria, Feminism.* New York: Columbia University Press, 1985.

Blackwell, Jeannine and Susanne Zantop, eds. *Bitter Healing: German Women Writers from 1700 to 1830: An Anthology.* Lincoln: University of Nebraska Press, 1991.

Bloom, Harold. *Ruin the Sacred Truths: Poetry and Belief from the Bible to the Present.* Cambridge: Harvard University Press, 1989.

Bottigheimer, Ruth B. *Grimms' Bad Girls and Bold Boys: The Moral and Social Vision of the Tales.* New Haven: Yale University Press, 1987.

Brennan, Teresa, ed. *Between Feminism and Psychoanalysis.* London: Routledge, 1989.

Broe, Mary Lynn, ed. *Silence and Power: A Reevaluation of Djuna Barnes.* Carbondale: Southern Illinois University Press, 1991.

Brownstein, Rachel. *Becoming a Heroine: Reading about Women in Novels.* New York: Penguin, 1984.

Bruch, Hilde. *The Golden Cage: The Enigma of Anorexia Nervosa.* Cambridge: Harvard University Press, 1978.

Butler, Jsudith. *Gender Trouble: Feminism and the Subversion of Identity.* New York: Routledge, 1990.

Butler, Octavia E. *Dawn: Xenogenesis.* New York: Warner, 1987.

Button, Karen Elias. "The Muse as Medusa." In *The Lost Tradition: Mothers and Daughters in Literature*, edited by Cathy N. Davidson and E.M. Broner, New York: Ungar, 1980.

Campbell, Joseph. *The Hero With a Thousand Faces.* 2nd ed. Princeton: Princeton University Press, 1968.

Carlson, P. M. *Murder Unrenovated*. New York: Bantam, 1987.

———. *Rehearsal for Murder*. New York: Bantam, 1988.

Carter, Angela. *The Passion of New Eve*. London: Virago, 1983.

———. *Nights at the Circus*. New York: Penguin, 1985.

Charnas, Suzy McKee. *Motherlines*. New York: Berkley, 1978.

Cherryh, C. J. *Well of Shiuan*. New York: Daw, 1978.

Chodorow, Nancy. *The Reproduction of Mothering: Psychoanalysis and the Sociology of Gender*. Berkeley and Los Angeles: University of California Press, 1978.

Chodorow, Nancy and Susan Contratto. "The Fantasy of the Perfect Mother." In *Rethinking the Family: Some Feminist Questions*. Edited by Barrie Thorne with Marilyn Yalom. New York: Longman, 1982.

Christ, Carol. *Laughter of Aphrodite: Reflections on a Journey to the Goddess*. San Francisco: Harper and Row, 1987.

Cixous, Hélène. "The Laugh of the Medusa." Translated by Keith Cohen and Paula Cohen. In *Signs* 1, no. 4 (1976): 875-99.

Clément, Catherine. *Opera, or The Undoing of Women*. Translated by Betsy Wing. Minneapolis: University of Minnesota Press, 1988.

Clifton, Lucille. *Good Woman: Poems and a Memoir 1969-1980*. Brockport, N.Y.: Boa, 1987.

Cluster, Dick. *Return to Sender*. New York: Penguin, 1988.

Cohn, Carol. "Sex and Death in the Rational World of Defense Intellectuals." *Signs* 12, no.4 (1987): 687-718.

Cook, Albert. *The Dark Voyage and the Golden Mean: a Philosophy of Comedy*. Cambridge: Harvard University Press, 1949.

Cornell, Drucilla. *Beyond Accomodation: Ethical Feminism, Deconstruction, and the Law*. New York: Routledge, 1991.

Cornillon, Susan Koppelman, ed. *Images of Women in Fiction: Feminist Perspectives*. Bowling Green, Ohio: Bowling Green University Popular Press, 1972.

Couzyn, Jeni, ed. *The Bloodaxe Book of Contemporary Women Poets: Eleven British Writers*. Newcastle-upon-Tyne: Bloodaxe, 1985.

Cross, Amanda. *The Theban Mysteries*. New York: Knopf, 1971.

———. *No Word From Winifred*. New York: Dutton, 1986.

———. *A Trap for Fools*. New York: Dutton, 1989.

———. *The Players Come Again*. New York: Random House, 1990.

Decker, Hannah S. *Freud, Dora and Vienna, 1900*. New York: Free Press, 1991.

Delany, Sheila. *Writing Woman: Women Writers and Women in Literature, Medieval to Modern*. New York: Schocken Books, 1983.

De Lauretis, Teresa. *Alice Doesn't: Feminism, Semiotics, Cinema.* Bloomington: Indiana University Press, 1984.

—————. *Technologies of Gender: Essays on Theory, Film, and Fiction.* Bloomington: Indiana University Press, 1987.

—————. ed. *Feminist Studies/Critical Studies.* Bloomington: Indiana University Press, 1986.

Derrida, Jacques. *Glas.* Translated by John P. Leavey, Jr., and Richard Rand. Lincoln: University of Nebraska Press, 1986.

Diamond, Irene and Quinby, Lee, eds. *Feminism and Foucault: Reflections on Resistance.* Boston: Northeastern University Press, 1988.

Dijkstra, Bram. *Idols of Perversity: Fantasies of Feminine Evil in Fin de Siècle Culture.* New York: Oxford University Press, 1986.

Dinesen, Isak. *Seven Gothic Tales.* New York: Modern Library, 1947.

Dinnerstein, Dorothy. *The Mermaid and the Minataur: Sexual Arrangements and Human Malaise.* New York: Harper and Row, 1976.

Doane, Mary Ann. *The Desire to Desire: The Woman's Film of the 1940's.* Bloomington: Indiana University Press, 1987.

Dobyns, Stephen. *The Balthus Poems.* New York: Atheneum, 1982.

Donovan, Josephine. "Towards a Women's Poetics." *Tulsa Studies in Women's Literature* 3, no.1/2 (1984): 99-110.

—————. *Feminist Theory: The Intellectual Traditions of American Feminism.* New York: Ungar, 1985.

—————. "Animal Rights and Feminist Theory." *Signs* 15, no.2 (1990): 350-375.

—————. ed. *Feminist Literary Criticism: Explorations in Theory.* Lexington: University Press of Kentucky, 1975.

Douglas, Mary. *Purity and Danger: An Analysis of Concepts of Pollution and Taboo.* New York: Praeger, 1966.

Edwards, Lee R. *Psyche as Hero: Female Heroism and Fictional Form.* Middletown, Conn.: Wesleyan University Press, 1984.

Ellmann, Mary. *Thinking About Women.* New York: Harcourt, Brace and World, 1968.

Feldstein, Richard and Harry Sussman, eds. *Psychoanalysis and. . . .* New York: Routledge, 1990.

Felman, Shoshana. *Jacques Lacan and the Adventure of Insight: Psychoanalysis in Contemporary Culture.* Cambridge: Harvard University Press, 1987.

Flax, Jane. *Thinking Fragments: Psychoanalysis, Feminism, and Postmodernism in the Contemporary West.* Berkeley and Los Angeles: University of California Press, 1990.

Gallant, Mavis. *A Fairly Good Time.* New York, Random House, 1970.

Gallop, Jane. *The Daughter's Seduction: Feminism and Psychoanalysis*. Ithaca: Cornell University Press, 1982.

Garber, Marjorie. *Vested Interests: Cross Dressing and Cultural Anxiety*. New York: Routledge, 1992.

Garner, Shirley Nelson, Claire Kahane, and Madelon Sprengnether, eds. *The (M)other Tongue: Essays in Feminist Psychoanalytic Interpretation*. Ithaca: Cornell University Press, 1985.

Gilbert, Sandra and Susan Gubar. *The Madwoman in the Attic: The Woman Writer and the Nineteenth Century Literary Imagination*. New Haven: Yale University Press, 1979.

————. *No Man's Land: The Place of the Woman Writer in the Twentieth Century*. 2 Vols. New Haven: Yale University Press, 1990.

————. eds. *Shakespeare's Sisters: Feminist Essays on Women Poets*. Bloomington: Indiana University Press, 1979.

————. eds. *The Norton Anthology of Literature by Women: The Tradition in English*. New York: Norton, 1985.

————. "The Mirror and the Vamp: Reflections on Feminist Criticism." Paper presented at the Center for Literary and Cultural Studies, Cambridge, Mass., November 1988.

Gilligan, Carol. *In a Different Voice: Psychological Theory and Women's Development*. Cambridge: Harvard University Press, 1982.

————. "Joining the Resistance: Psychology, Politics, Girls and Women." In *Michigan Quarterly Review* 23, no.4 (1990): 501-536.

Gilman, Charlotte Perkins. *Herland*. Edited by Ann J. Lane. New York: Pantheon, 1979.

Gimbutas, Marija. *The Civilization of the Goddess: The World of Old Europe*. New York: HarperCollins, 1991.

Grafton, Sue. *E is for Evidence: A Kinsey Millhone Mystery*. New York: Holt, 1988.

————. *F is for Fugitive: A Kinsey Millhone Mystery*. New York: Holt, 1989.

Grahn, Judy. *The Work of a Common Woman: The Collected Poetry of Judy Grahn, 1964-1977*. Oakland: Diana, 1978.

Gray, Francine du Plessix. *Adam and Eve and the City: Selected Non-Fiction*. New York: Simon and Schuster, 1987.

————. *Soviet Women: Walking the Tightrope*. New York: Doubleday, 1990.

Green, Diana. "An Asteroid of One's Own: Women Soviet Science Fiction Writers," *Irish Slavonic Studies* 8 (1987): 127-139.

Greenspan, Miriam. *A New Approach to Women and Therapy*. New York: McGraw Hill, 1983.

Griffin, Susan. *Woman and Nature: The Roaring Inside Her*. New York: Harper and Row, 1978.

Gubar, Susan. " 'The Blank Page' and the Issues of Female Creativity." In *The New Feminist Criticism: Essays on Women, Literature, and Theory*, edited by Elaine Showalter. New York: Pantheon, 1985.

Hartsock, Nancy. "Masculinity, Heroism and the Making of War." In *Rocking the Ship of State: Toward a Feminist Peace Politics*. Edited by Adrienne Harris and Ynestra King. Boulder Colo.: Westview, 1989.

Heilbrun, Carolyn. *Writing a Woman's Life*. New York: Norton, 1988.

Hejinian, Lyn, and Barrett Waẗten, eds. *Poetics Journal: Women and Language*, no.4 (May 1984).

Held, David. *Introduction to Critical Theory: Horkheimer to Habermas*. Berkeley and Los Angeles: University of California Press, 1980.

Hirsch, Marianne. *The Mother/Daughter Plot: Narrative, Psychoanalysis, Feminism*. Bloomington: Indiana University Press, 1989.

Hite, Molly. *The Other Side of the Story: Structures and Strategies of Contemporary Feminist Narrative*. Ithaca: Cornell University Press, 1989.

Howe, Florence and Ellen Bass, eds. *No More Masks! An Anthology of Poems by Women*. Garden City N.Y.: Anchor, 1973.

Hutcheon, Linda. *A Poetics of Postmodernism: History, Theory, Fiction*. London: Routledge, 1988.

Huyssen, Andreas. *After the Great Divide: Modernism, Mass Culture, Postmodernism*. Bloomington: Indiana University Press, 1986.

Irigaray, Luce. *This Sex Which is Not One*. Translated by Catherine Porter with Carolyn Burke. Ithaca: Cornell University Press, 1985.

———. *Speculum of the Other Woman*. Translated by Gillian C. Gill. Ithaca: Cornell University Press, 1985.

Jardine, Alice A. *Gynesis: Configurations of Women and Modernity*. Ithaca: Cornell University Press, 1985.

Johnson, Buffie. *Lady of the Beasts: Ancient Images of the Goddess and Her Sacred Amimals*. San Francisco: Harper and Row, 1988.

Jong, Erica. *Fear of Flying*. New York: Signal, 1974.

Kaledin, Eugenia. "Dr. Manners: S. Weir Mitchell's Prescriptions for an Upset Society." *Prospects*, no.11 (1987):199-216.

Kaplan, Marcie. "A Woman's View of DSM-111." *American Psychologist* 38, no. 7, (1983): 786-792.

Karlsen, Carol F. *The Devil in the Shape of a Woman: Witchcraft in Colonial New England*. New York: Norton, 1987.

Kauffman, Janet. *Places in the World a Woman Could Walk: Stories*. New York: Knopf, 1983.

Kearns, Martha, ed. *Voices of Women: 3 Critics on 3 Heroines*. New York: Midmarch, 1980.

Kingston, Maxine Hong. *The Woman Warrior: Memoirs of a Girlhood Among*

Ghosts. New York: Knopf, 1980.

Klein, Kathleen Gregory. *The Woman Detective: Gender and Genre*. Urbana: University of Illinois Press, 1988.

Knight, Kathryn Lasky. *Trace Elements*. New York: Norton, 1986.

Kolbenschlag, Madonna. *Kiss Sleeping Beauty Goodbye: Breaking the Spell of Feminine Myths and Models*. Garden City, N.Y.: Doubleday, 1979.

Krantz, Judith. *I'll Take Manhattan*. New York: Crown, 1986.

Kristeva, Julia. *Powers of Horror: An Essay on Abjection*. Translated by Leon S. Roudiez. New York: Columbia University Press, 1982.

————. "Women's Time." In *The Kristeva Reader*. Edited by Toril Moi. New York: Columbia University Press, 1986.

La Belle, Jenijoy. *Herself Beheld: The Literature of the Looking Glass*. Ithaca: Cornell University Press, 1988.

Lacan, Jacques. *Feminine Sexuality: Jacques Lacan and the École Freudienne*. Edited by Juliet Mitchell and Jacqueline Rose, translated by Jacqueline Rose. New York: Norton, 1982.

Lauter, Estella. *Women as Mythmakers: Poetry and Visual Art by Twentieth Century Women*. Bloomington: Indiana University Press, 1984.

Lefanu, Sarah. *In the Chinks of the World Machine: Feminism and Science Fiction*. Bloomington: Indiana University Press, 1989.

Le Guin, Ursula. *A Wizard of Earthsea*. Berkeley: Parnassus, 1968.

————. *The Tombs of Atuan*. New York: Atheneum, 1971.

————. *The Farthest Shore* New York: Atheneum, 1972.

————. *Always Coming Home*. New York: Bantam, 1987.

————. *Dancing at the Edge of the World, Thoughts on Words, Women, Places*. New York: Grove Press, 1989.

Lesser, Wendy. *The Life Below the Ground: A Study of the Subterranean in Literature and History*. Boston: Faber and Faber, 1987.

————. *His Other Half: Men Looking at Women Through Art*. Cambridge: Harvard University Press, 1991.

Lessing, Doris. *The Marriages Between Zones Three, Four, and Five (As Narrated by The Chroniclers of Zone Three). Canopus in Argos: Archives 2*. New York: Vintage, 1984.

————. *The Diaries of Jane Somers*. New York: Vintage, 1984.

Lochte, Dick. *Sleeping Dog*. New York: Warner, 1985.

Lorde, Audre. *Zami: A New Spelling of My Name*. Trumansburg, N.Y.: Crossing Press, 1983.

Lyotard, Jean François. *The Differend: Phrases in Dispute*. Translated by Georges Van Den Abbeele. Minneapolis: University of Minnesota Press, 1988.

Macleod, Charlotte. *The Silver Ghost*. New York: Mysterious, 1988.

McCorkle, Jill. *Crash Diet: Stories*. Chapel Hill, N.C.: Alquonquin, 1992.

McRae, Diana. *All the Muscle You Need: an Eliza Pirex Mystery*. San Francisco: Spinsters/Aunt Lute, 1988.

Mamonova, Tatyana, ed. *Russian Women's Studies: Essays on Sexism in Soviet Culture*. New York: Pergamon, 1989.

Marcus, Jane. "Laughing at Leviticus: 'Nightwood' as Woman's Circus Epic." In *Silence and Power: a Reevaluation of Djuna Barnes*, edited by Mary Lynn Broe. Carbondale: Southern Illinois University Press, 1991.

Marks, Elaine and Isabelle de Courtivron, eds. *New French Feminisms: An Anthology*. Amherst, Mass.: University of Amherst Press, 1980.

Michie, Helena. *The Flesh Made Word: Female Figures and Women's Bodies*. New York: Oxford University Press, 1987.

Middlebrook, Diane Wood. *Anne Sexton: A Biography*, Boston: Houghton Mifflin, 1991.

Miles, Margaret. *Carnal Knowing: Female Nakedness and Religious Meaning in the Christian West*. Boston: Beacon, 1989.

Miller, Jean Baker. *Toward a New Psychology of Women*. Boston: Beacon, 1976.

Miller, Nancy. *Subject to Change: Reading Feminist Writing*. New York: Columbia University Press, 1988.

Miner, Valerie. *Murder in the English Department*. New York: St. Martin's, 1983.

Moers, Ellen. *Literary Women*. Garden City, N.Y.: Doubleday, 1976.

Moi, Toril. *Sexual/Textual Politics: Feminist Literary Theory*. London: Methuen, 1985.

Morgan, Robin. *The Demon Lover: On the Sexuality of Terrorism*. New York: Norton, 1989.

Morgan, Susan. *Sisters in Time: Imagining Gender in 19th Century British Literature*. New York: Oxford University Press, 1989.

Mulvey, Laura. "Visual Pleasure and Narrative Cinema." *Screen* 16, no.3 (1975): 7-19.

————. "Changes: Thoughts on Myth, Narrative and Historical Experience." *History Workshop Journal*, no.23 (Spring 1987): 1-19.

————. *Visual and Other Pleasures*. Bloomington: Indiana University Press, 1989.

Napier, George. "Greek Art and Greek Anthropology: Orienting the Perseus-Gorgon Myth." Paper presented at the Center for Literary and Cultural Studies, Cambridge Mass., 1988.

Nochlin, Linda. *Women, Art, and Power, and Other Essays*. New York: Harper and Row, 1988.

Ostriker, Alicia Suskin. *Writing Like a Woman*. Ann Arbor, Michigan: University of Michigan Press, 1983.

————. *Stealing the Language: The Emergence of Women's Poetry in America*. Boston: Beacon, 1986.

Ozick, Cynthia. "Does Genius Have a Gender?." *Ms Magazine*. (December 1977): 56, 79, 80-81.

Paglia, Camille. *Sexual Personae: Art and Decadence from Nefertiti to Emily Dickinson*. New Haven: Yale University Press, 1991.

Paley, Grace. *Later the Same Day*. New York: Farrar, Strauss, Giroux, 1985.

Paretsky, Sara. *Indemnity Only: a Novel*. New York: Dial, 1982.

————. *Bloodshot*. New York: Bantam, 1988.

————. *Burn Marks*. New York: Delacorte, 1989.

Parnassus: Poetry in Review. 12, no.2/13, no.1.

Pfaff, William. "The Fallen Hero." *The New Yorker*, (May 8, 1989) 105-115.

Piercy, Marge. *Woman on the Edge of Time*. New York: Knopf, 1976.

Piesman, Marissa. *Unorthodox Practices*. New York: Pocket Books, 1989.

Poovey, Mary. " 'Scenes of an Indelicate Character': The Medical 'Treatment' of Victorian Women." *Representations* 14. (Spring 1986): 137-168.

Pratt, Annis, Barbara White, Andrea Lowenstein and Mary Wyer. *Archetypal Patterns in Women's Fiction*. Bloomington: Indiana University Press, 1981.

Rabine, Leslie W. *Reading the Romantic Heroine: Text, History, Ideology*. Ann Arbor: University of Michigan Press, 1985.

Raphael, Ray. *The Men from the Boys: Rites of Passage in Male America*. Lincoln: University of Nebraska Press, 1988.

Reddy, Maureen, T. *Sisters in Crime: Feminism and the Crime Novel*. New York: Continuum, 1988.

Redfield, James. *Nature and Culture in the Iliad: The Tragedy of Hector*. Chicago: University of Chicago Press, 1975.

Rich, Adrienne. *Of Woman Born: Motherhood as Experience and Institution*. New York: Norton, 1976.

Riviére, Joan. "Womanliness as a Masquerade." In *Formations of Fantasy*, edited by Victor Burgin, James Donald, and Cora Kaplan. London: Methuen, 1986.

Robinson, Marilynne. *Housekeeping*. New York: Farrar, Straus, Giroux, 1980.

Rose, Ellen Cronan. "Through the Looking Glass: When Women Tell Fairy Tales." In *The Voyage In: Fictions of Female Development*, edited by Elizabeth Abel, Marianne Hirsch and Elizabeth Langland. Hanover, N.H.: University Press of New England, 1983.

Rose, Jacqueline. *Sexuality in the Field of Vision*. London: Verso, 1986.

Rose, Phyllis. *Writing of Women: Essays in a Renaissance*. Middletown, Conn.: Wesleyan University Press, 1985.

Rubin, Gayle. *The Traffic in Women: Notes on the 'Political Economy' of Sex*. In *Towards an Anthropology of Women*, edited by Rayna R. Reiter. New York: Monthly Review Press, 1976.

Ruddick, Sara. *Maternal Thinking: Toward a Politics of Peace*. Boston: Beacon, 1989.

Russ, Joanna. *The Female Man*. Boston: Beacon, 1975.1

———. *Alyx*. Boston: Gregg, 1976.

———. *On Strike Against God: A Lesbian Love Story*. Brooklyn: Out and Out, 1980.

———. *The Adventures of Alyx*. New York: Baen, 1986.

Russo, Mary. "Female Grotesques: Carnival and Theory." In *Feminist Studies/Critical Studies*, edited by Teresa De Lauretis. Bloomington: Indiana University Press, 1986.

Sanford, Linda Tschirhart and Mary Ellen Donovan. *Women and Self-Esteem: Understanding and Improving the Way We Think and Feel About Ourselves*. New York: Penguin, 1985.

Scarf, Maggie. *Unfinished Business: Pressure Points in the Lives of Women*. New York: Ballantine, 1981.

Scheman, Naomi. "Missing Mothers/Desiring Daughters: Framing the Sight of Women." *Critical Inquiry* 15, no.1 (1988): 62-89.

Scott, Joan Wallach. *Gender and the Politics of History*. New York: Columbia University Press, 1988.

Scott, Rosie. *Glory Days*. Seattle: Seal Press, 1988.

See, Carolyn. *Making History*. Boston: Houghton Mifflin, 1991.

Sexton, Anne. *To Bedlam and Part Way Back*. Boston: Houghton Mifflin, 1960.

———. *Transformations*. Boston: Houghton Mifflin, 1971.

Showalter, Elaine. *A Literature of Their Own: British Women Novelists from Brontë to Lessing*. Princeton: Princeton University Press, 1977.

———. *The Female Malady: Women, Madness and English Culture, 1830-1980*. New York: Penguin, 1987.

———. *Sexual Anarchy: Gender and Culture at the Fin de Siècle*. New York: Penguin, 1991.

Sidel, Ruth. *On Her Own: Growing up in the Shadow of the American Dream*. New York: Viking, 1990.

Slonczewski, Joan. *A Door into Ocean*. New York: Arbor House, 1986.

Smith, Joan. *A Masculine Ending*. New York: Charles Scribner's Sons, 1988.
————. *Why Aren't They Screaming?* New York: Fawcett Crest, 1990.
Spero, Nancy. *Nancy Spero: Works Since 1950*. Edited by Dominique Nahas. Syracuse: Everson Museum of Art, 1987.
Starhawk. *Truth or Dare: Encounters with Power, Authority, and Mystery*. San Francisco: Harper and Row, 1987.
Stasio, Marilyn. "What's Happened to Heroes Is a Crime," *New York Times Book Review* (October 14, 1990) 1, 57-58.
Sturgis, Susanna J., ed. *Memories and Visions: Women's Fantasy and Science Fiction*. Freedom, CA: Crossing Press, 1989.
Suleiman, Susan Rubin. *Subversive Intent: Gender, Politics, and the Avant-Garde*. Cambridge: Harvard University Press, 1990.
————. ed. *The Female Body in Western Culture: Contemporary Perspectives*. Cambridge: Harvard University Press, 1986.
Thurston, Carol. *The Romance Revolution: Erotic Novels for Women and the Quest for a New Sexual Identity*. Urbana: University of Illinois Press, 1987.
Tiptree, James, Jr. [Alice B. Sheldon]. "The Women Men Don't See" in *The New Women of Wonder: Recent Science Fiction Stories by Women About Women*, edited by Pamela Sargent. New York: Vintage, 1978.
————. "Houston, Houston, Do You Read?" In *Her Smoke Rose Up Forever*. Sauk City, Wisc.: Arkham House, 1990.
Turner, Frederick. *Beyond Geography: The Western Spirit Against the Wilderness*. New York: Viking, 1980.
Vance, Carole S. *Pleasure and Danger: Exploring Female Sexuality*. Boston: Routledge and Kegan Paul, 1984.
Wallach, Anne Tolstoi. *Women's Work: A Novel*. New York: New American Library, 1981.
Weldon, Faye. *The Life and Loves of a She-Devil*. New York: Ballantine, 1985.
Winnicott, D. W. *Maturational Processes and the Facilitating Environment: Studies in the Theory of Emotional Development*. New York: Norton, 1977.
Winterson, Jeannette. *Sexing the Cherry*. New York: Atlantic Monthly, 1989.
Wittig, Monique. *Les Guérillères*. Translated by David Le Vay. Boston: Beacon, 1985.
Wolf, Christa. *Cassandra: A Novel and Four Essays*. Translated by Jan van Heurck. New York: Farrar, Straus, Giroux, 1984.
Wolf, Naomi. *The Beauty Myth: How Images of Beauty Are Used Against Women*. New York: William Morrow, 1991.
Yaeger, Patricia. *Honey-Mad Women: Emancipatory Strategies in Women's Writing*. New York: Columbia University Press, 1988.

Acknowledgments

Grateful acknowledgment is made to the following for permission to reprint material copyrighted or controlled by them:

Excerpt from "In Celebration Of My Uterus," *Love Poems* by Anne Sexton. Copyright © 1967, 1968, 1969 by Anne Sexton. Reprinted by permission of Houghton Mifflin Company. All rights reserved.

Selections from "In Celebration of My Uterus," reprinted by permission of Sterling Lord Literistic, Inc. Copyright © by Anne Sexton.

Selections from "My Sisters, O My Sisters," from *The Lion and the Rose* by May Sarton reprinted by permission of Russell & Volkening as agents for the author. Copyright © 1948 by May Sarton, © renewed in 1976 by May Sarton.

Selections from "My Sisters, O My Sisters" reprinted from *Collected Poems 1930-1933* by May Sarton with the permission of W. W. Norton & Company, Inc. Copyright © 1993, 1988, 1984, 1980,1974 by May Sarton.

"The Muse as Medusa" reprinted from *A Grain of Mustard Seed* by May Sarton, with the permission of W. W. Norton & Company, Inc. Copyright © 1971 by May Sarton.

Excerpt from "Katia Reading," *Balthus Poems* by Stephen Dobyns. Copyright © by Stephen Dobyns 1981, 1982. Reprinted by permission of Harold Ober Associates, Inc.

Excerpt from "From the House of Yemanja," reprinted from *The Black Unicorn* by Audre Lorde, with the permission of W.W. Norton & Company, Inc. Copyright 1978 by Audre Lorde.

"Song For Ishtar" by Denise Levertov from *Poems 1960-1967*. Copyright © 1962 by Denise Levertov Goodman. Reprinted by permission of New Directions Publishing Corporation.

Excerpts from "The Goddess" from *Collected Earlier Poems 1940-1960*. Copyright © 1959 by Denise Levertov. Reprinted by permission of New Directions Publishing Corporation.

Excerpts from *The Passion of New Eve* copyright © by Angela Carter 1977. Published by Virago Press 1982.

Excerpts from "Letter From a Far Country" from *Selected Poems*, copyright © 1985 by Gillian Clarke, by permission of Carcanet Press Limited.

Art Acknowledgments

Hydria, Meikirch/BE, Grächwil, bronze, 6th century BC: Collection of the Bern Historical Museum, Switzerland.

Mosaic Floor with Head of Medusa in Center. Collection of the J. Paul Getty Museum, Malibu, California.

Woman and Animal by Paul Klee. Besitzerhinweis, Nom du propriétaire Paul Klee-Stiftung, Kunstmuseum, Bern.

Death and the Maiden, 1510–11, by Hans Baldung. Collection of the Lazaro Galdiano Museum, Madrid.

The Abandoned Doll, 1921, oil on canvas 51" by 32" by Suzanne Valadon (French, 1865–1938), The National Museum of Women in the Arts. Gift of Wallace and Wilhelmina Holladay.

Repose, oil on canvas, 1895, by John White Alexander. The Metropolitan Museum of Art, Anonymous Gift, 1980 (1980.224).

The Wyndham Sisters, oil on canvas, 1899, by John Singer Sargent. The Metropolitan Museum of Art, Wolfe Fund, Catharine Lorillard Wolfe Collection, 1927.

Lucas van Uffele, oil on canvas, by Sir Anthony Van Dyck. The Metropolitan Museum of Art, Bequest of Benjamin Altman, 1913.

Gloria Steinem. Reproduced by Special Permission of *Playboy* magazine. Copyright © 1973 by Playboy. Photo by Frank Eck.

Charcot Lecturing on Hysteria at the Salpêtrière, anonymous: etching, after a painting by André Brouillet. Courtesy: The Wellcome Institute Library, London.

Mistress and Maid by Johannes Vermeer. Copyright The Frick Collection, New York.

Interior, oil on canvas, 1868–69, by Edgar Degas. Philadelphia Museum of Art: The Henry P. McIlhenny Collection in memory of Frances P. McIlhenny.

Nude Descending a Staircase, No. 2, oil on canvas, 1912, by Marcel Duchamp. The Philadelphia Museum of Art: The Louise and Walter Arensberg Collection.

The Peacock Skirt, black ink on white paper, 1894, by Aubrey Beardsley. The Harvard University Art Museums: Bequest of Grenville L. Winthrop.

Toilet of Venus ("Rokeby Venus") by Diego Velazquez. Reproduced by courtesy of the Trustees, The National Gallery, London.

Snake Goddess, Minoan from Crete, ca. 1600-1500 BC, Gold and ivory, H. 6 1/2". Gift of Mrs. W. Scott Fitz, Musuem of Fine Arts, Boston.

Index